CW00731054

BLOOD AND STEEL

Other Books by Donald E. Graves

And All Their Glory Past: Fort Erie, Plattsburgh and the Last Battles in the North
(Robin Brass Studio, 2013)

First Campaign of an A.D.C.: The War of 1812 Memoir of Lt. William Jenkins Worth, U.S. Army (Old Fort Niagara Press, 2012)

Dragon Rampant: The Royal Welch Fusiliers at War, 1793–1815
(Frontline Books & Robin Brass Studio, 2010)

Fix Bayonets! A Royal Welch Fusilier at War, 1796–1815
(Robin Brass Studio & Spellmount Publishing, 2007)

Century of Service: The History of the South Alberta Light Horse (The South Alberta Light Horse Regiment Foundation & Robin Brass Studio, 2005)

More Fighting for Canada: Five Battles, 1760–1944 (Robin Brass Studio, 2004)

Another Place, Another Time: A U-boat Officer's Wartime Album
(with Werner Hirschmann; Robin Brass Studio, 2004, 2011)

In Peril on the Sea: The Royal Canadian Navy and the Battle of the Atlantic
(Canadian Naval Memorial Trust & Robin Brass Studio, 2003)

Quebec, 1759: The Siege and the Battle (by C. P. Stacey; edited and with new material by Donald E. Graves; Robin Brass Studio, 2002)

Guns Across the River: The Battle of the Windmill, 1838
(Friends of Windmill Point & Robin Brass Studio, 2001, 2013)

Fighting for Canada: Seven Battles, 1758–1945 (Robin Brass Studio, 2000)

Field of Glory: The Battle of Crysler's Farm, 1813 (Robin Brass Studio, 1999)

The Incredible War of 1812: A Military History (by J. Mackay Hitsman; updated by Donald E. Graves; Robin Brass Studio, 1999)

South Albertas: A Canadian Regiment at War (South Alberta Regiment Veterans Association & Robin Brass Studio, 1998, 2004)

Where Right and Glory Lead! The Battle of Lundy's Lane, 1814
(Robin Brass Studio, 1997)

Soldiers of 1814: American Enlisted Men's Memoirs of the Niagara Campaign
(Old Fort Niagara Press, 1996)

Redcoats and Grey Jackets: The Battle of Chippawa, 1814 (Dundurn Press, 1994)

Merry Hearts Make Light Days: The War of 1812 Journal of Lieutenant John Le Couteur, 104th Foot (Carleton University Press, 1993; Robin Brass Studio, 2012)

Normandy 1944: The Canadian Summer
(with W. J. McAndrew and M. J. Whitby; Art Global, 1993)

BLOOD AND STEEL

The Wehrmacht Archive:
Normandy 1944

Donald E. Graves

Frontline Books, London

Blood and Steel:
The Wehrmacht Archive: Normandy 1944

First published in 2013 by Frontline Books,
an imprint of Pen & Sword Books Ltd,
47 Church Street, Barnsley, S. Yorkshire, S70 2AS

www.frontline-books.com

Copyright © Donald E. Graves, 2013

The right of Donald E. Graves to be identified as the author
of this work has been asserted by him in accordance with
the Copyright, Designs and Patents Act 1988.

ISBN: 978-1-84832-683-5

All rights reserved. No part of this publication may be reproduced,
stored in or introduced into a retrieval system, or transmitted,
in any form, or by any means (electronic, mechanical, photocopying,
recording or otherwise) without the prior written permission of the publisher.
Any person who does any unauthorized act in relation to this publication
may be liable to criminal prosecution and civil claims for damages.

CIP data records for this title are available from the British Library

For more information on our books, please visit
www.frontline-books.com, email info@frontline-books.com
or write to us at the above address.

Printed and bound by CPI Group (UK) Ltd, Croydon, CR0 4YY

Typeset in 11/13.5 point Minion Pro Regular

Contents

Panzer Divisions on the Western Front, 6 June 1944 1; Order of
Commanding Officer, 46th Luftwaffe Field Regiment, 16th Luftwaffe Field
Division, Prior to Going into Action, 2 July 1944 5; Battle Experience,
3rd Parachute Division, July 1944 7; Report on Battle Experience, 10th
SS Panzer Division 'Frundsberg', July 1944 14; German Experience of the
Invasion Battles 20; Battle Experience of Recent Operations by 2nd Panzer
Division, Whose Sector Is Being Taken Over by 36th Infantry Division 22;
Diary of 1st Platoon, 5th Company, 1st SS Panzer Grenadier Regiment,
1st SS Panzer Division, 9 July to 29 July 1944 30; Lack of Radio Discipline,
July 1944 33; Operation Order, 1056 Grenadier Regiment, 89th Infantry
Division, 4 August 1944 33; Führer's Orders to the Commander of the
St. Malo Garrison, 9 August 1944 36; Order for Deployment, 85th Infantry
Division, 12 August 1944 37; Report of the Strength of the Divisional
Formations under the Command of Seventh Army, 31 July 1944 38;
Appreciation of the Situation of Seventh Army, 10 August 1944 40; Allied
Evaluation of the Combat Worthiness of 12th SS Panzer Division 'Hitler
Jugend,' 18 August 1944 41

The Enemy Has Landed: Seventh Army Attempts to Deal with the Invasion,
6 June to 11 June 1944 44; *Feldmarschall* von Kluge Deals with Operation

List of Plates

Generalfeldmarschall Gerd von Rundstedt inspecting a German unit. *(Courtesy Service Publications)*
Generalfeldmarschall Rommel visits 21st Panzer Division. *(Courtesy Service Publications)*
A leFH18 105mm howitzer mounted on a French Lorraine ammunition vehicle. *(Courtesy Service Publications)*
French Somua half-track armed by the Germans with multiple 80mm mortars.
(Courtesy Service Publications)
A le FH16 105mm howitzer on the chassis of a British Mk VI light tank. *(Courtesy Service Publications)*
A regiment of self-propelled 105mm guns on parade at Versailles. *(Courtesy Service Publications)*
The Tiger I. *(Drawings by Christopher Johnson, reproduced with permission from Brian Reid,* No Holding Back: Operation Totalize, Normandy 1944*)*
A knocked-out gun position on the Normandy coast. *(Canadian Army Intelligence Summaries)*
The Tiger II. *(Canadian Army photo, Author's collection)*
A Panther of I/12th SS Panzer Regiment. *(Library and Archives of Canada, PA-114983)*
The Jagdpanther mounted the deadly 88mm gun. *(Canadian Army Intelligence Summaries)*
The Mk IV medium tank, work horse of the panzer divisions. *(Drawings by Christopher Johnson, reproduced with permission from Brian Reid,* No Holding Back: Operation Totalize, Normandy 1944*)*
Map: The Normandy Theatre, 1944.

Goliath remote-controlled demolition vehicle. *(Canadian Army Intelligence Summaries)*

Sherman of the Canadian 1st Hussars. *(Courtesy R. T. Leslie)*

Panzer grenadiers of the Panzer Lehr Division in their SPW 251 half-track. *(Courtesy Uwe Feist)*

The PAK 40 75mm, the standard German divisional anti-tank gun. *(Drawings by Christopher Johnson, reproduced with permission from Brian Reid,* No Holding Back: Operation Totalize, Normandy 1944*)*

American soldiers examine an 88mm Panzerschreck. *(United States Army)*

Panzerfaust 30 launcher and projectiles. *(Canadian Army Intelligence Summaries)*

German 150mm howitzer. *(Canadian Army Intelligence Summaries)*

German vehicle columns under air attack during the battle for the Falaise Gap, August 1944. *(Author's collection)*

The 2nd French Armoured Division prepares to move forward in August 1944. *(United States Army)*

American troops fighting in the hedgerows, July 1944. *(United States Army)*

A German column surrenders, St. Lambert-sur-Dives, 19 August 1944. *(Library and Archives of Canada, PA-111565)*

'HIWIs' captured by American forces. *(United States Army)*

Introduction

In early June 1944, despite the heavy damage to their cities caused by Allied bombing, the war remained distant for most Germans. Although there had been major defeats in Russia, the Eastern Front was still more than 500 miles from Berlin and Allied armies were only painfully clawing their way up the Italian peninsula. The Third Reich still stretched from the Ukraine to the Spanish border and from the Arctic to the Mediterranean. Most intelligent German soldiers and civilians believed that the most serious threat was in the west as it was inevitable that the Western Allies would attempt to invade France. They hoped that, if this landing could be defeated, it might then be possible to reinforce the Eastern Front and perhaps force a military victory or, at the least, create conditions that might lead to a negotiated end to the war. As one German officer put it:

> The days of shining victories were gone. Since the start of 1943, there were almost only failures. If the Anglo-Americans were successful with their invasion in the West, the war would be lost. Should the invasion be repulsed, it would create a new situation that could perhaps allow a political solution, with hopes for a bearable termination of the war. Therefore, every effort had to be made to thwart the invasion.[1]

As defeating the forthcoming invasion was crucial for the survival of Nazi Germany, the strength of the Wehrmacht in western Europe was gradually increased to sixty divisions, including eleven panzer or panzer-grenadier formations. The numbers may have been impressive but, as an appraisal of the panzer divisions deployed in the west (Document 1/1) illustrates, many were unprepared for battle. As a case in point, the elite 1st SS Panzer Division, the *Leibstandarte Adolf Hitler*, which had been 'bled white' in Russia and was unable to replace its losses, was regarded as only

---

1. Heinz Günther Guderian, *From Normandy to the Ruhr. With the 116th Panzer Division in World War II* (Bedford, 2001), 19.

marginally ready for action. Ready or not, on 6 June 1944, Allied forces began landing in Normandy and for the next twelve weeks the Wehrmacht was engaged in heavy fighting – at first to throw the invaders back into the sea, later to prevent them advancing and, finally, to struggle for survival.[2]

Blood and Steel is not a history of this campaign but an attempt to depict the German side of the 1944 campaign in France from the beachhead to the Belgian border based on the observations of German eyewitnesses and military documents. The greater part of this material is taken from the daily intelligence summaries of First Canadian Army, which also contain material from other Allied formations such as First and Fifth United States Armies and Second and Eighth British Armies as well as their constituent corps and divisions. These summaries constitute a rich source of data on the German side of the Normandy battle and the state of the Wehrmacht in 1944.[3]

As an example of their contents, consider Summary No. 30 issued at 2200 hours on 29 July 1944, which consists three parts. Part I, the work of the senior intelligence officer, is a summary of enemy activity on the American, British and Canadian fronts, as well as a report on German activity, including air and reserves, and an assessment of German intentions. The second part is a summary of the latest intelligence on German tactics, various units and formations, unit organization, biographies of senior officers and includes completed translated documents or parts thereof. In Summary No. 30, this part contains information on German *Werfer* brigades; an order from 22nd SS Panzer Grenadier Regiment on how to man a defence line; information on the destruction of German supply depots; information on a change of command in Panzer Group West and an order from the new commander, General Heinrich Eberbach, dated 13 July; the table of organisation for an SS Panzer Division; excerpts from the letters of German soldiers; the identification of the location of German units based on interrogation, deserters, actual contact and documents and insignia found on corpses. This part ends with a note of humour that the enemy has apparently been reduced to using British Stokes mortars from the First World War as a number of dud rounds

---

2. On German dispositions in the west in 1944, see Chester Wilmot, *The Struggle for Europe* (London, 1952), 201–7.
3. The Daily Intelligence Summaries of First Canadian Army are presently located in Record Group 24 of the Canadian national archives in Ottawa. I feel it only fair to remark that this is the second book to appear based on this material. The first was *Defeat in the West*, written by Milton Schulman, a former intelligence officer in the Canadian army, and published in 1947.

from that weapon had recently landed in Allied positions. The third and final part consists of technical intelligence and includes a memo from the Inspector of Armoured Troops on the strengths and weaknesses of the Panzer Mark V Panther; a description and particulars of the Soviet 76.2mm howitzer being used by the Wehrmacht; extracts from a German pamphlet on how to aim the *Panzerschreck* anti-tank weapon; and a description of cast steel fittings and shutters for concrete emplacements.

It must be stressed that these are wartime documents and reflect both the primary interests and the period prejudices of Allied intelligence officers. For example, they were pre-occupied with the organization of Wehrmacht formations and units and the capabilities of its weapons, particularly armoured and anti-armoured weapons. The bewildering variety of German organization was a source of great mystery to the Allied intelligence community and they worked very hard to clarify it. It is not surprising that there was also great interest in German tanks and anti-tank weapons because it was matter of survival. Today, fortunately, there are a number of dependable texts on German divisional organisation and on German armour and anti-armour weapons.[4] As for prejudices, I have excluded the most egregious comments by wartime officers.

Overall, the Wehrmacht was not particularly impressed with the fighting quality of its opponents. 'The enemy,' reported 3rd Parachute Division (Document 1/3) 'uses his great arms superiority in the fighting' and 'is a hard fighter only as long as he has good support from the artillery and mortar units.' 'The morale of the enemy infantry is not very high,' noted 10th SS Panzer Division (Document 1/4), it 'depends largely on artillery and air support' with artillery, being the 'main arm of the attrition and annihilation tactics' and 'well organized and manifold'.

The Germans, however, respected the Allies' immense manpower and materiel superiority. Veterans of the Eastern Front were taken aback by the intensity of artillery bombardment and air attack that they experienced in Normandy. 'I fought in Poland, France, the Balkans and Russia,' stated one prisoner who could 'honestly say that I have never in the whole of my experience as a soldier experienced anything which remotely compared to British artillery fire' (Document 14/1). 'I have fought on all fronts,' another German remarked, 'but I have never seen

---

4. There are numerous well-researched and reliable titles – too many to list here – on every type of German armoured vehicle that saw action in the summer of 1944. On Wehrmacht organization in France, the best single reference is Niklas Zetterling, *Normandy 1944. German Military Organization, Combat Power and Organizational Effectiveness* (Winnipeg, 2000).

such artillery.' (Document 14/1). General von Lüttwitz of the 2nd Panzer Division reported (Document 1/6) that

> The incredibly heavy artillery and mortar fire (of the enemy) is something new, both for the seasoned veterans of the Eastern front and the new arrivals from reinforcement units. Whereas the veterans get used to it comparatively quickly, the inexperienced reinforcements require several days to do so, after which they become acclimatized. The average rate of fire on the division sector per day is 4,000 artillery rounds and 5,000 mortar rounds per day. This is multiplied many times before an enemy attack, however small. For instance, on one occasion when the British made an attack on a sector of only two companies they expended 3,500 rounds in two hours. The Allies are waging war regardless of expense. In addition to this, the enemy have complete mastery of the air. They bomb and strafe every movement, even single vehicles and individuals. They reconnoitre our area constantly and direct their artillery fire. Against all this the GAF [German Air Force or Luftwaffe] is conspicuous by its complete absence. During the last four weeks the <u>total</u> number of German aircraft over the division area was six.

Allied air attacks were unceasing, the 3rd Parachute Division stating (Document 1/3) that the enemy fighters

> do not attack in formations, but peel off singly while the others keep on observing. The planes which come down to attack fly out of the sun or alongside the hedges and then jump across them. The enemy considers columns moving to the front better targets than the front itself.

The result was constant disruption in the delivery of supplies and a lengthening of the times to conduct major movements, which had to be done at night. It also resulted in much emphasis being put on camouflaging positions and equipment. The 10th SS Panzer Division stressed (Document 1/4) that armoured vehicles 'must be completely camouflaged, so that even low flying planes cannot recognize the type of vehicle'. Most German units adopted the tactical methods of the 277th Infantry Division which ordered (Document 7/4) that 'Low flying aircraft will be engaged by every man and every MG'. There were so many complaints about the absence of German aircraft that the Luftwaffe high command felt compelled to issue a statement (12/6) that soldiers complaining about lack of air support should be made aware that they cannot see how supply ships and troop transports are sunk or damaged, so that the enemy troops, tanks and supplies on them never reach the battle zone, causing the enemy considerable losses and lightening the weight of the enemy along the whole of our front. Care must be taken therefore that this is explained, in order to avoid a misunderstanding between the different services.

This would have been cold comfort to the average German *Landser* huddling in a slit trench watching endless Allied aircraft flying overhead.

Allied air superiority was bad enough but many Germans thought that their artillery was even more dangerous. The sheer weight of fire, as von Lüttwitz noted, was unnerving and it was worse on sectors where the Wehrmacht faced Commonwealth formations as they were using a recently-introduced system which could very quickly deliver a heavy volume of fire on a target. Known as the Parham System after its creator, Brigadier F. J. Parham, RA, it was based on that officer's belief that, in mobile warfare, pinpoint accuracy was hard to attain and, in any case, the same result could be obtained by simply drenching the area of the target with fire. It was his belief that 'the shock of a large number of rounds arriving simultaneously was far greater than that of a prolonged bombardment' and his solution was 'to fire every gun that could bear as soon as it could be laid and loaded'.[5] The key to the Parham system was an efficient communications system based on radio. The gun positions would be fed target information from static OP (Observation Point) officers or mobile FOOs (Forward Observation Officers), located with the forward troops, or AOP (Air Observation Post) aircraft. These relatively junior officers would identify a target, give its approximate location (often based on a six-digit map reference) and the level of fire (that is, the number of guns to be used and rounds to be fired). An observation officer could bring down fire from a troop of four guns up to, if he believed it necessary, every gun within range. The result could be devastating. One German artillery prisoner stated (Document 7/5) that enemy counter-battery fire was inevitably received 'before our troops could fire more than 4–5 rounds' To many Germans, it seemed as it did to one soldier (Document 4/4) that the enemy 'has a vast quantity of artillery [and] to send over to us, 1,000 rounds is for him a matter of minutes'.

Faced with an enemy superior in airpower and artillery, the Wehrmacht was forced to alter its defensive tactics. German doctrine held that defensive warfare was 'based primarily on firepower' and the defender 'must try to

---

5. Shelford Bidwell and Dominick Graham, *Fire-Power. British Army Weapons and Theories of War, 1904-1945* (Boston, 1985), 200.

produce the maximum fire effect'.[6] The Wehrmacht therefore organized its defences on firepower deployed in depth and the field of fire dictated the choice of a defensive position with easily-concealed locations offering good fields of fire prized above all others. Wherever possible, defences were laid out in three distinct lines or belts. Advance positions were placed on forward terrain features to deny 'the enemy observation and to force him to deploy unnecessarily early'.[7] Next came a line of battle outposts 'sited to act as a buffer in front of a defended area as well as to deceive the enemy as to the site of the main defensive belt'. Finally came that main belt (the *Hauptkampflinie* or HKL), defended 'primarily by means of the schematically planned fire of all arms', which was strong enough to bring an enemy assault to a halt. Any part of the HKL that was evacuated had to be 'regained by immediate or deliberate counterattack' but the object was to destroy an enemy assault by fire before it reached the HKL.[8] Even if Allied armour breached the HKL, German doctrine held that enemy success was 'not guaranteed' if the defenders 'use their weapons to cut off the tanks of the armoured spearhead from the follow-up infantry . . . since a tank unit by itself cannot hold ground for any length of time'.[9] German manuals emphasized that the determination 'to hold a position must not be shaken by the appearance of enemy AFVs' as soldiers 'caught within the effective range of AFVs who attempt to run away, will certainly be killed'.[10] The Germans would separate enemy infantry from any tanks that approached close to the HKL and, once this was done, tank hunters would move in to deal with the tanks using hand-held weapons, mines, grenades and demolition charges.[11] One Commonwealth armoured squadron commander reported (Document 9/4) that the Germans waited until his tanks 'were right in among them and then they came out of their dugouts with every type of anti-tank weapon and opened up with grenades and PIATs [*sic*: *Panzerfausts*] at ranges as low as 10 yards' causing the loss of six tanks and eight tank commanders.

To counter Allied materiel superiority, the Wehrmacht changed its

---

6. Bruce Condell and David Zabecki, eds., *On the German Art of War. Truppenführung* (Boulder, 2001), 119. *Heeresdienstvorschrift 300 Truppenführung* (Unit Command) was the Wehrmacht's standard doctrinal manual during the Second World War.
7. *Tactics of the German Army. Vol. 1. Defence and Withdrawal. 1944.* War Office (London, 1944), 1.
8. *Tactics of the German Army. Vol. 1. Defence and Withdrawal. 1944,* 1–2, 4–17.
9. Memorandum, 1 May 1943, in James Lucas, *War on the Eastern Front. The German Soldier in Russia* (London, 1991), 119.
10. *German Infantry in Action (Minor Tactics),* War Office (London, 1941), 23.
11. *Vorläufige Richtlinien für den Einsatz von Panzerabwehrwaffe in der Verteidigung* (Berlin, OKH, May 1944), 21.

defensive tactics. A report from 10th SS Panzer Division (Document 1/4) summarizes these alterations. To cut down casualties from artillery fire, the three defence lines were only thinly held but, behind each sector,

> local reserves are to be kept ready, each group linked to the next by means of tanks. After the enemy artillery fire lifts from the MLR [HKL], these reserves will immediately take position. They will then counter-attack the enemy who is very sensitive about close combat, and flank assaults at his weakest moment – the moment when he is forced to fight without artillery support.

'Whoever puts most of his men into the HKL,' noted Panzer Group West (Document 5/12) 'will have high casualties without being able to prevent a break-in of the enemy.'

Firepower arrayed in depth was the key to the German defensive system and the Wehrmacht possessed the weapons systems – particularly tanks and other armoured vehicles, anti-tank guns and handheld anti-tank weapons – capable of delivering that firepower. Allied intelligence officers devoted much time and energy to gaining information about these weapon systems and there are many documents below devoted to them. Chapter 7 contains information on German ant-tank guns and the hand-held weapons such as the *Panzerfaust* and *Panzerschreck* while Chapter 8 contains information on the strengths and weaknesses of the Panther, Tiger, Jagdpanther and Hornet AFVs from German documents. Chapter 9 has information on that humble and much-neglected weapon, the mine, as well as data on the range and rate of fire of all German anti-tank weapons. An interesting study in that chapter (Document 9/2) is a British analysis of Sherman 75mm tank casualties suffered in Normandy during the first month of the campaign which was compiled by a British Operational Research Unit. Its authors note the propensity for almost every Allied soldier to identify any German high-velocity direct fire weapon as one of the feared '88s' when it was more often the humbler but more numerous 75mm Pak gun. They add the somewhat ironic comment that many Allied tankers 'reported that they had been knocked out by 88mm, when in fact it had been 75mm shot, while the reverse mistake had not yet been discovered'.

In Normandy, weapons such as these, combined with the German defence in depth, curtailed the ability of Allied armour to successfully support their infantry. Intelligence officers in 4th Canadian Armoured Division analyzed the result of an Allied assault against a German defensive position. All crossroads and major intersections were covered by towed or self-propelled anti-tank guns sited in positions of all-round fire, extremely well camouflaged, and protected by mines. The German defences were centred around these weapons and they were supported by infantry in company or platoon strength dug in around the gun positions. As Allied tanks advanced, the German anti-tank gunners would hold their fire until the last possible moment and then engage them frontally. They would fire only a few rounds, in order not to give their position away, as spotting the muzzle flash of high-velocity weapons was difficult, and visibility was further obscured by the ever-present clouds of dust. If Allied tanks did locate and engage the enemy anti-tank guns from the front, their vulnerable side armour would come under fire from German tanks in positions on their flanks. While the enemy tanks were firing, the towed anti-tank guns would move to new, but previously prepared, positions from which they would re-engage. If the Allied tanks tried to work around a flank, German *Jagdpanzers*, positioned at the rear of the defence position, would fire several rounds before moving to previously selected positions while the towed guns opened up again. And so it went, anti-tank guns, tanks and *Jagdpanzers* firing, moving, and covering each other until heavy Allied tank losses brought forward momentum to a halt. While all this was going on, the German infantry would use heavy automatic weapons fire to force the Allied infantry to go to ground and, with both arms immobile and on terrain strange to them, the Germans would then launch savage counter-attacks, usually from a flank. Inevitably, the Allied attack would fail.[12]

In Normandy, the Wehrmacht not only faced enemy superiority in arms, it also suffered shortages, primarily of fuel but also other vital requirements. Prisoner interrogations revealed a shortage of ammunition, food, medical supplies and weapons. So dire was the loss of small arms that one of the first general orders issued by *Generaloberst* Heinz Guderian after he was appointed *Chef des Generalstab des Heeres*, effectively commander of the army, in August 1944 threatened disciplinary action for any officer or enlisted man who lost his weapon without sufficient excuse (Document 11/1). Punishments included the loss of leave for up to one year or the loss of the tobacco ration and the cost of the weapon was to be deducted from the miscreant's pay. Thus, we learn that an MP 44 assault rifle was valued at 80 Reichsmarks (£6.15s in 1944) while a Walther P38 pistol was valued at 30 RM (£2.10s).

---

12. Library and Archives of Canada, War Diary, 4th Canadian Armoured Division, August 1944, Intelligence Summary No. 4, 7 August 1944.

German losses were constant and heavy, and combat effectiveness was adversely affected by casualties. Up until the summer of 1944, although it had been severely strained by heavy losses sustained in three years of fighting on the Eastern Front, the German training and replacement system had functioned effectively. The losses suffered in western Europe during that summer, when added to the 300,000 Wehrmacht casualties inflicted during the Soviet offensive against Army Group Centre in June and July, caused the system to break down. It has been reliably estimated that 640,000 men served in German ground combat units in Normandy and the most probable figure for German losses is about 210,000 killed, wounded and missing. Very few replacements were received during the campaign, one author estimating that only about 40,000 men had reached Normandy by 13 August or were on their way. To put the manpower situation in perspective, on 25 July 1944, the day that the American Operation COBRA commenced, 1,452,000 Allied soldiers were facing no more than 380,000 German soldiers in Normandy – a ratio of 3.8 to 1, yet another aspect of Allied superiority.[13]

What replacements did arrive in Normandy were inadequate not only in terms of numbers but also in their level of training. Many were recent transfers from the Luftwaffe, men previously exempt from military service because of age or disability or so-called 'volunteers' or *Hilfswillige* (HIWIs). One conscripted Alsatian, who had served in the French army in the first year of the war, was amazed to find himself sent to the same German division he had fought against in 1940 (Document 3/1). Obtaining replacements was particularly difficult for the Waffen SS units, which suffered high casualties in Normandy, as they did throughout the war.[14] Both the 1st and 12th SS Panzer Divisions, nominally elite formations, received low-grade replacements in Normandy. A *Marschbataillon* of 250 men, half of them *Volksdeutsche* from the Luftwaffe or convalescents, was sent to the *Hitlerjugend* division in July (Document 13/5) and one company of the 26th SS Panzer Grenadier Regiment of that formation, which suffered nearly 50 per cent casualties during that month in July, had a sizeable proportion of Ukrainians in its ranks (Document 13/1). For its part, the *Leibstandarte Adolf Hitler* received a thousand former men from the 9th

---

13. Figures for German troop strengths, losses and replacements in Normandy and Russia from Zetterling, *Normandy 1944*, 27–34, 77–83, and Richard Evans, *The Third Reich at War* (New York, 2009), 619–21.
14. It has been estimated that of the 900,000 men who served in the Waffen SS during the war, 34 per cent were killed in action, see Rüdiger Overmans, *Deutsche Militärische Verluste in Zweiten Weltkrieg* (Munich, 1999), 257.

Panzer Division, 90 per cent of whom were non-German (Document 13/5). Not only was the combat effectiveness of such replacements low, many seized the first opportunity to desert. It is likely that, in most divisions that received them, such men were employed as they were in the 271st Infantry Division, which was 'to dig slit trenches, carry ammunition, and bring up food from the kitchen' (Document 13/2). By the last days of August and the early days of September, the manpower shortage had reached such a crucial stage that it saw the creation of units like the 276th Fortress Machine Gun Battalion, composed of men 'aged 35-40, with little or no training and 90 per cent were in the physical category for only garrison duty at home with the balance coming straight from the hospital' including 'one man with a stiff arm and another with a glass eye' (Document 13/6).

During their interrogations, many German PWs (Prisoners of War) complained about their officers. To a certain extent, this was probably the normal griping of enlisted men about their superiors but it may also have partially resulted from a decline in the quality of leadership in the Wehrmacht owing to heavy wartime casualties. From 1939 to 20 January 1944, the German army lost 47,581 officers killed or missing of whom 24,109 were lieutenants and captains (Document 13/3). The highest officer losses were, not surprisingly, suffered by the infantry followed, in order, by armoured, engineer and artillery units. Although there was a desperate need for junior officers, there must have been problems with the quality of some new entrants into the officer corps as it was directed that they should 'not be immediately employed under trying battle conditions' but 'at first, must be carefully directed, even if the posts of company commanders must be filled by NCOs' (Document 13/3). Nonetheless, the training of senior officers was only marginally affected by wartime conditions. For example, although there were only 1,054 qualified officers available for the 1,900 general staff positions in the army, the 17th wartime General Staff course, which commenced on 1 August 1944, was scheduled to last eighteen months, ending only on 1 February 1946 (Document 10/1).

Equipment shortages and human losses impacted on morale and German officers devoted much time and energy to boosting it, using a variety of methods. Some officers drew on historical examples from the past such as Frederick the Great's triumphs during the Seven Years' War (Document 12/9). Others made exaggerated claims concerning the introduction and effect of the *Vergeltungswaffen* or retaliation weapons such as the V-1 and V-2. One officer blithely informed his men that V-2 missiles had already sunk several Allied battleships and cruisers, that a V-3 missile existed, which was even more deadly, and a V-4 weapon was in development which had the 'ambitious' purpose of sinking the British Isles! (Document 12/4). A company commander in the 276th Infantry Division assured his men in early July that they would soon take part in a great counter-offensive, supported by 3,000 aircraft, which would 'eject the Anglo-American tools of Bolshevism' by the 21st of that month (Document 12/5). This same officer claimed that V-1 missiles had killed twelve million people in Britain and that much of the southern part of that country was on fire! Rumours were spread that the new ME-262 jet fighters had destroyed 400 Allied aircraft on their first day in action (Document 3/3). A more traditional method of increasing the spirit of the German soldier was a generous policy of awarding decorations – by 1944 a division commander was permitted to award 100 Iron Crosses 2nd Class per month during a quiet period, and up to 500 such decorations per month during periods of heavy fighting (Document 12/12).

There was, of course, the use of fear as an incentive. Propaganda emphasized that the defeat of Nazi Germany would mean the loss of 'Honour, Freedom and Bread' (Document 12/7). German workers would 'be sent as slaves to Siberia,' German intellectuals 'castrated or killed,' German youth 'educated to communism by Jewish teachers' and German women would become 'easy prey' for Allied occupation troops. 'Only an iron will to resist and endure,' claimed the commander of the 276th Infantry Division, 'will save us and lead us to victory, which in spite of everything is perhaps closer than we think' (Document 12/3). The men of this division 'must believe this, as the Führer believes it' and any soldier who 'does otherwise is a scoundrel and a traitor, for he believes the enemy rather than his own commanders.' *Generalleutnant* Richard Schimpf expressed his certainty to the men of the 3rd Parachute Division that 'we will finish this war victoriously' and that his formation 'will never cease to fight and will do its duty unvanquished to the end of the war' (Document 12/10). 'Whoever thinks or speaks differently,' warned Schimpf, 'will be slapped across the face.'

A slap across the face was by no means the only punishment German soldiers might receive if they spoke of defeat. They could be charged with *Wehrkraftzersetzung* or 'undermining military power', a charge that might result in a variety of punishments, including execution. The Wehrmacht did not spare the death penalty and it has been estimated that 21,000 German servicemen were executed during the Second World War, compared to forty-eight in the First World War.[15] There is some evidence that the Wehrmacht did experience discipline problems in Normandy but it seems that the majority of these problems occurred among the rear echelons. This is implied by a confidential order issued by Panzer Group West on 16 July (Document 12/1) that complains of men 'idling about behind the front', an increased incidence of looting, the improper use of vehicles to 'organize' (i.e. loot) things or to 'cultivate some female acquaintance', improper dress and a lack of saluting.

But despite the odds against them, many German soldiers continued to fight to the bitter end. For every German who engaged in looting before they retreated, as narrated in the Epilogue, there were many more like the officer who still firmly believed (Document 4/5) that, if 'we can still hold out a few weeks more, we will soon be advancing again', In the end the Allied armies were forced to use overwhelming air and artillery superiority to 'grind' soldiers like these down in a campaign of attrition that the Germans could not win. That Allied victory in the summer of 1944 was due to materiel strength does not reflect badly on the fighting qualities of Allied soldiers because there is no 'elegant formula for the overthrow of a powerful opponent' and the 'vast expenditure of steel and high explosive had this supreme justification' of saving lives.[16] The Allies were in a position to substitute steel to save blood; the Wehrmacht did not have that option.

Donald E. Graves
'Maple Cottage',
Valley of the Mississippi,
Upper Canada

---

15. Information on German disciplinary measures and executions from Evans, *Third Reich*, 502.
16. Bidwell and Graham, *Fire-Power*, 190–1.

A Note to the Reader

The First Canadian Army Daily Intelligence Summaries, from which most of the documents below were taken, were the product of many different hands working under extreme pressure (and perhaps the occasional artillery round or aerial bomb). The result is that there was little consistency in format and terminology from one summary to the next. Some translators and typists retained the original German document format; others simply transcribed them as they thought best. Even the translations of words or titles can vary from document to document and, thus, the 12th Waffen SS Panzer Division can be referred to as the *Hitlerjugend*, *Hitler Jugend* or Hitler Youth Division.

This lack of consistency made the task of editing the following manuscript not only laborious but also very difficult. There was also the consideration that the imposition of a strict but artificial consistency on the documents would have, in some cases, adversely affected their period 'flavour'. Therefore, editorial work was kept as minimal as possible. Obvious mistakes in times, names and dates were silently corrected. The titles and identifications of formations and units were anglicized in the document titles and preliminary comments but left as they appeared in the text of the original document. German words and phrases that appear in the text were italicized except for such words as Luftwaffe, Panzer and Wehrmacht that have become so common in English that they are very near part of that language. I should mention that Wehrmacht is used below – as, indeed, it was during the war – to indicate German land forces although it actually encompassed all three German services.

Editorial or prefatory comments by wartime intelligence officers have been put in italics as have comments by the present editor.

One final point is that the Wehrmacht identified corps by Roman numerals, divisions and regiments by Arabic numerals, battalions by Roman numerals and companies by Arabic numerals. Thus, the 5th

Company of the II Battalion of the 979th Infantry Regiment of the 271st Infantry Division was part of the LVIII Panzer Corps.

D. E. G.

Acknowledgements

I would be very remiss if I did not acknowledge the assistance given to me in the preparation of this book by Uwe Feist, John Furst, Christopher Johnson and Ron Volstad. And, of course I must again render thanks to my wife, Dianne, who is the unsung partner in all my writing work.

D. E. G,

German Ranks and their Equivalents

German Army	Waffen SS	British/American
Generalfeldmarschall		Field Marshal/ General of the Army
Generaloberst	*Oberstgruppenführer*	General
General der Infanterie*	*Obergruppenführer*	Lieutenant-General
Generalleutnant	*Gruppenführer*	Major-General
Generalmajor	*Brigadeführer*	Brigadier/ Brigadier-General
Oberst	*Oberführer*	Colonel
	Standartenführer	Colonel
Oberstleutnant	*Obersturmbannführer*	Lieutenant-Colonel
Major	*Sturmbannführer*	Major
Hauptmann	*Hauptsturmführer*	Captain
Oberleutnant	*Obersturmführer*	First Lieutenant
Leutnant	*Untersturmführer*	Second Lieutenant
Stabsfeldwebel	*Sturmscharführer*	Sergeant-Major Master Sergeant
Oberfeldwebel	*Hauptscharführer*	Technical Sergeant
Feldwebel	*Oberscharführer*	Staff Sergeant/
Unterfeldwebel	*Unterscharführer*	Sergeant
Unteroffizier	*Rottenführer*	Corporal
Stabsgefreiter	*Sturmmann*	Lance-Corporal/PFC
Obergefreiter	*Sturmmann*	Lance-Corporal/PFC
Gefreiter	*Sturmmann*	Lance-Corporal/PFC
Obersoldat/Obergrenadier	SS-*Oberschütze*	Private
Soldat/Grenadier	SS-*Schütze*	Private

* Or *der Artillerie, der Panzertruppen* etc.

Source: War Department, *Handbook on German Military Forces* (Washington, 1945).

Abbreviations and Acronyms
Used in Text and Notes

AA	anti-aircraft
ADMS	Assistant Director, Medical Services
AP	armour-piercing
APCBC	armour-piercing, capped ballistic cap (shell)
AV (Tech)	Armoured Fighting Vehicles (Technical)
C of S	Chief of Staff
CG	Commanding General
CGS	Chief of the General Staff
CO	Commanding Officer
COS	*See* C of S
CP	Command Post
CRA	Commander Royal Artillery
DAAG	Deputy Assistant Adjutant General
DAQMG	Deputy Assistant Quartermaster General
DF (SOS)	Defensive Fire (SOS)
DSD	Director, Staff Duties
DTD	Directorate of Technical Development
flak	anti-aircraft
FAO	Forward Artillery Observer (US)
FEB	*Feld Ersatz Bataillon*
FDL	Forward Defence Line
FOO	Forward Observation Officer (UK)
FPN	*Feldpostnummer*
GAF	German Air Force, *Luftwaffe*
GHQ	General Head Quarters
GS 1 (A)	General Staff Officer 1 (Armour)
HE	high explosive
HF	harassing fire
HKL	*Hauptkampflinie* (*see* MLR)

i/c	in charge or in command, depending on context
Int	Intelligence
ISUM	First Canadian Army Intelligence Summary
KIA	Killed in action
MG	Machine-gun
MDS	Main Dressing Station
MLR	Main Line of Resistance
MT	Motor Transport
NAAFI	Navy, Army and Air Force Institutes
NSF	*Nationalsozialistischer Führungsstab des Heeres*
NSFO	*Nationalsozialistischer Führungsoffizier*
OB West	*Oberbefehlshaber* West.
OC	Officer Commanding
OKH	*Oberkommando des Heeres* (army high command)
OP	observation post
ORs	Other Ranks (i.e. NCOs and enlisted men)
pdr.	pounder
pdv	Probability Directional Value
PFC	Private First Class
PIAT	Projector, Infantry, Anti-Tank
POL	Petrol, Oil and Lubricants
PW	Prisoner of War, both singular and plural
Q.	Quartermaster
REME	Royal Electrical and Mechanical Engineers
RM	Reichsmark
RP	rocket projectile
RSO	*Raupenschlepper Ost*
R/T	Radio/Telephone
SFH	*Selbsfahrlafett-Feld-Haubitze* (self-propelled gun)
SHAEF	Supreme Headquarters Allied Expeditionary Force
SMG	submachine-gun
SP	self-propelled
SS	*Schutzstaffel*
VD	Venereal Disease
WIA	Wounded in action
WO	Warrant Officer or War Office, in context
WT	Wireless Telegraphy

Chapter 1

The German Experience of Battle

Formations and Units

Document 1/1[1]

Panzer Divisions on the Western Front, 6 June 1944

1. Estimate of Panzer-Type Divisions,
   Western Front, 6 June 1944

Panzer Group West could give orders to the Waffen SS on training matters only. The activation or re-forming of Panzer-type divisions in the West was not the same for the *Heer*[2] as it was for the Waffen SS. The Waffen SS had priority as a result of the aid and resources of Himmler or sometimes because of overriding the orders of Hitler. The principal advantage accruing to the Waffen SS was priority on replacements and matériel. On the other hand, the Waffen SS was short of officers and NCOs. Army officers did not wish to join the Waffen SS. The *Heeres Personalamt*,[3] under Schmundt,[4] Hitler's chief aide-de-camp, interposed by order to provide the 12th SS Panzer Division with the bare minimum of company grade officers necessary for training. The same method was sometimes applied to procure general staff officers.

---

1. Extracted from 'History of Panzer Group West (Mid 1943–5 July 1944)' by *General der Panzertruppen* Leo, *Freiherr* Geyr von Schweppenburg. This is Report B-466 in the Foreign Military Studies collection, Record Group 338, National Archives and Records Administration.
2. *Heer* or army, as opposed to Waffen SS.
3. The army personnel department.
4. *General der Infanterie* Rudolf Schmundt (1896–1944), chief of the *Personalamt*. Schmundt died of wounds received in the 20 July bomb explosion.

The cadre of officers and NCOs was rather small and somewhat poor in quality. A few casualties or changes in the roster of an SS division might mean a great deterioration in fighting value. This value was largely based on the presence of a few 'personalities'. For instance, the performance of the 12th SS Panzer Division depended on Witt[5] (killed during the invasion), Meyer[6] (his successor) and a few battalion commanders.

The number of SS divisions and the activation of more greatly exceeded the number of corresponding personnel available. It became more and more evident that Hitler was not concerned with wearing down the *Heeres* Panzer divisions in the East. While these divisions were burned out fighting the Russians, the SS divisions were sent to France for reorganization.

The selection by the Berchtesgaden staff, of divisions for a strategic reserve in France was characteristic: 1st SS Panzer Division (*Leibstandarte*), 12th SS Panzer Division (*Hitlerjugend*), Panzer Lehr Division, and 17th SS Panzer Grenadier Division (*Götz von Berlichingen*). I would have chosen from a military standpoint, on the basis of efficiency, the 2nd Panzer Division, 12th SS Panzer Division, 11th Panzer Division or 9th SS Panzer Division, and the Panzer Lehr Division.

The allotment of material was made by the *Generalinspektion der Panzertruppen* (General Inspectorate of Panzer Troops), strongly influenced by Hitler. The latter knew <u>nothing</u> about training and based his evaluation on '*Geist*' (spirit). He believed this '*Geist*' to be superior in the SS. In the Fall of 1943 and the Spring of 1944, there were a large number of battle-seasoned tank battalions in France which had come from the Eastern front and were re-formed. These battalions waited several months for their matériel, whereas some of the SS Panzer divisions had already received their matériel, despite a lack of sufficient personnel and trained crews. However, it is only fair to say that in training as well as fighting, the SS divisions did their best to pull their full weight.

The SS officer corps was far more varied in origin, education and character than that of the *Heer*. One could find the ruthless mercenary, the 'just a soldier' type, and the responsible officer side by side. For those who had come to dislike service in the Waffen SS, there was no 'way back'. Himmler, in a case with which I am familiar, left no doubt to a highly responsible and very able officer what would happen.

5. *Brigadeführer* Fritz Witt (1908–44), commander of 12th SS Panzer Division. KIA, Normandy, 14 June 1944.
6. *Standartenführer* Kurt Meyer (1910–61), commander of 25th SS Panzer Grenadier Regiment and later of the 12th SS Panzer Division.

The conclusion to be drawn is that the staying and recovery power during and after weeks and months of fighting was bound to be superior in the *Heeres* divisions. The standard and thoroughness of the tactical education of subordinates was also superior in *Heeres* divisions. The following is a thorough estimate of the comparative combat efficiency of all Panzer-type formations between 1939 and 6 June 1944. The list has been compiled after interrogating my most experienced corps and division commanders. The average efficiency varies from 30 to 40 per cent of the average division performance in 1939. This percentage does not apply to training methods, to which I would give greater credit because of modernization.

Order of Combat Efficiency

A. 2nd Panzer Division
9th SS Panzer Division
12th SS Panzer Division
Panzer Lehr Division

B. 11th Panzer Division
2nd SS Panzer Division
21st Panzer Division

C. 9th Panzer Division
17th SS Panzer Grenadier Division
116th Panzer Division (probably)

D. 10th SS Panzer Division
1st SS Panzer Division

(Estimate is of 6 June 1944, no matter what performance the divisions made later on.)

2. Remarks

2nd Panzer Division: The division commander[7] was a good leader in the field, but less experienced in training. The division was well backed with personnel and matériel by the *Generalinspektion*. *Generaloberst* Guderian[8] was in command of this division before the war.

---

7. *General der Panzertruppen* Heinrich, *Freiherr* von Lüttwitz (1896–1969), commanding general, 2nd Panzer Division.
8. *Generaloberst* Heinz Guderian (1888–1954), Inspector-General of Armoured Troops in 1944.

9th SS Panzer Division: The performance of this division depended on the commanding military personality of its commander, *Obergruppenführer* Bittrich,[9] who was a first class trainer. The division was especially efficient against airborne operations (proved at Arnhem) and in teamwork.

12th SS (Hitlerjugend) Panzer Division: This commander[10] was also good in training and possessed a will and a passion for advanced methods. The quality of conscripts was high, but that of the subordinate officers and NCOs was poor.

Panzer Lehr Division: The division was well provided for by the *Generalinspektion*. The commander[11] was very modern in his thoughts and methods. There were deficiencies in infantry tactics and teamwork (combined arms.)

11th Panzer Division: The commander[12] was well experienced in mobile warfare. The division was thoroughly schooled in higher training methods. It had an adequate cadre of seasoned subordinate officers and was augmented by conscripts from 273rd Reserve Panzer Division.

2nd SS Panzer Division: The remnants of this division, which in 1944 was re-formed in France, still had sufficient veterans from the period when its first commander (*Oberstgruppenführer* Paul Hausser)[13] had given the division very high standards. The division had the best tank battalion in the West.

21st Panzer Division: The division was reorganized after the African campaign with undesirable personnel from a large number of divisions. Even very thorough and experienced training could never overcome this basic fault. Part of its matériel was manufactured in French factories.

9th Panzer Division: There were too many changes in division

---

9. *Obergruppenführer* Wilhelm Bittrich (1894–1979), commanding general II SS Panzer Corps. Bittrich was succeeded as commanding general of the 9th SS Panzer Division on 29 June 1944 by *Standartenführer* Thomas Müller.
10. *Brigadeführer* Fritz Witt (1908–44), commanding general, 12th SS Panzer Division, killed in action 14 June 1944.
11. *Generalleutnant* Fritz Bayerlein (1899–1970), commanding general, Panzer Lehr Division.
12. *Generalleutnant* Wend von Weitersheim (1900–75), commanding general, 11th Panzer Division.
13. *Oberstgruppenführer* Paul Hausser (1880–1972), commander of Seventh Army late in the Normandy campaign.

commanders[14] and their principal staff officers and too much interference with training by employing the troops to build fortifications and so forth.

17th SS Panzer Grenadier Division: Its performance depended on two men, *Brigadeführer* Ostendorff,[15] its first commander, and *Standartenführer* Fick,[16] commander of the Panzer Grenadier regiment. The matériel was poor. The division, which was organized and trained in haste, was quite efficient but deteriorated rapidly after Ostendorff was wounded in Normandy.

10th SS Panzer Division: The division was unlucky in its assignment of division commanders.[17]

1st SS Panzer Division: A type of 'Praetorian Guard,' the division was bled white in Russia and was unable to refill the gaps resulting from casualties and sending out cadres (the 12th SS Panzer Division was formed by a cadre from the 1st SS Panzer Division). Discipline was a sham; the NCOs were poor. The division did not have time for thorough training before the invasion.

Document 1/2[18]

Order of Commanding Officer, 46th Luftwaffe Field Regiment, 16th Luftwaffe Field Division, Prior to Going into Action, 2 July 1944

The hour has struck for the regiment to assert itself. For the first time, since its formation, the regiment is going into action with the task of holding the sector to which it has been allotted against all attacks.

---

14. *Generalleutnant* Erwin Joliasse was commanding general of this division in the early summer of 1944.
15. *Brigadeführer* Werner Ostendorff (1903–45), commander of 17th SS Panzer Grenadier Division.
16. *Standartenführer* Jakob Fick (1912–2004), commander of 37th SS Panzer Grenadier Regiment.
17. *Brigadeführer* Heinz Harmel (1906–2000), commander of 10th SS Panzer Division.
18. ISUM 26, 25 July 1944.

I expect from all leaders, subleaders and soldiers of the regiment that they will do everything to accomplish this task under all circumstances and so ensure that our young regiment joins the ranks of the battle experienced old regiments.

The enemy opposing us, the 51 English Division,[19] is an experienced formation, which has been tested in many theatres of war. They fight hard, make use of all possible tricks and means of deception and are very well equipped. Due to his present air superiority the enemy constantly looks into and behind our positions. No movement by day is missed by him. By constant reconnaissance he is looking for weak spots in our positions, so as to attack these very areas. He avoids, however, our fire and withdraws from it.

Therefore, the following points arise in the conduct of our fight:

(1) During all activity, there must be the most careful camouflage and cover against air reconnaissance.

(2) Battle and dug out positions must be constructed with the greatest care to prevent observation by enemy aircraft.

(3) Enemy reconnaissance activity must be harassed and prevented by continuous reconnaissance of our own.

(4) Enemy patrols and assault parties must be repulsed by heavy fire. Traps for enemy patrols must be prepared so as to attack them, to surprise them, to destroy them or to take them prisoner.

(5) Each and every enemy stroke is to be answered whenever possible by a heavier counter stroke. For this purpose fire concentration of all weapons is to be ready.

The superior battle morale of the German soldier in our regiment has to surpass the seemingly technical superiority of the foe. Our regiment will then achieve successes equal to those of old and experienced troops.

Each in his own task can and must contribute to this end.

---

19. 51st Highland Division.

Document 1/3[20]

Battle Experience, 3rd Parachute Division, July 1944

Secret

A. Operations 10–20 July 1944

1. 10 July 1944 was quiet on the entire front.

2. On 11 July, shortly after midnight, assault troops of the 5th Parachute Regiment attacked successfully in the direction of Berigny. Two companies of the regiment supported by engineers attacked with a limited objective. The purpose was to straighten out the lines but was unsuccessful. During the day the Americans had assembled to attack St. Lô and our troops, and upon contacting this strong resistance, were compelled to retreat.

3. After this the enemy opened up with his artillery in preparation for his attack which started in the early morning. The Americans were successful right along. They succeeded in penetrating the road St. Lô-Bayeux after breaking through St. Georges d'Elle. They also gained ground south and west of St. Andre.

4. The Parachute Regiments 5 and 90, and especially the 2nd Company of Regiment 9 suffered heavy losses owing to the enemy's enormous superiority of materiel. The division was compelled to commit first the 12th Assault Gun Brigade and then the division reconnaissance company in order to halt the breakthrough. When these reserves were found insufficient, the 3rd Company of the 8th Parachute Regiment was thrown into battle. However, all these combined forces were only able to stem the advance near the main road. It was impossible to reach the old MLR.[21]

5. After enemy penetration had widened the gap in the old CP area of the 9th Parachute Regiment, the division was compelled to commit the 3rd Parachute Engineer Battalion as a last reserve. By dark we had succeeded with all these forces in forming and holding a new MLR, at the same time retaking an area in the sector of the 5th Parachute

---

20. Library and Archives of Canada, Record Group 24, C17, volume 13645, Annex to Periodic Report, No. 55.
21. MLR, Main Line of Resistance.

Regiment, northwest of Berigny, stretching along the road to La Boulaye and from there to the northwest.

6. More attacks followed at 0600 12 July after heavy artillery and mortar fire. The enemy tried all day long to advance on the left flank of the new MLR in the sector where he had gained ground the previous day. However, after transferring the 2nd Company of the 9th Parachute Regiment behind the 3rd Engineer Battalion, a new MLR was held against all attacks. Despite their continuous artillery barrage, the Americans did not succeed in piercing this line.

7. The 13th was like the previous day. Notwithstanding their superior materiel and heavy weapons the Americans did not gain any ground. In the evening the 9th Parachute Regiment was relieved by the 8th Parachute Regiment. The 3rd Parachute Signal Battalion added a quickly formed company.

8. 14 July was a quiet day. Because of the bad weather it was possible to relieve units during daylight.

9. On 15 July the Americans again attacked after very heavy artillery bombardment in the direction of St. Lô. By evening the 3rd Parachute Engineer Battalion had beaten off eleven attacks under repeated artillery fire. The twelfth enemy attack succeeded in gaining ground after inflicting casualties on the Engineer Battalion. The enemy penetrated into the main line of resistance and advanced up to Martinville. Although we counter-attacked we were unable to break through owing to nightfall and the weakness of our reserves. A counterattack during the night by the 8th Parachute Regiment was also without success.

10. Small scale attacks by the Americans during the day against the left flank of the 9th Parachute Regiment and 1st Company of the 5th Parachute Regiment were fruitless.

11. With daybreak on 16 July we attacked again and slowly cleaned the enemy out of Martinville. We were unable, however, to reach the old MLR. At this point the CO of the 8th Parachute Regiment on division order took over command of the 9th Parachute Regiment, and in turn the CO of the 9th Parachute Regiment took over on the right flank of the division. More attempts during the afternoon to clean the enemy out of his breakthrough were of no success.

12. On the following day the enemy renewed his attacks. After several attacks against the 2nd Company of the 5th Parachute Regiment, the 1st Company of the 8th Parachute Regiment and the 3rd Parachute Engineer Battalion, the enemy succeeded in breaking through on the front of the 2nd Company of the 8th Parachute Regiment. This time the enemy gained ground all through Martinville and south to the village of La Madeleine. The available reserves were too weak in order to beat back the advancing troops. All our counterattacks during the day were unsuccessful.

13. With great difficulty we succeeded in occupying the MLR by noon and holding off all attacks. We also accomplished contact with the units to our left. The continuous, agile, harassing fire by the Americans aggravated our already tired troops. In the afternoon the Americans took La Rocque for the second time after throwing in reserves as well as using tanks. Again we succeeded in stemming the enemy and throwing him back across the big road. At the same time the foe succeeded in advancing on our left to St. Lô. After having lost contact on the left flank, owing to the enemy penetration and the danger of being fired upon from the rear, the MLR had to be pulled back beyond the road St. Lô–Bayeux. After building up a weak flank support we succeeded in holding off the coming decisive breakthrough to the south of St. Lô, and in forming a new MLR with the troops on the left. Only the 3rd Parachute Engineer Battalion in an advance position blocked all traffic east to west on the main road.

14. After establishing a new MLR on the flank in the night of 18 July, the Americans were satisfied by taking St. Lô and only local fighting took place on 19 and 20 July.

B. Enemy Situation and Strength

1. The General Front

a. The first days of July were quiet on the front. With the exception of continuous artillery fire from the Second American Army there was no activity. Then the First American Army began an offensive which, on the 12th of July, was extended by the Second British Army when it began a large scale attack east of the Orne.

b. Several attacks of the U.S. VIII Corps on the right flank anticipated the main attack of the First U.S. Army eastward of Carentan, with the intention to cross the Vire river west and southwest of Isigny, and then to pass in a direction southwest of St. Lô to cut over to the west coast near Coutances and there to cut off the troops of the LXXXIV Corps.

c. By switching and adding the 2nd Panzer Division, LXXXIV Corps was able to frustrate the enemy's intention to push deep into the southwest even though it was unsuccessful in throwing the enemy back across the Vire.

2. Our own front

a. While the enemy limited himself in the first days of July to front line thrusts and reconnoitring as a basis for the coming attack on St. Lô, he finally attacked on 11 July, after regrouping and bringing up the newly identified 35th Division.

b. We expected the attack to begin on the V Corps front, but instead it took place on the XIX Corps front (with the 29, 35, 30 and parts of the 32nd Division, 3rd Armoured Division and Corps troops), the 29th Division at the strongpoint, along a line stretching from St. Quentin, St. Georges d'Elle, Bretel. The attack started with heavy artillery shelling, especially on the right flank and going eastward towards St. Georges d'Elle.

c. According to captured American documents it was the mission of the XIX Corps to break through west of St. Quentin and first to take the sector south of the Bayeux – St. Lô road, Hill 192, St. André and Laluzerne, and as a second objective to occupy Hills 150 and 147, south and southwest of St. André and from there to push into St. Lô.

d. With the fall of Caen and St. Lô, 21 Allied Army Group has reached key points and will now try to capture Coutances as a third strongpoint in order to start new attacks from there.

C.   American Tactics and Strategy

1. General

a. The enemy uses his great arms superiority in the fighting. At the strongpoints the employment of artillery, mortars and the air force reached an all time high.

b. The enemy not only employed heavy artillery and mortar fire for his attacks, but also used this strong fire to support assault and reconnaissance missions of company strength.

c. The enemy overcomes the difficulty of hedgegrown country by employment of artillery air observers. They fly over the battle zone in regular reliefs and their reconnaissance is followed by strong, short bursts of fire with considerable ammunition expenditure. In sectors where there are only few AA guns these planes sweep down to a low level in order to direct the fire to picked targets.

2. Offensive Tactics

a. The enemy supports his attacks in relatively small areas with tanks, fighters and heavy artillery. He starts his attacks by accurate shelling and destruction of our weapons. This barrage usually ploughs up the area in which the attack is to be made. This process is carried on by fighter-bombers.

b. The infantry follows up the rolling barrage in order to occupy the disputed area. At the smallest resistance the infantry stops and retires and a new artillery bombardment takes place in order to stamp out the remaining resistance.

The attacking infantry advances along the roads and hedges under artillery protection. Sharpshooters up in the trees and heavy infantry arms are employed so that hedges etc. are under continuous fire. All captured territory is prepared immediately for defensive action, disregarding the fact that the attack may be continued. In so doing mines are laid and then they are picked up again just before the unit leaves the area.

3. Defensive Tactics

a. In defence as well as in offence the enemy is excellent in camouflaging. He is a hard fighter only as long as he has good support from the artillery and mortar units. During long and strong resistance and fire he falls back to his alternate position where he gets support from units moving up. He is not afraid [*here two lines are illegible*].

4. Use of Artillery

The enemy artillery is distinguished by accuracy of fire and man-oeuvrability. Employment in depth, changes of position, self-propelled guns – during infantry attacks close to the main fighting line – is the doctrine followed. A great number of observation planes makes it possible, by using considerable ammunition, to fire effectively even on small targets. The employment of fire and phosphorus bombs as well as H.E. ammunition with white smoke has been frequently observed. They cause stomach trouble and headaches.

5. Use of Tanks

a. As yet tanks have not been committed as a closed formation for the purpose of breaking through. So far tanks have only been committed as support for the infantry, about 20 tanks to every battalion. Those tanks have advanced up to the MLR, fired and then retired in order not to be attacked by tank destroyers. From there on they support further attacks of the infantry by firing from the flank. In many instances it has been noticed that the tank is being used as a mobile observation post.

b. So far tank crews do not show much enthusiasm for a fight between tanks. They respect anti-tank guns and dislike close-combat weapons.

D.   Air Attacks

1. For attacking troops on roads, in the battle zone and supply echelons, the enemy is employing the following types of planes: Thunderbolts, Typhoons, Lightnings, Spitfires, Mustangs

2. All planes attacking road movements fly at altitudes up to 3,000 metres. At this level they are out of range of light and medium flak, and besides they have good observation of terrain and roads and they can also identify columns and single vehicles.

3. The number of planes is variable, the highest number observed is 24. The formations used permit observation of large strips and at the same time of secondary roads.

4. The fighters do not attack in formations, but peel off singly while the others keep on observing. The planes which come down to attack fly out of the sun or alongside the hedges and then jump across them. The enemy considers columns moving to the front better targets than the front itself.

5. Road movements and activity in fields are recognised from the air as follows:

   a. By day:
     (1) Dust clouds which are noticeable both in hedgerow and wooded country.
     (2) The blinking of bare parts especially when the sun is low (windshield).
     (3) Using wrong shading and camouflage colours (tan coloured vehicles in woods, or green vehicles in open country).
     (4) New paths; persons walking around in the open.
   b. By night:
     (1) Raising of dust clouds.
     (2) Not properly dimmed tail lights.
     (3) Vehicles on bright surfaced roads.

E. Enemy Information

1. The average age of the infantry is from 21–23. Losses are replaced quickly.

2. The enemy has built up his landing facilities, making it possible for him to bring in all his supplies on the beaches. However, he is still not independent of the weather. It is of great importance to the enemy to have a good port.

3. In order to mark the front lines the enemy uses orange coloured panels. Paratroopers and glider troops use phosphorus, scarves and arm bands.

4. In several cases time shells have exploded 14 hours (some of heavy calibre) after they were fired.

5. Dummy positions have been attacked by the enemy, using considerable ammunition.

6. To mark targets, the enemy so far has been using orange, red and green coloured smoke shells and bombs.

7. In order to clear mines, it is said, the enemy uses a special tank with some kind of a roller in the front which tears up the ground with steel rods.[22] The tank is supposed to have additional armour in front. These tanks are attached to special tank units and are separately attached to units making an attack. In his own lines the enemy has been using

---

22. This is a description of the Sherman Flail tank equipped with a roller with weighted chains, which thrashed the ground ahead of the tank to explode any mines.

cattle for discovering mine fields. The enemy pays careful attention to dummy mine fields.

8. In several cases the enemy has used radio in an attempt to confuse us. He has tried by radio to misdirect tanks and artillery and the direction of fire.

9. Several cases of unfair fighting have been observed.
   a. Requests for stretcher bearers to pick up the dead and then opening of fire on them.
   b. Misuse of the Red Cross emblem by supply-carriers and construction workers.
   c. Advance patrols which raise their hands and hold a white sheet, indicating they want to surrender, and then fire on approaching German soldiers.

Document 1/4[23]

Report on Battle Experience, 10th SS Panzer Division 'Frundsberg', July 1944

SS Panzer Grenadier Regiment 21, 10 SS Division 'Frundsberg'

The combat methods of English and American fighting units, and especially their complete air-superiority, make it essential that we learn from the following experiences.

No unit must be committed on the Western or Southern front without having been carefully trained on the basis of our recent experience.

The March

(i)   One must now figure at least three times the amount of time than previously allowed.

(ii)   If the tracked vehicles travel by rail, it is advisable to arrange the route in such a manner that the wheeled vehicles are close to the tracked vehicles in case rail transport is interrupted.

---

23. ISUM 58, 24 August 1944, from First US Army, G-2 Periodic Report No. 74.

(iii)   It is most essential to arrange road marches so that the main body reaches the march-objective before daybreak. The march may be started one or two hours before dark, because it will be completely dark before the enemy can exploit his air reconnaissance results.

(iv)   In case a larger unit is to be transferred along a route where no ground contact with the enemy is expected, the march will be more fluid if the unit marches in small serial instead of in one great column. The smallest group permissible, however, is the company.

(v)   Armoured vehicles must be completely camouflaged, so that even low flying planes cannot recognize the type of vehicle.

(vi)   In case of enemy air activity, especially when fighter-bombers appear, each vehicle will seek cover independently. All marching motion must cease completely so that the enemy does not realize a large unit is on the move.

(vii)   Bivouac areas will be revealed, therefore stay away from villages and civilians.

(viii)   The march will continue only as long as darkness allows, and not as far as figured out previously on maps. March only on side roads which must be well marked.

(ix)   Send strong road-reconnaissance groups far ahead and keep another one in reserve with the main body.

(x)   No lights are allowed at night.

(xi)   If a march in daylight is unavoidable keep an interval between cars of at least 200 yards.

(xii)   Each vehicle must have an air sentinel facing the rear.

(xiii)   Change the location of your CP frequently. In doing so avoid villages and the various sections far apart.

Combat

Basic Tactical Rules

(i)   Enemy combat action will be preceded by a thorough reconnaissance, mainly by planes and tanks. Planes are used for strategic as well as for tactical reconnaissance. The reconnaissance is usually supported by intense harassing fire. The fire is directed by a forward observer, who rides in a tank or accompanies the infantry.

(ii)   Enemy attacks usually take place only after heavy artillery preparation.

(iii)   Combat activity of the infantry at night is limited to individual patrols.

Conclusions:

(i)   The MLR is to be thinly occupied (observers at the most important points, roads and places overlooking the terrain are sufficient). Hereby the casualties from enemy artillery fire are cut down.

(ii)   Behind each sector local reserves are to be kept ready, each group linked to the next by means of tanks. After the enemy artillery fire lifts from the MLR, these reserves will immediately take position. They will then counter-attack the enemy who is very sensitive about close combat, and flank assaults at his weakest moment – the moment when he is forced to fight without artillery support.

(iii)   The reserves formed for the counterattack are to be committed by the commander of the respective main force.

(iv)   The commitment of the local reserves will immediately be reported to the next higher commander.

(v)   The terrain to the immediate front of our positions is to be mined by engineers. Dummy mines mixed in with live ones will accomplish this purpose.

(vi)   Digging in deeply is the first duty. In order to be protected against tree-bursts, recesses have to be built into the dugouts.

(vii)   Recognition of the MLR by the enemy should be made impossible by the use of reconnaissance patrols to the front of our lines and by excellent camouflage.

(viii)   Erection of our CP should be, as a rule, to the rear of our sector, but never outside of it.

Infantry:

(i)   The morale of the enemy infantry is not very high. It depends largely on artillery and air support.

(ii)   Infantry combat reconnaissance moves with great caution. In several cases strong detachments with machine guns have attempted to infiltrate through our lines. An uncontrolled, strong concentration of fire has been used to create panic and leave our forward troops under the impression they had been encircled and cut off.

(iii) Assembly areas for the attack are located at a considerable distance from the MLR. Enemy digs in and keeps tanks far to the front to protect his assembly areas.

(iv) The attacks have been launched on very narrow sectors with intermediate objectives. As soon as intermediate objectives were reached the enemy came to a halt to reorganize his troops, in order then to continue his planned attacks. The enemy endeavours rather to occupy terrain than to fight for it.

Conclusions:

(i) Do not be influenced by small local penetrations. At such moments do not spare the ammunition.

(ii) Leave infiltrated tanks to the men in the rear of the front line.

(iii) In a crisis employ all available weapons in order to stop the drive of the enemy attack.

(iv) Move to the front line only in places which are not under enemy observation.

(v) Relief of troops, ration supply and delivery of ammunition should be conducted at night only.

Artillery:

(i) The main arm of the attrition and annihilation tactics of enemy reconnaissance, it is well organized and manifold . . . Main effort of artillery fire is always in the area where the penetration is to take place. Strong interdicting fire on supply routes continues by day and night.

(ii) Artillery ammunition: Highly sensitive percussion fuze with very heavy shrapnel effect, but poor penetration power.

Conclusions:

(i) Dig in deeply.

(ii) Avoid all bunching up.

(iii)   Own attacks to advance in loose formations. Dig in at once after reaching intermediate objectives.

(iv)   Keep only very few vehicles behind the first line. (Dig in to protect tires and motors.)

(v)   Put warning markers at important crossroads and points which are constantly under artillery fire.

Tanks:

(i)   Good combat spirit; together with artillery they form support for the infantry. Skilled exploitation of terrain even off roads and highways. Always two tanks for reconnaissance thrusts. Accompanying infantry protects the tanks against anti-tank units.

(ii)   Enemy attacks have occurred mostly in groups of three to five tanks, thrust almost exclusively along roads. Tanks employed in support of infantry attack had only a few rifle men accompanying them. Mission of these tanks was to roll up the most forward line and cause confusion and panic in the rear areas by heavy firing. Their mounted machine guns are as a rule being used by the tanks for that purpose.

Own Employment:

(i)   Battle area consists of wavy terrain with poor visibility. In many cases terrain-waves cannot be crossed by tanks, therefore, with a few exceptions, tanks are road-bound. S-curves necessitate heavy use of deflection gear. Employment of tanks must be confined to the support of the infantry. Close contact and liaison from both sides are necessary. Paramount is the timely selection of trap positions to enable our own tanks to put attacking enemy armour out of action.

Conclusions:

(i)   Let enemy tanks approach. Fight at close quarters.

(ii)   If destruction is not possible let the tanks pass and try to destroy them in the rear areas. Separate infantry from tanks at this moment.

(iii)   Anti-tank defences must be employed in depth. (Mobile reserves.)

(iv)   Anti-tank units must be ready for immediate action. Of two approaching tanks, let the first one pass and attack the second one first.

(v)   Lay mines in front of our MLR.

(vi) Our own advancing tanks rely on mutual assistance and correct driving. First tank gives fire protection and guards the terrain to get a quick view of road, (recon, technique). When advancing with the infantry (always desirable) rifle-men proceed to the left and to the right of the road ahead of the tanks to eliminate surprises from the flanks.

(vii) Experience proves that many actions requiring lengthy preparations were failures, because the enemy had a chance to find out our intentions. He then employed his artillery and his air force and smashed our well planned attack. The best counter-measure discovered so far, is an inconspicuous filtering into the enemy sector which is only weakly occupied by his infantry. The troops should be divided into numerous small detachments, and good use of terrain waves and hedgerows must be made. At the same time, though, terrain which the enemy is in a position to observe and cover with fire must be avoided.

Air Force:

(i)   Owing to the fact that the enemy air force controls the air it does heavy damage to our supply system. Losses are created mostly by low flying planes (strafing and rocket-projectiles).

(ii) The biggest nuisance, though, are the slow-flying spotter planes which in utter calmness fly over our positions and direct fire, while our infantry weapons cannot reach them.

(iii) As [his] latest innovation the enemy employs low-flying planes at night which use searchlights, search out supply roads and knock out our trucks.

10 SS Panzer Division   Division C.P. 29 July 1944
'FRUNDSBERG'

The above report will be sent to all units for their information and exploitation.

For the Divisional Commander
The 1st General Staff Officer
signed
S. Wagner
SS. *Obersturmbannführer*
(lieutenant-colonel)

19

Document 1/5[24]

German Experience of the Invasion Battles

Wartime Intelligence Officer's Comments

The following is a translation of a German secret pamphlet issued 18 July 1944 dealing with the landings in Normandy . The precis is based on a report issued by Heeresgruppe 'B' on 30 June 1944.

1. Elimination of Defensive Weapons.

a) Flame-Throwers

Built-in flame-throwers of every kind never came into action because they were either prematurely eliminated by carpet bombing and artillery fire or outflanked by attack from the rear.

b) Mines

Mines in front of the fortifications were exploded by carpet bombing and artillery fire [and] thus rendered useless for the defenders. On the other hand, minefields in the rear areas proved very effective though German counter attacks were sometimes hampered by insufficient knowledge of their extent. Minefields must therefore be extended to great depth and guides provided for piloting reserves.

c) Goliath Tanks[25]

Remote control tanks (Goliath) were unable to go into action because they were either destroyed by carpet bombing and artillery fire or could not move in the cratered ground. They should rather be employed with operational reserves along big roads which Allied aircraft usually leave intact for future use by own troops, and to destroy bridges. They must be launched close to their target (200 to 300 metres) at the utmost.

---

24. ISUM 103, 11 October 1944.
25. The Goliath was a remote-controlled tracked demolition vehicle powered by either a gasoline engine or a small electric motor. It carried approximately 200lb of explosive which was detonated by remote control.

2.   Reserves

As a result of Allied air supremacy, Panzer and motorized divisions cannot be used by day if the weather is clear, and armoured battle groups only if sufficient anti-aircraft artillery protection is available.

Because Allied air superiority has thus made any timing impossible, mobile reserves must be kept well forward, and operational reserves will be employed for prepared counter attacks.

3.   Anti-aircraft Defence

As the majority of Allied air attacks are directed against targets behind the front line, anti-aircraft weapons, especially light anti-aircraft guns, must be echeloned in depth in the rear area. Headquarters, reserves, supply troops and telephone connections are not to be located in villages.

Headquarters and units will always dig slit trenches. Alternative battle positions will be provided. Attention must be paid to camouflage and air alerting.

4.   Defence against Airborne Forces.

Mass airborne enemy landings near or in the middle of own attacking troops are particularly unpleasant, and occasion high losses. An anti-aircraft barrage of all arms, even in the Line of Communications area also, must therefore be prepared. 2 cm fire, directed at descending paratroops, has proved the most effective method. Anti-aircraft-landing stakes have destroyed many gliders but in most cases inflict losses on the crews only if they are mined.

The organization of a close observation net, and protection of all important objectives, are vital. Mobile raiding parties must be held in readiness at all Headquarters and formations, including supply troops and columns, in order to carry out immediate counter attacks and thus prevent the formation of strong airborne striking forces.

5.   Supply

The transport of supplies is only possible at night. All officers responsible for supply, and all column commanders, must know their routes and detours by heart. Every driver who does not know the road must be provided with a sketch giving route and destination.

6. Traffic

Strict traffic control is necessary. Roads must be marked by signs. In the Line of Communication area, every unit commander must know all roads and paths without maps. Main roads will be avoided. On each journey, air sentries will be appointed. Slit trenches will be dug by the side of every road. For clearing and repairing roads, especially in villages, special forces (Engineers and civilians) will be employed.

Document 1/6[26]

Battle Experience of Recent Operations by 2nd Panzer Division, Whose Sector Is Being Taken Over by 36th Infantry Division

Characteristics of Fighting

The fighting of the Division on the invasion front is characterized by:

(a) The special nature of the country of Normandy

The country in which the fighting is taking place consists of meadow and bush land enclosed squarely by hedges, with embankments and sunken roads. This does not lend itself to engagements over large areas. All engagements soon resolve themselves into shock-troop and individual engagements. The possession of 'dominating heights' is often not as decisive as the possession of traffic junctions. Often the former cannot be exploited because hedges and trees limit visibility and field of fire, whereas road traffic arteries are essential, since it is only by roads that the heavy weapons, artillery and tanks can be brought forward. Nevertheless certain features always retain their dominating role, whereas conversely some traffic junctions can be dispensed with.

---

26. ISUM 37, 3 August 1944.

(b) The great material superiority of the enemy, even on so-called quiet fronts

The incredibly heavy artillery and mortar fire (of the enemy) is something new, both for the seasoned veterans of the Eastern front and the new arrivals from reinforcement units. Whereas the veterans get used to it comparatively quickly, the inexperienced reinforcements require several days to do so, after which they become acclimatized. The average rate of fire on the division sector per day is 4,000 artillery rounds and 5,000 mortar rounds per day. This is multiplied many times before an enemy attack, however small. For instance, on one occasion when the British made an attack on a sector of only two companies they expended 3,500 rounds in two hours. The Allies are waging war regardless of expense. In addition to this, the enemy have complete mastery of the air. They bomb and strafe every movement, even single vehicles and individuals. They reconnoitre our area constantly and direct their artillery fire. Against all this the GAF [German Air Force or Luftwaffe] is conspicuous by its complete absence. During the last four weeks the total number of German aircraft over the division area was six.

From the operations point of view, our own offensive operations by day, after completed assembly etc. – i.e. attacks prepared all 'according to the book', have little chance of succeeding. The assembling of troops is spotted immediately by enemy reconnaissance aircraft, and smashed by bombers, fighter bombers and artillery directed by aircraft; and if, nevertheless, the attacking troops go forward they become involved in such dense artillery and mortar fire, that heavy casualties ensue and the attack peters out within the first few hundred metres. The losses suffered by the infantry are then so heavy that the impetus necessary to renew the attack is spent.

Better results have been obtained by attacks prepared down to the last detail by assault detachments operating by night on a broad front. These penetrate the enemy positions noiselessly and in each individual case surprise and overcome the enemy, without the enemy artillery or air force having a chance to intervene. The primary condition for this is that each individual assault detachment be fully acquainted with its task and knows what to do in various circumstances, is in close liaison with its neighbours, and that the heavy weapons and artillery know exactly when to come into operation (usually only in the case of local failure when the element of surprise has not been achieved). The direction of such operations is less a question of large-scale elaborate planning than that of practical instruction and reminders. The mere fact that 'assembly has been completed before the attack begins' is of less importance than the fact that every company and platoon commander has thought of everything necessary to ensure the success of the operation of his assault detachment. It is an essential duty of the staff planning the operation to put everyone down to the lowest ranking commanders completely in the picture. An attack of this nature attains no far-distant objective, but proceeds only by small stages, night after night. But in the end it reaches its objective without paying a heavy toll in manpower. The more cunning and variable the fighting, the more successful the operation. This 'infiltration' has proved its worth in every case hitherto, as far as this division is concerned.

The fact that modernly equipped Panzer Divisions with two tank battalions and two (infantry) battalions with armoured half-tracked vehicles is not necessary for such fighting methods is another question.

In defence we must reckon with the fact that the attacking enemy simply smashes down the forward battle area with his massed artillery fire and aircraft. Hitherto the enemy has always succeeded, usually after a very short time, in occupying our main line of defence after a heavy barrage of this kind. It is, therefore, essential to maintain reserves in at least every battalion sector, which come forward immediately after the barrage had ended. Large masses of troops are not needed for this, but only a few assault detachments. The enemy infantryman is no fighter in our sense of the term, and consequently only a few machine guns are necessary to hold him – but these must be there at the right time. The divisional reserves must be employed immediately without waiting for the 'All Clear' in order to throw back the enemy, assault-troop fashion, in immediate counter-attack. In any case, when the enemy are firing a lot of smoke from weapons of all calibres everything is hidden in a blinding pall and a clear picture is impossible. But once the enemy has brought up his anti-tank guns and FOOs[27] and dug himself in, it is usually too late. Then the only remedy is to infiltrate on the following night. After several abortive attempts the British become cautious and finally discontinue their attacks.

---

27. FOO, Forward Observation Officer, was a British term for an officer who called down artillery fire from an observation post, which was connected by radio or land line to an artillery unit. The American equivalent would be a Forward Artillery Observer, or FAO.

Individual Arms

1. Panzer Grenadiers

The Panzer Grenadiers must be able to withstand the heavy artillery fire of the enemy. This is the decisive factor. They must therefore be dug-in deeply. Since the enemy use a very sensitive fuze,[28] overhead protection is necessary against shells which explode on striking trees. During the barrage the weapons must also remain under cover, or else they get clogged with mud and rendered useless.

Our soldiers enter the battle in low spirits at the thought of the enemy's enormous material superiority. They are always asking 'Where is the GAF?' The feeling of helplessness against enemy aircraft operating without any hindrance has a paralyzing effect, and during the barrage this effect on the inexperienced troops is literally 'soul shattering' – and it must be borne in mind that four-engine bombers have not yet taken part in attacking ground targets in this division's area. It is, therefore, essential for troops to be lifted out of this state of distress the moment the counter-attack begins. The best results have been obtained by the platoon and section commanders leaping forward uttering a good old-fashioned 'hurrah', which spurs on the inexperienced troops and carries them along. The revival of the practice of sounding a bugle call for the attack has been found to answer the purpose, and this has been made a divisional order. Moreover, the use of the bugle in territory where visibility is restricted enables the troops to know when and where the attack is taking place. An attack launched in this manner is an experience which new troops will never forget, and stimulates them into action again.

The Panzer Grenadiers fight as assault detachments, in this more depends on the NCOs than ever before. Only an energetic commander will get his men to go forward. For weaklings there is every inducement and opportunity to hide in the hedges. Close-combat weapons (flame throwers, anti-tank close-combat weapons, mines and explosive charges) are specially effective in country of this nature. In defence it may be expedient to deplete the front line in order to maintain sufficient reserves for counter-attack. Specially efficient NCOs should be selected for this.

The battle outposts and outlying piquets of all kinds must change their positions frequently and at irregular intervals. The enemy, especially the Americans, are experts in creeping up under cover of the hedges, and

---

28. This is not a reference to the proximity or VT fuze as it was not deployed in land fighting in Europe until late in 1944.

making frequent attempts to dislodge our piquets. They then cover their withdrawal with heavy mortar and artillery defensive fire.

The heavy weapons are compelled by the heavy fire to change their positions frequently. The enemy get their range very soon. It is not unusual to change positions ten times during the day. Therefore heavy and light infantry guns use only their 'roving' guns (see para 4). The evaluation and employment of enemy tactics has proved profitable. In one instance a counter-attacking company succeeded in turning the enemy mortars and firing smoke on the enemy, with the result that the enemy was misled into believing that a penetration had been achieved on the breadth of front covered by smoke, and brought down heavy artillery fire on his own troops.

2. Tanks

There is no question of tank employment in the true sense of the term. They can only be employed to accompany infantry. Their mobility is limited by the sunken roads and hedges. They can only penetrate the square areas enclosed by hedges at certain points, and these points are registered by the enemy anti-tank guns. Therefore the anti-tank weapon must be neutralized before the tanks advance again. Since the country favours close anti-tank combat, each single tank must have strong flank protection. It is unprofitable to employ more than one troop of tanks at the time. On sunken roads, which are often the only places where tanks can move, the first and last tanks of the column get knocked out and those in between are wedged in. Therefore the tanks must work in the closest cooperation with their infantry. The tanks must give HE[29] and MG[30] covering fire along the ridge of the hedgerow until the infantry have reached it by passing along the hedgerow running at right angles to it. The infantry then mop up, and then the tanks make another bound forward to the next hedgerow and the process is repeated. In this case the actual punch is delivered by the infantry and the fire power supplied by the tanks, and thus the control of the operation lies with the infantry.

3. Anti-tank

(a) SP – The employment of self-propelled anti-tank guns is extremely limited in country of this kind. Their low structure is a disadvantage, and in many cases they are unable to shoot over hedges and walls. Since the turret cannot be traversed, SP guns are completely helpless on

---

29. HE, High Explosive.
30. MG, Machine-gun.

sunken roads. The best method of employing them is to have them in a concealed position at the side of main roads. Therefore SP anti-tank guns should be kept back as reserves in order to intercept enemy thrusts along the main roads in the event of an armoured break-through.

(b) Tractor drawn[31] – There are not enough of these available. If it were possible to employ these regardless of loss (see News Sheet for Tank Troops, Issue No. 12, page 19[32]) they would be the best weapon in the main defensive line, since they can be properly camouflaged and dug in and can destroy enemy tanks at closest range and inflict severe casualties on the enemy infantry in the hedgerows by HE fire. But then they cannot get away again, and their loss has to be reckoned with as a matter of course. Losses and damage inflicted by enemy artillery fire must also be taken into account. The enemy uses his anti-tank guns in this way, but the German can no longer afford to do so. Therefore tractor-drawn anti-tank guns have been withdrawn and placed in depth in the main battle area, where they form the backbone of the main defence zone. The only available anti-tank weapons in front line proper are the close-combat weapons.

4. Artillery

The highest demands are made on the elastic use of artillery. Since our own artillery can only fire one tenth of the amount fired by the enemy, success can only be achieved by closest concentration and best possible ground observation. Therefore, forward observers must be placed well forward. Ample provision of means of communication are essential. Even in counter-attack the forward observers must be well forward. It is essential to maintain ample reserves of forward observers in order to avoid loss of all forward observers and their equipment during the enemy barrage. The allotment of 'SOS'[33] tasks which can be brought down

---

31. The American equivalent would be 'towed', meaning anti-tanks guns drawn by a towing vehicle. In the British army, any vehicle used to tow guns was designated a 'tractor'.

32. *Nachrichtenblatt der Panzertruppen*, a monthly pamphlet issued by the *Generalinspekteur der Panzertruppen*. Issue 19, dated June 1944, contains on page 19 an article titled '*Anlage und Augbau eines russischen Pak-Schewerpunktes*', describing how Soviet anti-tank units laid out their defences.

33. 'SOS tasks' is a Commonwealth artillery term for a defensive fire tactic. Properly termed DF (SOS) or Defensive Fire (SOS) it was the target deemed most critical and usually covered the most dangerous probable enemy approach route. Loaded guns would be laid on it, when not engaged on other tasks, and all an FOO had to do was request 'SOS Fire' and rounds would immediately come down on the SOS target.

automatically during an enemy attack has proved profitable. The artillery must change its position frequently, since it is spotted very rapidly and engaged with the aid of observation from the air. Good results have been achieved by 'roving' artillery troops and 'roving' guns which mislead the enemy as to the siting and strength of our own guns. Every attempt at harassing fire on the part of our artillery is promptly repaid many times over by the enemy. The artillery must take up different positions by day and by night. Here on the Western front, too, the siting of the artillery for all-round defence is the chief support for the main battle area.

5. Anti-Aircraft

The AA cannot protect everything. It is better to concentrate all the light and heavy troops on the point of main effort instead of scattering over the whole division area in troops and sections. In bad weather the AA can be used successfully in an artillery role. In this case, but in this case only, they are placed under command of the artillery. The siting of light AA troops in concealed positions close behind the main line of defence is with the sole task of engaging any artillery-spotting aircraft. By this means the division succeeded in shooting down two enemy aircraft in the course of a few days, and now the enemy spotting-aircraft keep a safe distance of approximately three kilometres from the main line of defence, whereas formerly they used to fly right over it.

6. Engineers

The engineers have been particularly successful in an infantry role in this terrain, thanks to their good training in assault and close combat methods. Since they are limited in their employment as infantry they must, however, be restricted to exceptional cases, as, owing to their numerical inferiority in this close country, their technical engineering tasks in front of and in the main defensive area, and the consolidation of positions in the rear, are of special importance. The commander of the engineers must exercise control over all engineers employed, including all engineer platoons. Owing to the limited means available, this is the only way whereby points of main effort on the part of the engineers can be created. Since the whole operation in this territory demands special skill, the construction of obstacles must be carried out with resource and variety. In this cut-up territory it is impossible to construct a continuous line of obstacles which can be covered by our own fire from medium and long range. The improvised anti-personnel mine S150[34] issued to the engineers has proved unsatisfactory, since the chemical igniter is unreliable. In order not to waste the effort of the engineers in purely labour tasks the division has combed out all surplus personnel from the supply columns to provide labour for consolidating the main battle area and rear positions. This method, adopted from the Eastern front, has also proved successful here.

7. Reconnaissance

This is performed exclusively as battle reconnaissance. The best results are achieved by bringing back PW,[35] even if these scarcely disclose anything. Signals interception within the division area scarcely provides any results, since the enemy hardly carries on any WT traffic and if he does, it is impossible to determine if this is taking place in front of our own sector. Listening in has so far produced no results. It is only done for monitoring our own traffic.

8. Signals

The principle remains the same. The division avoids WT traffic as far as possible. No enemy attempts at direction-finding have yet been confirmed, but this must still be reckoned with. There are signs that the enemy is monitoring our WT traffic.

9. Supplies

The entire supply system, including the receiving, works by night. The time is very short, with the results that losses are constantly incurred due to journeys made in the daytime (also by moonlight). The supply of ammunition is insufficient. Hitherto it has been out of the question to engage the enemy artillery. The enemy, too, is gradually realizing this, and is, therefore, moving up closer and closer in order to take full advantage of the range to disrupt our communications in the rear. Consequently our supply lines are under constant artillery fire, even at night. Our supplies of POL[36] are adequate, since the division is in a fixed position. The use of MT[37] traffic is reduced to a minimum. The supplies of food obtained from

---

34. The *Behelfs-Schützenmine* s.150, known as the 'pot mine', a cheap variant of the standard anti-personnel mine, was introduced late in the war.
35. PW, or Prisoner of War, is a Commonwealth military term, the American army used POW or PoW. Note that PW can be singular or plural in context.
36. POL is 'Petrol, Oil and Lubricants,' the supply of which is necessary for a modern mechanized army to move and fight.
37. MT is 'Motor Transport', soft-skinned vehicles.

the land are very good, but those obtained through supply channels are mediocre.

The question of spare parts and tyres is a serious problem. The division has to fetch everything over distances of hundreds of kilometres, so that in spite of the division being engaged in static warfare, its mobility gradually becomes less and less.

The enemy's air superiority presents an almost insolvable problem with regard to supplies.

Signed: *Freiherr* von Lüttwitz

Above battle experience of 2nd Panzer Division forwarded herewith for information and exploitation.

Signed: Marcks
GSO 1
for Commander 326 Infantry Div

Document 1/7[38]

Diary of 1st Platoon, 5th Company, 1st SS Panzer Grenadier Regiment, 1st SS Panzer Division, 9 July to 29 July 1944

Wartime Intelligence Officer's Comments

The following are extracts from a war diary kept by 2nd Section of 1st Platoon of 5th Company, 1st SS Panzer Grenadier Regiment of 1st SS Panzer Division. It indicates some of the formations and tactics used at company and platoon level within the past three weeks by this division. From 9 July – 29 July 1944 casualties in 1 Platoon had been four killed, four wounded and one missing. Total strength, exclusive of casualties on 29 July, was 40 All Ranks.

---

38. ISUM 37, 3 August 1944.

9 July 1944

Expecting general British offensive. Received order to get ready to disengage from the enemy. Company withdrew along railway lines, direction Bretteville 9866 – Louvigny 0065. In the afternoon II Battalion[39] of 1 SS Panzer Grenadier Regiment is relieved by 2 SS Panzer Grenadier Regiment. Move into rest area in wood SE of Louvigny. Digging in.

10 July 1944

0300 hrs. Receive order to relieve Reconnaissance Company 1000 metres north of rest area. Harassing enemy artillery fire. During morning there is a tank battle on our left. In the afternoon enemy attack repulsed. Our company supported by assault guns and three Anti-tank guns. Assault guns remain with our company. During night supplies do not arrive. Company without food.

11 July 1944

Harassing fire during night and morning. Intermittent barrage one hour at a time. At noon British attack with tanks and our company and 7 Company are involved. 7 Company withdraws. 2 Section in reserve counter attacks immediately, supported by two assault guns. We retake the old positions of 7 Company and advance a further 200 metres. During this counter attack one assault gun blows up. The English are driven back by our fire concentration. Mopping up section (*Sicherungsgruppe*) of I Battalion 2 SS Panzer Grenadier Regiment moves up. 2 Section withdraws having completed its task. 2 Section in first class spirits after their first hand-to-hand fight. Three stragglers come in from 3 Company 1 SS Panzer Grenadier Regiment. During night enemy rocket projector fire[40] on our positions. No casualties.

12 July 1944

Quiet. Engineers laying mines at night in front of 5 Company positions.

14 July 1944

Own rocket projectors firing on our positions. No casualties. Otherwise quiet day. We are to be relieved tonight.

---

39. The Wehrmacht designated battalions within regiments by Roman numerals, as in I, II, III, etc.
40. This is an interesting statement as the first Allied rocket weapons did not enter service until later in the war. It might well be that this was a case of 'friendly' fire from a German *Nebelwerfer* unit.

15 July 1944

At last relieved! The problem is, however, to leave our positions without casualties, as we have to cross a bridge which is under continuous artillery fire. Bridge crossed successfully on the double.

16 July

Rest area.

19 July 1944

Order received to move. 1 Platoon 2 Section of 3 Platoon and MMG section, form a 'battle company'. We are Corps reserve and move into a wood near Fresny 0040. Stay the night at Fresny, then move to the front. Company digs in. Pillboxes are built.

21 July 1944

During night building defence positions.

23 July 1944

Send out standing patrol at 0000 hrs, consisting of 1 MG section and two riflemen. We relieve standing patrol of 6 Company on height 135.

28 July 1944

Move in direction of road Caen–Falaise. Relieve II Battalion 2 SS Panzer Grenadier Regiment at 0130 hrs 29 July.

29 July 1944

Our first fatal casualty. Panzer Grenadier Habicht hit by a shell splinter.

Document 1/8[41]

Lack of Radio Discipline, July 1944

Top Secret,
29 July 1944

Army Group 'D', 2123 hrs[42]

Contrary to the orders of C-in-C West a panzer division has used its R/T[43] during its move to take up new positions.

This is a gross neglect of R/T discipline. It is especially necessary to refer the newly arrived formations to the Special Order Number 20 and to impress on them the danger and damage that are caused by R/T during the moving up of units, the taking up of battle positions, and the movement of troops to the front or to the rear.

Signed: Gimmler[44]
Lt. Gen

Document 1/9[45]

Operation Order, 1056 Grenadier Regiment, 89th Infantry Division, 4 August 1944

Wartime Intelligence Officer's Comments

This operational order was issued by 1056th Grenadier Regiment of 89th Infantry Division regarding the relief of 2 SS PGR on 2 Cdn Corps front during the night of 4/5 August 1944.

---

41. ISUM 45, 13 August 1944.
42. Army Group D or *Heeresgruppe* D was commonly called *Oberbefehlshaber* West, usually contracted to OB West.
43. R/T, Radio/Telephone or radio.
44. *Generalleutnant* Gimmler was the chief signals officer for OB West.
45. ISUM 43, 11 August 1944, from *2nd Canadian Corps Intelligence Summary*, No. 29, 9 August 1944

Grenadier Regiment 1056   Regimental HQ 4 August 1944
MUST NOT FALL INTO ENEMY HANDS

<u>Regimental Order for the Def of the Orne Sector south of Caen</u>
1. Not particularly highly trained Canadian troops are holding the general line St Martin–Tilly. The presence of armoured formations behind the enemy's front line has been established.

2. The regiment will relieve 2 SS Regiment after dark during the night of 4/5 August and will defend the general line, junction of R Laize and R Orne–May sur Orne–Verrières.

(*Here follow the exact Regimental Boundaries, Main Defence line and FDLs[46]*).

> Dispositions
> > RIGHT: Third Battalion
> > LEFT: First Battalion

Inter-battalion boundary: (*Here follow place names, inclusive and exclusive to the two battalions*).

4. The relief is to be prepared in good time by personal liaison between commands concerned and the withdrawal of the necessary battle outposts.

   Third battalion (1056 GR) will relieve second battalion 2 SS Regiment on the right following which first battalion (1056 GR) will relieve third battalion 2nd SS Regiment.

5. Existing Battle Instructions and fire plans for heavy weapons will be taken into effect.

   The tank destroyer units at present under command of battalions will remain so and will be fitted into the presently existing anti-tank plan.

   The second battalion after completion of its first task will act as protection for the artillery areas along the general line Cramesnil–southern edge Clinchamps. One company will be echeloned forward along the line Fontenay–le Val de Laize. This battalion will carry out patrols and will be prepared to act as a counter attack force in the event of enemy infiltration into the forward battalion positions. Its point of

---

46. FDL is Forward Defence Locality. The actual positions were not included in the original document.

maximum effort will be Verrières. In addition this battalion will afford protection for the artillery behind it.

All battalions will maintain contact with flanking units and will conform with the established signals network. All boundary areas will be secured.

6. Upon confirmation by the SS Divisional heavy weapons at present in position will remain so until our own weapons arrive.

Upon completion of the relief, which will be reported to Reg HQ, 2 SS Regiment will leave rear parties with the relieving battalions until [and] including the evening of 5 August. They will be made use of to the utmost in established battle positions and battle tasks.

7. 13 Company will take over the battle tasks of the troops being relieved and will position the heavy platoon in such a way that fire can be brought to bear both on Verrières and on the area west of St Martin. Defensive fire tasks in the areas named will be laid on.

14 Company will take up its position in depth in the main defence line so as to be able to repel enemy armoured attacks which may have their '*schwerpunkt*'[47] between Verrières and St Martin.

8. The Engineer platoon will revert to regimental command and will await further orders in the Forêt de Cinglais north of Point 121.

Platoon commander will report to Regimental HQ for orders.

9. Regiment Signals platoon will lay line to the three battalions. The two forward battalions will also be provided with wireless communication. OC Signals platoon will liaise with flanking formations regarding communications. The method of communication with third battalion of 189 Artillery Regiment will be considered and a report will be submitted to Regimental HQ forthwith.

10. Equipment such as transport, and offices not required for battle will be held south of the general line Grainville–St Germain–Cingal–Bois Halbout.

Above all, horses not engaged in the immediate battle will not be brought forward. Riding horses will be held in rear areas at all times.

11. Supply routes will be reconnoitred and marked as usual, as also will routes for reporting back. Regarding these last particular consideration

---

47. Lengthy books have been written about the German word *Schwerpunkt*, and its meaning and interpretation in the military context. Most simply, it might be translated as the 'centre of gravity', or critical area of a military operation.

will be given to the facilities of movement of runners, since the smallest movement picked up by Tactical Reconnaissance leads to immediate shelling.

Traffic will be reduced to the minimum, otherwise no unshelled routes will remain for communication purposes. Unit Camouflage officers are responsible for seeing that these orders are carried out to the letter.

12. I forbid the looting of deserted villages. Fodder and root crops will only be collected on the orders of unit commanders.

13. The Regimental Engineer Platoon will collect and dump in a park, all wire necessary for the building of defences. Battalions will strengthen the defence system currently.

14. All traces, minefield plans etc. will be taken over on relief.

15. Until a division main casualty station has been established the Regiment will provide for wounded and will establish an ambulance park in Fresney Le Puceux.

The Medical Company will be on call to the third battalion upon request by telephone.

Document 1/10[48]

Führer's Orders to the Commander of the St. Malo Garrison, 9 August 1944

Following instruction issued by the Führer to the Fortress Commander[49] of St. Malô is to be made known to all Fortress Commanders as a directive.

(1) Fortresses to be held as long as there is a single man and weapon available.

(2) A court is to be set up in St. Malô so that every inhabitant loses once and for all the desire for rebellion.

---

48. ISUM 56, 24 August 1944.
49. The fortress commander at St. Malô was *Oberst* Andreas von Aulock (1893–1968). He surrendered after an American siege lasting nearly three weeks.

(3) If there are any reliable *Osttruppen* there they can be given a completely free hand in these and similar situations in Brittany to act as counter-terrorists[50] and suppressors.

Document 1/11[51]

Order for Deployment, 85th Infantry Division, 12 August 1944

85th Infantry Division   CONFIDENTIAL

Ia (Operations)   *Division Battle HQ, 12 August 1944*
Order for the Employment of the Division in the Area North of Falaise

1. <u>Enemy</u> has stopped his strong attacks on our divisional front, due to heavy losses and successful counter-attacks by 1055 Grenadier Regiment. But this lull is only temporary, and it is to be expected that supported by strong tank formations in area St. Sylvain–Cintheaux–Grainville – he will renew his attack, so as to break through our positions.

2. <u>85th Infantry Division</u> is under command of 1 SS Panzer Corps. It will take over the sector of the SS Division *Hitler Jugend* and parts of the sector of 89. Infantry Division. It will defend the high ground NW of Maisieres–Quilly le Tesson. The HKL[52] running on general line of the heights close now to Le Bû-sur-Rouvres north edge of woods NW Rouvres and north of Quesnay.

3. <u>Infantry</u>. The following units will be employed:
   right 1053 Grenadier Regiment
   left 1054 Grenadier Regiment.

4. <u>Divisional Reserves</u>. 85th Division Fusilier Battalion.

---

50. The Germans referred to resistance fighters as 'terrorists'.
51. ISUM 48, 20 August 1944.
52. HKL or *Hauptkampflinie* was the German term for the Commonwealth term Main Line of Resistance or MLR. The HKL had to be defended at all costs.

Document 1/12[53]

Report of the Strength of the Divisional Formations under the Command of Seventh Army, 31 July 1944

(1) 2nd Parachute Corps

3rd Parachute Division

Has fought very well. Casualties have been covered partly by reinforcements from 2 Parachute *Ersatz u Ausb. Regiment*.[54] Fighting strength in infantry approx 2,500 men.

(2) 47th Panzer Corps

(a) 352nd Infantry Division

Has been engaged since the beginning of the invasion. In consequence of the heavy battles in which it has participated the division consists only of slender remnants. It has lost one artillery battalion. Odd elements still lacking.

(b) 2nd Panzer Division

Well-praised division with high fighting value. Had considerable casualties in the heavy fighting since 29 July, particularly in Panzer Grenadier company commanders.

(c) 116th Panzer Division

First time in battle. On that account been a little slow up to now. (Note: 2 August reported to have 15 Assault Guns, 50 [Mark] IVs, 52 {Mark] Vs [Panthers].)

(d) Panzer Lehr Division

Suffered considerably in consequence of casualties in personnel and equipment in defensive fighting west of Caen and west of St. Lô. Remaining elements two Panzer Grenadier companys [*sic*], one company reconnaissance battalion, artillery 4 guns, 10 tanks. (Note: 2 August tank strength reported to be 6 Vs [Panthers])

---

53. ISUM 56, 24 August 1944.
54. 2. *Ersatz-und-Ausbildungs-Regiment* was the training and replacement unit for the II Parachute Corps.

(e) 2nd SS Panzer Division

Division HQ and Signals Battalion efficient. Infantry: Grenadier Regiment *Deutschland*, I and II weak, III suffered high casualties [in] men and equipment. Tanks: Not known. Artillery: I Battalion (SP) <u>no guns</u>. IV [battalion] serviceable. II and III [battalions] have so far reported only slight losses. Panzer Jäger: 14 Assault guns. Reconnaissance: Heavy losses in equipment. Engineer: 1 company lost completely as far as equipment concerned. The other companys [*sic*] already withdrawn for rest and refit.

(3)   84th Corps

(a) 17th SS Panzer Grenadier Division

Division HQ not completely serviceable in either in men or equipment. Battle group being commanded by 2 SS Panzer Division Signals Battalion: Only W/T [Wireless or Radio] company serviceable. Infantry: Approximately three knocked out [knocked about?] battalions. Flak: Probably 65% losses. Artillery: Two battalions each with five guns. Heavy battalion with 5 SFH[55] [self-propelled howitzers] and 2 guns 10.5 [cm calibre] Engineer and Reconnaissance: Suffered heavy casualties in men.

(b) Battle Group 243 Infantry Division

Division HQ very efficient, although without signals communications and equipment. Complete fighting strength including engineers, artillery and signals so far reported as approximately 200 men.

(c) 353rd Infantry Division

Division HQ efficient. Infantry: 941 Grenadier Regiment strength 11 officers, 31 NCOs, 164 men and including HQ and HQ units. 942 Grenadier Regiment 14 officers, 40 NCOs, and 162 men. Artillery: 2 battalions each with 8 guns. I and IV with 91 Infantry Division Engineers: In operation with 2 SS Panzer Division. Supply Troops: 50 tons m/t [motor transport]. 120 tons horse drawn.

d) Battle Group 91st Infantry Division

Few details.

(e) 5th Parachute Division

In consequence of insufficient training and lack of experienced nucleus with the exception of 15 Para Regiment, it has not stood up to the burden of heavy fighting. Division has been split up by the fighting and is now

---

55. SFH is an acronym for *Selbstfahrlafett-Feld-Haubitze* or self-propelled gun. In this case a field howitzer and not an anti-tank weapon.

in various groups with other divisions or battle groups. Division HQ not engaged. 6 Parachute Regiment fought well but has suffered heavy casualties through continuous fighting. No figures available.

(f) 275th Infantry Division
Insufficient equipment. Heavy losses in personnel.

In 352nd Division and the SS divisions units are considerably mixed from 265, 266, and 275 Divs.

Document 1/13[56]

Appreciation of the Situation of Seventh Army, 10 August 1944

Teleprint Dated 10 August from Seventh Army to Army Group B Appreciating the Operation Situation on that Date

In the present situation there are only two possibilities. Either to stick to the operation already planned and ordered by the Führer, i.e., an attack with strong *Panzergruppe*[57] towards Avranches and thrust with the flank of the enemy attacking frontally, or to fight the Army's way eastwards out of its present situation, maintaining a strong Southern flank on both sides of the general line Domfront–Alençon in order to regroup itself by constructing a North to South front. The second possibility does not depend on the Army decision. It can only be envisaged within the framework of the whole situation by the higher command. As long as this is not the case the Army will apply itself with all means to the offensive operation already planned. Any delay in the present situation must lead to destruction.

---

56. ISUM 56, 24 August 1944
57. In this context, *Panzergruppe* is not a higher formation but an armoured *Kampfgruppe* or battle group.

Document 1/14[58]

Allied Evaluation of the Combat Worthiness of 12th SS Panzer Division 'Hitler Jugend', 18 August 1944

The recent capture of some helpful PW of this division has given some indication of what is left of this once formidable formation. Moving into the Normandy battle on D-Day, its strength was whittled down gradually but effectively, until now nothing but isolated remnants remain to carry on the struggle. The survivors have been grouped together into a number of battle groups designed to carry out a last-ditch stand where necessary, but whose primary function at present seems to be the keeping of infantry divisions in the line. These battle groups are as follows:

WUNSCHE[59]   OC 12 SS Panzer Regiment

WALDMULLER[60] OC I Battalion, 25th SS Panzer Grenadier Regiment

KRAUSE[61]   OC I Battalion, 26th SS Panzer Grenadier Regiment

OLBOETER[62]   OC III Battalion, 26th SS Panzer Grenadier Regiment

At the beginning of July, after a month's hard fighting, the division was withdrawn for a rest in the area of Falaise. The interlude was short-lived and about 20 July the division was ordered to form battle groups which were to be held ready for immediate action. When 21st Panzer Division moved west from Caen what was left of 25th SS Panzer Grenadier Regiment was put into the line south of Emieville 1365 intermingled with two battalions of 731st Grenadier Regiment of 711th Division.

Placing together interrogation reports and identifications seems to indicate that early on August 25th SS Panzer Grenadier Regiment consisted of two battalions. I Battalion, not having been seriously committed before this date, was still well up to strength with 450 men. II Battalion was being reorganised and probably contained the remains

---

58. ISUM 50, 18 August 1944.
59. *Standartenführer* Max Wunsche (1914–95), commander of 12th SS Panzer Regiment.
60. *Obersturmbannführer* Hans Waldmüller (1912–44), commander of 25th SS Panzer Grenadier Regiment, KIA, 8 September 1944.
61. *Obersturmbannführer* Bernhard Krause (1910–45), commander of I Battalion, 26th SS Panzer Grenadier Regiment.
62. *Sturmbannführer* Erich Olboeter (1917–44), commander III Battalion, 26th SS Panzer Grenadier Regiment. KIA 2 September 1944.

of both II and III Battalions of 25th SS Panzer Grenadier Regiment. Even this amalgamation failed to provide sufficient personnel, and a *Marsch Battalion*[63] from Germany provided an additional 35 reinforcements, giving this unit approximately 300 men. With those two battalions and about 20 tanks, the battle group Waldmüller was formed to meet the Canadian attack of 7/8 August. By the night of the 8 August II/25th SS Panzer Grenadier Regiment had about 30 men left, and I Battalion fared little better. So badly beaten was this *Kampfgruppe*[64] that since the 9 August nothing has been heard of it and prisoners from 25th SS Panzer Grenadier Regiment unattainable. Subsequent PW from 25th SS Panzer Grenadier Regiment believe that Gruppe Waldmüller was either absorbed by the other divisional battle groups or it is reforming somewhere far behind the lines.

For the next phase of the battle south of Caen, battle group; Wünsche comes into prominence. As OC of 12 Panzer Regiment he apparently took over what was now left of the Hitler Jugend. Under him were two battle groups utilizing the remaining battalions of 26th SS Panzer Grenadier Regiment, I and III Battalions.

Group Krause had about 250 men, while Olboeter was given some 250 to 300 men. These two groups, together with 30 to 35 Mk IVs and some Tigers, the latter of which were probably provided by 101 SS Heavy Tank Battalion of 1 SS Panzer Corps, comprised Group Wünsche. Mounted in armoured half-track vehicles and protected from the air by 5 x 2 cm AA-Anti-tank three-barrelled guns (*Drillinge*), this was to provide the backbone of the defence against our attack of 14 August.

In addition to acting as a counter-attack force, this party had the task of keeping the Army Infantry Divisions in the line. Thus Group Krause held a line of 600 metres, about 1000 metres behind 271 Infantry Division. As one PW put it, they were put there to 'boost the morale' of 271st Division. The Olboeter Group was apparently doing the same morale boosting for 85th and 89th Divisions in the neighbourhood of Quesnay Woods 1047. Wünsche and his tanks constituted the only real counter-attack element available to the division.

After our victorious drive of the last three days, what is left of battle group Wünsche can best be determined by a count of the SS dead lying in the fields and hedges between Quesnay and Falaise. A company of

---

63. *Marschbataillon*, a temporary unit formed for the purpose of moving replacements to the front.
64. A *Kampfgruppe* or battle group was an *ad hoc* unit formed for a single operation or mission. The German army was very skilled at forming these temporary units.

Group Krause which went into battle with 54 men had about 17 left on the morning of 15 August. The SS Panzer Grenadier who volunteered the information claimed that the rest of Krause had suffered a similar fate. From reports of mopping up operations in Falaise it would seem that the Olboeter party had received the same sort of treatment. Our tank claims should eliminate the bulk of the tank strength of Wünsche.

Today it may conservatively be said that 12th SS Panzer Division Hitler Jugend as a fighting divisional formation, no longer exists. That it may be reformed and regrouped is very probable. But it is most unlikely that such a reorganization can have any serious effect on the present battle south of the Seine.

Chapter 2

Defending Normandy

Extracts from the Telephone Log of Seventh Army and Fifth Panzer Army, June, July and August 1944

Document 2/1[1]

The Enemy Has Landed: Seventh Army Attempts to Deal with the Invasion, 6 June to 11 June 1944

Wartime Intelligence Officer's Comments

In the Seventh Army files captured by the Polish Armoured Division was found a telephone journal meticulously listing all conversations held by the Command and the Chief of Staff of Seventh Army with both lower and higher formations. It has given a remarkable insight into the problems that faced the enemy staff and the steps taken to meet them. Herewith are some extracts from the aforementioned journal. Remarks in brackets did not appear in the original text.

6 June 1944

0925 <u>Chief of General Staff,[2] Seventh Army to General Marcks,[3] Commander of LXXXIV Corps</u>

General Marcks urgently requests mobile reserves for the west of Caen,

---

1. ISUM 59, 27 August 1944.
2. The chief of staff of Seventh Army on this date was *Generalleutnant* Max-Josef Pemsel (1897–1985).
3. *General der Artillerie* Erich Marcks (1891–1944), commander, LXXXIV Corps. KIA 12 June 1944.

since 21st Panzer Division is committed to the right of the Orne. He would like to have 12th SS Panzer Division.

1655 Chief of Staff reports situation to Chief of Staff Western Command[4]
Chief of Staff, Western Command (Rundstedt's HQ[5]) emphasizes the desire of Supreme Command (Hitler) to have the enemy in the bridgehead annihilated by the evening of 6 June, since there exists a danger of additional sea and airborne landings for support. In accordance with an order by General Jodl,[6] all units will be diverted to the point of penetration in Calvados. The beach-head there must be cleaned up by not later than tonight. The Chief of the General Staff declares that such would be impossible. The Commander of Army Group 'B' (Rommel)[7] states that 21st Panzer Division must attack immediately regardless of whether reinforcements arrive or not. The Supreme Command has ordered that the bad weather conditions of the night of 6–7 June be utilized for the bringing up of reserves.

2240 Commander of Seventh Army (*Generaloberst* Dollmann)[8] reports to Field Marshal Rommel
Seventh Army Headquarters has repeatedly requested air support at Riva Bella without success. Field Marshal Rommel answers that Air Force units are just on the point of changing location.

2400 Chief of Staff of Seventh Army to Commanders of 21st Panzer Division and 716 Infantry Div
716th Infantry Division is still defending itself at strong points. Communications between Division, Regimental and Battalion Command Posts, however, no longer exist, so that nothing is known as to the number of strong points still holding out or of those liquidated . . . The Chief of General Staff gives the order that the counter-attack of 7 June must reach the coast without fail, since the strongpoint defenders expect it of us.

---

4. The chief of staff at OB West at this time was *General der Infanterie* Günther Blumentritt (1892–1967).
5. *Generalfeldmarschall* Gerd von Rundstedt (1875–1953) was the *Oberbefehlshaber West* (OB West), and had Army Groups B and G, responsible for the defence of France, under his command.
6. *General der Infanterie* Alfred Jodl (1890–1946), the chief of staff of *Oberkommando der Wehrmacht* (OKW), the armed forces high command.
7. *Generalfeldmarschall* Erwin Rommel (1891–1944), commander of Army Group B, responsible for the defence of the Channel coast.
8. *General der Artillerie* Friedrich Dollmann (1882–1944), commander of Seventh Army. Dollmann died on 28 June 1944.

Wartime Intelligence Officer's Comments

These conversations show that the High Command intended to defeat the invasion on the beaches. It was to this end that both 12th SS Panzer Division and 21st Panzer Division were committed in the first 24 hours.

8 June 1944

0840 Chief of Staff to Army Group 'B'
An English operational order has been recovered from the water. Contents will be transmitted by telegraph.

0810 Chief of Staff Army Group 'B'[9] to Seventh Army
An urgent demand for information on the situation by order of Field Marshal Rommel, since the report telegraphed this morning has not yet come through.

(a) Extracts are given from the operation order of VII American Corps, according to which the following units are committed:

> On the Right: VII American Corps with four divisions.
> Mission: To attack northward from the Carentan–Quineville bridgehead and to take Cherbourg from the land side.
> On the Left: V English Corps, with four English divisions and two American divisions in the Calvados sector.
> Mission: To take Bayeux and join up with the American VII Corps at Carentan.

(b) Our own situation:
> Bayeux in the enemy hands. Attack by I SS Panzer Corps, because of the situation in the air, was not possible until this morning. Direction of the attack: north and north-west of Caen, in the direction of the coast. Field Marshal Rommel interrupts and orders I SS Panzer Corps to initiate a point of main effort on the left as quickly as possible, taking all three divisions.

0830 Chief of General Staff to Field Marshal Rommel
The western coast of Cotentin is clear of the enemy and as a consequence the necessity arises to direct II Parachute Corps either towards Bayeux or Cherbourg. Field Marshal Rommel orders that the right wing of II Parachute Corps, with two divisions, be advanced first of all, toward St. Lô. On inquiry, the Chief of General Staff makes it known that there

---

9. *Generalleutnant* Hans Speidel (1897–1984) was the chief of staff of Army Group B.

still exists no communications with the HQs of II Parachute Corps and the divisions, so that nothing is known as to the present location of the Corps units. The Corps has been ordered to set up radio communications with Seventh Army Headquarters immediately. The establishment of communications appears to have been delayed by air attacks, particularly in the Avranches area.

Wartime Intelligence Officer's Comments

Our superiority in the air was so great that despite the capture of these Operation Orders, Seventh Army was unable to take immediate, effective action against the bridgehead.

9 June 1944

1730 Conversation of Field Marshal Rommel, in Army HQ, with the Commanding General and Chief of Staff, Seventh Army

(1) The Chief of Staff acquaints those present with the situation as just reported by the Commanding General LXXXIV Corps on the Cotentin Peninsula. The essential point is that the enemy has not succeeded, until now, in effecting a junction with the Carentan Bridgehead, by means of his attack from Isigny toward the west. 6 Parachute Regiment, which has fought better than expected, has been given the order to hold Carentan to the last man.

(2) Field Marshal Rommel orders that the enemy must be prevented at all costs from:
    (a) Getting the fortress of Cherbourg and harbour, in his hands
    (b) Establishing the connection between both bridgeheads; that west of the Orne and that west of the Vire.

(3) The Chief of Staff expresses the opinion that the enemy, because of the increased resistance south of Montebourg, will commit more airborne troops in order to take possession of Cherbourg rapidly. Field Marshal Rommel does not share this opinion, since the Supreme Command expects a large landing on the Channel Coast within the next few days, and therefore the enemy will not have more airborne troops available.

(4) As to future operations, the Commanding General, Seventh Army, is of the opinion that he will only go over to the attack when II Parachute Corps is ready for commitment and when the attack can be coordinated with the counter-attack of I SS Panzer Corps.

Field Marshal Rommel concurred with this opinion. However, the defence of Cherbourg is to be conducted independently and started immediately, with the greatest vigour.

2400 <u>General Marcks acquaints the Chief of Staff with the unfavourable development at the Ste. Mère Eglise bridgehead</u>

The enemy has broken out, both to the west, across the inundated land and also in a northerly direction towards Montebourg. In the west he has reached Font L'Abbé. In the north he has crossed the road Montebourg–Quineville. The Commanding General, LXXXIV Corps, believes that tomorrow will be the decisive day for the battle of the Cherbourg fortress. He has given strict instructions that the line reached this evening must be held at all costs. General Marcks makes the following demands:

(1) Exceptional reinforcements, of our own Air Force, to combat the enemy superiority
(2) Likewise, the sending in of a large amount of Anti-tank weapons
    He maintains that the units brought up have been most inadequately equipped and that, particularly, the 'stove-pipes'[10] (Bazookas), etc. are effective against enemy tanks only at a few metres' range . . .

Wartime Intelligence Officer's Comments

Here Rommel himself indicates that the handling of the situation west of the Orne was governed largely by the appreciation of the High Command that further large landings were expected on the Channel Coast.

10 June 1944

1100 <u>General Meindl, Commander II Parachute Corps,[11] reports to Chief of Staff</u>

3 Parachute Division must be brought forward piecemeal, because of lack of fuel. At the present time one regiment is located approximately east of St. Lô. The main body of the division is still in Brittany.

77th Infantry Division is, in the opinion of General Meindl, with its advance elements already in the area of Valognes, and the remainder in the region of Avranches.

---

10. 'Stove pipe' or *Ofenrohr* was the nickname of the *Panzerschreck*, an 88mm anti-tank rocket launcher modelled on the early bazooka. It was a highly effective weapon and much feared by Allied tank crews.
11. *General der Fallschirmjäger* Eugen Meindl (1892–1951), commander of II Parachute Corps.

1245 Commander, LXXXIV Corps, talks to the Chief of Staff
The advance units of 17 SS Panzer Grenadier Division are stuck in the St. Lô area because of lack of fuel.

The Chief of Staff underlines the fact that it is not only a question of preventing a junction of the two enemy groups in the area of Bayeux and Carentan, but the main task is that of preventing the enemy from cutting off the Cotentin peninsula by a further advance to the west and south-west.

HQ LXXXIV Corps and their intentions thereto: The object is not merely preventing the enemy from taking possession of roadways, but to destroy and wipe out the enemy.

1700 Chief of Staff informs Army Group 'B'
Panzer Group West has sustained enemy attack and is now engaged in local counter-attacks. It is evident, from reports, that Panzer Group West has been prevented from carrying out its basic mission. He points out that according to existing orders, traffic regulations in combat are governed by C in C, West. It has been shown, however, that this can be done properly and effectively only by Seventh Army.

Chief of Staff Army Group 'B' presents the views of the Supreme Commander of the Armed Forces (Hitler) that there should be neither a withdrawal, fighting to the rear, nor a disengagement rearward to a new line of resistance, but that every man will fight and fall, where he stands . . .

2330 Chief of Staff to Quartermaster-General
Orders given to draw off 65% of the Anti-tank, close defence weapons (*Panzerfaust*[12] and *Panzerschreck*), from 265 and 266 Infantry Divisions and the remaining elements of 275 Infantry Divs, as well as 5 Parachute Division. These weapons are to be sent, at once, to the St. Lô area (Camp Michel) and put at the disposition of LXXXIV Corps.

Wartime Intelligence Officer's Comments

Despite the lack of fuel, the shortage of Anti-tank weapons necessitating the divisions in Brittany being milked of theirs, and an ever-worsening tactical situation, the finger in Berchtesgaden underlines the words 'No withdrawal'.

---

12. The *Panzerfaust*, or 'armoured fist' was a disposable anti-tank weapon consisting of a launching tube and a missile with a shaped charge.

11 June 1944

0520 General Marcks LXXXIV Corps to Chief of Staff Seventh Army
He asks when 17 SS Panzer Grenadier Division will be ready for commitment, since the situation on the right flank is critical. 352nd Infantry Division now only has a very small combat value; gaps between them and their right flank neighbour become constantly larger. Communications with this division no longer exist.

0920 Chief of Staff informs Army Group 'B'
Nothing is known as to whether the enemy has effected a union across the Vire. Panzer Group West has been knocked out by a direct bomb hit on its HQ; command has been given to I SS Panzer Corps. Road traffic must be dictatorially governed, directly, by Seventh Army through the employment of road commanders.

Wartime Intelligence Officer's Comments

The losses in men, the disruption of communications and the traffic problems are only some of the mounting problems now facing Seventh Army.

Document 2/2[13]

Feldmarschall von Kluge
Deals with Operation Cobra, 31 July

Wartime Intelligence Officer's Comments

The following extracts are from telephone conversations of Field Marshal von Kluge Commander in Chief, West,14 dated 31 July 44. They deal with the period when the Americans were exploiting their success west of St. Lô designed to cut off the balance of the Cotentin Peninsula. Having taken

---

13. ISUM 59, 27 August 1944.
14. *Generalfeldmarschall* Hans-Günther von Kluge (1882–1944). Von Kluge replaced Rundstedt at OB West but committed suicide when he was in turn replaced by Field Marshal Model in August 1944.

Coutances and Granville they were now proceeding towards Villedieu and Avranches, which finally fell on the night of 31 July. Since D-Day General Marcks of LXXXIV Corps has been killed and replaced by Lt-Gen von Choltitz,[15] *while General Hausser has filled the vacancy as Commander of Seventh Army, created by the death of General Dollman. Field Marshal von Kluge has taken over the unprofitable job of Commander in Chief West from his weary predecessor, von Rundstedt.*

31 July 1944

0100 <u>With Lieutenant-General Speidel,[16] Chief of Staff Army Group 'B'</u>
LXXXIV Corps receives orders to withdraw to line Villedieu–Avranches, whether orders are still coming through is questionable.

The High Command is to be informed that the left flank has collapsed.

0145 <u>With General Farmbacher, Commander XXV Corps[17]</u>
Two companies of 266 Division are moving toward area south of St. Malô as well as one weak battalion of the Parachute Infantry Training Regiment.

General Farmbacher requests a most forceful order to the Navy, whose cooperation is insufficient.

He can only carry the responsibility if he can issue orders and does not have to ask for everything.

0920 <u>With Lieutenant-General Speidel</u>
The enemy has reached Avranches, our assault guns were obviously pushed back by the enemy. Intervention by 77th Infantry Division is unknown. LXXXIV Corps has already ordered withdrawal to the line Villedieu–Avranches. Infantry Regiment 957 of 363rd Infantry Division has apparently not moved owing to hitherto unprecedented enemy fighter-bomber activity. Enemy tank advances on Granville and Avranches were preceded by an umbrella of enemy fighter-bombers. This made any movement almost impossible.

All in all, the situation in the area Villedieu–Avranches is completely unclear. The troops have suffered high losses in men and equipment by strong air activity and the morale has greatly suffered.

---

15. *General der Infanterie* Dietrich von Choltitz (1894–1966) assumed command of the 84th Corps after Marcks was killed in action.
16. See note 9 above.
17. *General der Artillerie* Wilhelm Farmbacher (1880–1970), commander XXV Corps and commandant of the Lorient fortress.

On the left flank of Panzer Group West no clear picture. Situation absolutely unclear. The responsibility for the great crisis which has occurred here lies with the order of the Seventh Army to try, against the will of LXXXIV Corps, to break through to the south and south-east. 91st Infantry Division has established a thin line of resistance along the line Cerences–Brehal. As a consequence of the breakthrough of enemy armoured spearheads near Cerences the whole Western front has been ripped open, the key point Avranches has been taken by the enemy and Villedieu is threatened. Villedieu, springboard for the east and south as well as Avranches, is the anchor point for Brittany, [and] has to be held under all circumstances or else has to be recaptured.

To accomplish this, on our own, with the troops in their present conditions, is impossible. Air reconnaissance has to clarify the situation in the area Villedieu–Avranches immediately.

Question: What forces can be thrown in immediately?

Answer: 708th Infantry Division can be there in about eight days. This division is therefore out of the question for clarification of the situation. A second regiment of 363rd Infantry Division must be brought up immediately with all available transportation. What is important is the sealing off of the roads from Villedieu to the east and south as well as from Avranches to the south. Sealing off in Pontaubault, south of Avranches, is probably possible. The situation must be controlled under all circumstances, because this is the decisive phase. The seriousness of the situation must be explained to the Army High Command.

0935 <u>With Chief of Staff Seventh Army, Colonel von Gersdorff</u>[18]
Yesterday's heavy fighting was successful for the enemy only because he paralysed all our movements by employing fighter-bombers on an unprecedented scale.

The greatest worry of the Field Marshal is Villedieu as a key point for enemy operation towards the east and south. Whether or not Villedieu is occupied by the enemy has not been established. The Field Marshal therefore agrees to the withdrawal of 2nd SS Panzer Division to line Percy–Villedieu. Obviously the enemy is still very weak in Avranches. We are dealing with an advanced armoured spearhead there. We have to throw in whatever possible. The intention is to bring up 89 and 84 Infantry Divs.

1000 <u>With Commander XXV Corps</u>
Commander in Chief West informs General Farmbacher about the

---

18. *Oberst* Rudolf, *Freiherr* von Gersdorff (1905–80), chief of staff, Seventh Army.

situation, especially as far as the sector Villedieu–Avranches is concerned. It is necessary to close the Avranches gap by stripping the area of St. Malô of forces as far as possible in order to prohibit the influx of the enemy into Brittany.

General Farmbacher mentions that in spite of the weakness of the army, a great number of troops of the navy and air force remain unemployed within the corps area; a situation which appears unjustifiable. This personnel, however, does not come under the jurisdiction of the Commanding General.

1045   With General Warlimont (Hitler's representative)[19]

The Commander in Chief West gives the situation within the XLVII Panzer Corps and especially the LXXXIV Army Corps. The enemy is in Avranches and maybe also in Villedieu. These key positions for future operations must be held at all costs. Another advance of the enemy out of Avranches into Brittany was sealed off at Pontaubault. All available forces from St. Malô were brought up. The idle forces of the navy and air force which are absolutely needed for the decisive fight, the price of which is the future or the end of the situation in the bridgehead, are, according to Commanding General XXV Corps, not obtainable. General Warlimont agrees to refer this suggestion to the Führer.

Commander in Chief, West describes the seriousness of the situation with impressive eloquence. Whether the enemy can be stopped at this point is still questionable. The enemy air superiority is terrific, and smothers almost every one of our movements. Every movement of the enemy, however, is prepared and protected by its air force. Losses in men and equipment are extraordinary. The morale of the troops has suffered very heavily under constant murderous enemy fire, especially, since all infantry units consist only of haphazard groups which do not form a strongly coordinated force any longer. In the rear areas of the front, terrorists, feeling the end approaching, grow steadily bolder. This fact and the loss of numerous signal installations makes an orderly command extremely difficult. LXXXIV Corps has reached a certain degree of disintegration. Part of the responsibility for the present situation rests with the order of Seventh Army for the northern front to break through towards the south and south-east. Commander in Chief West has, as soon as he was informed thereof, changed this order to reconstitute the front with the forces at hand. Fresh troops must be brought up from the

---

19. *General der Artillerie* Walter Warlimont (1894–1976), deputy chief, OKW Operations Staff.

Fifteenth Army or from somewhere else. Commander in Chief West recalls herewith the World War I example, in which Parisian buses were used to bring up troops to the Allied front. Now, as then, all available means must be exhausted. It is, however, still impossible to determine whether it would be possible to stop the enemy.

Document 2/3[20]

The End in Normandy: Telephone Log of Seventh Army, 6 August to 7 August 1944

Wartime Intelligence Officer's Comments

These extracts concern frantic calls put through to Seventh Army on the 6th and 7th August 1944, during the abortive attempt of the armoured elements to break through at Mortain and reach Avranches.

The attack was undertaken by XLVII Panzer Corps, having under command the bulk of the available German armour in the west, including 1st SS Panzer Division which had just been switched from the Caen area. The staggering effect of Allied fighter-bombers against this armour is testified to by Colonel Reinhard in his conversation to the Chief of Staff of Seventh Army on the 7th August 44. The tenseness of the situation, as the attack had obviously failed and the American counter-attack was succeeding, must have been considerably increased at midnight when the first news of the commencement of the Canadian Operation TOTALIZE reached the ears of the Seventh Army Commander to add to all his troubles.

6 August 1944

2140 Chief of Staff to G-3, Colonel Helmdach[21]

Today has been characterized by strong attacks against the LXXXIV Corps. As a whole, the penetrations could be sealed off. Our own losses

---

20. The telephone log of Seventh Army for 6 to 16 August was extracted from the following Intelligence Summaries: 84, 22 September; 90, 28 September; 119, 27 October; 123, 1 November; and 132, 9 November. The transcripts of the log were originally circulated in SHAEF Intelligence Summaries in October and November 1944.
21. *Oberst* Erich Helmdach was the IA, or Operations Officer, of Seventh Army.

were great. Under all circumstances must replacements be made available for LXXXIV Corps. A replacement battalion must at once be made available for LXXXIV Corps. This is especially important and decisive.

2200 CG XLVII Panzer Corps to CG Seventh Army:
Those elements of Wisch which were to participate as the first in '*Lüttich*' (codename for the counter-attack towards Avranches) were only sighted in Tinchebray at 2120 hrs. von Lüttwitz, CG 2nd Panzer Division, did not receive the units promised to him by 116th Panzer Division. The Commanding General XLVII Panzer Corps requests that the Division Commander of 116th Panzer Division (von Schwerin[22]) be relieved. This division practically always mucks up the situation. Von Lüttwitz still lacks Panthers, the Assault Gun Brigade and the motorized artillery of II Parachute Corps. Therefore, the attack along the right wing will probably be delayed for hours.

CG Seventh Army: This does not alter the fact the '*Lüttich*' be executed as ordered.

CG Seventh Army: I have to admit this is a bad start. Let us hope that the loss of time this evening can be made good by fog tomorrow morning.

7 August 1944

1430 CG LXXXIV Corps to Chief of Staff:
The Commanding General reports an enemy penetration of 600 m. from the north towards St. Germain. Details are not known as yet. It can not yet be determined what units the local Commander has committed at the point of enemy penetration.

1445 Chief of Staff to General Bulowius:[23]
A radio message from XLVII Panzer Corps reports to Army unusually strong fighter-bomber activity over their area of attack. The Corps makes an urgent request for air support. General Bulowius informs Chief of Staff that his planes are over the area of attack now, with the mission to concentrate on fighter-bombers.

---

22. *Generalleutnant* Gerhard, *Graf* von Schwerin (1899–1980), commander of the 116th Panzer Division. Schwerin was removed from command for his actions during the Mortain counter-offensive.
23. *Generalleutnant* Alfred Bülowius (1892–1968), commander of II *Fliegerkorps*.

1500 Colonel Reinhard, XLVII Panzer Corps to Chief of Staff:[24]

The Colonel inquires about our air support. The Chief of Staff says that according to General Bulowius, our planes should be over the area of attack now. Colonel Reinhard claims that he has not seen a German plane all day. The activities of the fighter-bombers are said to be almost unbearable. The *LEIBSTANDARTE* (1st SS Panzer Battalion) also reports that fighter-bomber attacks, of such calibre, have never before been experienced. The attack of the *LEIBSTANDARTE* has been stopped. Five of their tanks are out of action.

1540 CG of the 7th Army speaking from LXXXIV Corps to the Chief of Staff:

The situation on the left wing, in the area of the 116th Panzer Division (von Schwerin), is absolutely unclear. Call [Major] Guderian[25] [Chief of Staff 116th Panzer Division] and inform him that he will have von Schwerin establish his Command Post with him.

1600 Chief of Staff to Commanding General LXXXI Corps:

CG LXXXI Corps reports: Nothing new in the north. 90th US Division with 357th Brigade has been identified in the centre. Nothing special between Mayenne and Domfront. Enemy has penetrated into Suzanne.

1700 Chief of Staff to Colonel Wiese, LXXXI Corps:[26]

Chief of Staff: Would it be of any value to enlarge the sector toward Angers? I believe that it is necessary to bring the whole sector under one command.

Wiese: We have neither the communications nor the command facilities necessary, however, uniform command seems to serve our purpose.

Chief of Staff: You would have to use Colonel Helmdach as operational Headquarters. He and his signal communication facilities, plus his auxiliary units are at your disposal. You will be in command.

1720 Chief of Staff to G-3, Colonel Helmdach:

Chief of Staff: We must bring the entire left sector under uniform command. LXXXI Corps will take command of the area extending to the left boundary of the Army. You and your communications will be

---

24. *Oberst* Walter Reinhard was the chief of staff of XLVII Panzer Corps. He replaced *Graf* von Schwerin as commander of the 116th Panzer Division when Schwerin was removed from command.

25. Major Heinz-Günther Guderian (1914–2004), IA or chief of staff, 116th Panzer Division.

26. *Oberst* R. Wiese was the chief of staff of LXXXI Infantry Corps.

under the command of Gen. Kuntzen,[27] that is, you will submit your proposal for the conduct of the operation to him for decision. Has General Kuntzen any signal communication facilities?

G-3: He has.

Chief of Staff: The Commanding General, Army will not let the Division (*Götz von Berlichingen*) be dissolved. That was a misunderstanding. The report on stragglers and their condition has been approved.

1740 Colonel von Scholz, Air Force, to Chief of Staff:[28]

von Scholz: Is there a change in the bomb line?

Chief of Staff: No.

von Scholz: Our own fighter units have been pursued by enemy fighters, as soon as they took off and as a result they could not reach their target.

1800 Chief of Staff to Colonel Reinhard, Commander XLVII Corps:

Our fighters have been engaged in aerial combat from the time of take-off and were unable to reach their actual target area. They hope, however, that their aerial engagements helped, just the same.

Colonel Reinhard: There was no noticeable relief. There are no reports that the operation of enemy fighter-bombers has decreased.

Chief of Staff: Has Schwerin started to attack?

Colonel Reinhard: Yes, at 1630. There are no reports as yet and as a result, I do not know if they were able to advance. One moment, another message is coming in. 20 Tanks attacking Mortain from the west.

1812 Colonel von Criegern, LXXXIV Corps to Chief of Staff:[29]

Chief of Staff: Did you have the impression that enemy attacks are as strong as yesterday.

Colonel von Criegern: That is hard to tell, however, he continues to attack. I believe his attack seems as strong because our troops are weak. Three penetrations near Vire, on the left flank of 353rd Infantry Division, and in the vicinity of Bois de la Haye. An unconfirmed report reached us that the enemy keeps rolling up our front with his tanks, from the north, and strong fighter-bomber activity. I again stress that this is unconfirmed.

Chief of Staff: Have you heard from Schwerin?

Colonel von Criegern: No, we have no communications with them any longer. The troops are disappointed at the absence of our planes.

---

27. *General der Panzertruppe* Adolf-Friedrich Kuntzen (1889–1964), commander of LXXXI Corps.
28. This officer cannot be further identified from the information given.
29. *Oberst* Friedrich von Criegern (1904–45), chief of staff, LXXXIV Corps.

1815 Chief of Staff to Colonel Tempelhoff, Army Group B:[30]

Chief of Staff: There must be some misunderstanding about the message regarding the dissolution of units. The Commanding General, Army, says that the case of 17th SS Panzer Grenadier Division does not come under his jurisdiction and that *Reichsführer* SS has to make the decision. The Division will remain as a combat Group within 2nd SS Panzer Division.

1835 G-3 to . . .:

I have 125 Mk 4s' and 95 Mk 5s' at my disposal. It must be established who needs them and where the necessary personnel can be obtained. The tanks must be repaired.

1900 G-3, Colonel Helmdach, to Chief of Staff:

G-3: Enemy tanks have been observed in Suzanne and are reported to be advancing toward the east. It still appears that enemy tanks are on the road Laval–Le Mans.

Chief of Staff: There is only one possibility for remedying the situation and that is the thrust we are planning. It will bring far-reaching relief.

1930 Colonel Tempelhoff to Chief of Staff:

Chief of Staff: This is the situation on the extreme southern wing of the Army: Strong enemy forces in the direction of Alençon–Le Mans. One Division (90th US Infantry Division) has been identified near Mayenne and probably one or two divisions further south. It must be assumed that the enemy operates here with from three to four Divisions. We have to realize that the forces we put against them are not strong enough to nail him down. There are three possibilities:

   (1) To hold the position to the last man;

   (2) To withdraw to the east and protect Le Mans. In this there is danger that the enemy will succeed in breaking through the gap, into the left flank of the Army.

   (3) Withdrawal in a northerly direction, whereupon Le Mans will have to be given up.

1940 CG, Army Group West, to Chief of Staff:

Chief of Staff: Army has decided on the third alternative. However, inasmuch as the situation affects the decision of Army Group, they are asked for a decision on the future conduct of the battle.

---

30. *Oberst* Hans-Georg von Tempelhoff (1907–85), operations officer, Army Group B.

Gen Speidel, Army Group West: A combat directive cannot be given as yet. The decision rests with the Field Marshal.

Chief of Staff: The actual attack has not made any progress since 1300 because of the large number of enemy fighter-bombers and the absence of our own Air Force. Army has ordered that the attack be continued as soon as the air situation permits.

1945 Gen Kuntzen, CG LXXXI Corps, to Chief of Staff:
The General requests a combat directive and continues: I estimate the enemy strength to be one panzer division.

Chief of Staff: I hope to have a decision from Army Group by tonight.

1950 Chief of Staff to Colonel von Criegern, LXXXIV Corps:
Col von Criegern: The situation near Gathemo is: Enemy has penetrated with Infantry and Armour (from Champ du Boult). Gathemo is still in our hands. The right wing of the LXXXIV Corps has been pushed back. Near La Vogerie we have no connection with the left. The liaison officer has not yet returned. Strong fighter-bomber activity. We hope to be able to hold the essential line. The time has come when weak characters desert and the remaining good men cannot hold the wide front any longer.

2000 Lieutenant-Colonel von Kluge to Chief of Staff:[31]
Chief of Staff: According to latest report, the situation on the southern wing of LXXXI Corps is becoming increasingly difficult. An enemy tank formation is advancing from the south toward Suzanne. Another tank threat from Suzanne toward the east. The Chief of Staff mentions the three alternatives and asks for a decision, inasmuch as General Kuntzen has already ordered Regiment to withdraw to the hills on both sides of Sille. We have outlined our plans to you and request a decision, for the overall situation concerns Army Group.

Lieutenant-Colonel von Kluge promises to talk to the Commanding General, Army Group West, immediately.

2035 General Funck, XLVII Panzer Corps, to CG Seventh Army:[32]
There is bitter fighting in the Mortain area. General Funck says: The situation of our tanks is becoming very alarming. Schwerin has not advanced one step to-day; neither have the other units.

---

31. *Oberstleutnant* von Kluge was the son of the field marshal.
32. *General der Panzertruppe* Hans, *Freiherr* von Funck (1891–1973), who had just assumed command of XLVII Panzer Corps.

2040 <u>Colonel Kleinschmidt, Army Group, to Chief of Staff</u>:[33]
Request that one Battalion of 275th Infantry Division be left near Barenton and attached to us for AA protection. The situation has become so bad that it may have a great influence on the general condition of things. Every unit, down to a Company, should be made fully aware of what is at stake.

Wartime Intelligence Officer's Comments

As the battle of Mortain continued to go badly, the mounting problems of insufficient manpower, poor leadership and lack of fuel provided a vivid picture of an army in defeat. In less than 24 hours Field Marshal von Kluge heard that two Commanders, von Schwerin and Kuntzen, had been dismissed; that LXXXI Corps would have to hold an entire front with four battalions and three batteries; that Laval and Le Mans had fallen, and Mayenne was soon likely to follow suit; and that a breakthrough had occurred at both St. Germain and Vire. Then to top the day's bad news, the significance of the Canadian Operation TOTALIZE began to make itself felt, and the Field Marshal had to announce that 'a breakthrough has occurred near Caen the like of which we have never seen'. With the finger of the Führer constantly pointing in his direction, and with twenty more days of news similar to this, it is small wonder that by the time his troops reached the Seine Field Marshal von Kluge felt that suicide was a happy way out of his troubles.

7 August 1944

2050 <u>Commanding General, 7th Army to Commanding General XLVII Panzer Corps</u>:
We must come to a decision on the matter of personnel.
General Funck: The Field Marshal asked me about that and also stated that we would have to wait. He said he would come to a decision tonight. I would like to know who is coming here.
Commanding General Army: With the permission of the Field Marshal, I have decided to let R[einhard] take over the division and put him ('him' probably refers to the officer whose place Reinhard is taking[34]) into the officers' pool, to be sent on leave.

---

33. This officer cannot be further identified from the information given.
34. That is to say, Schwerin.

2110 G-3, XLVII Panzer Corps to G-3 Lieutenant-Colonel Ziegelmann:[35]
While checking the line, my Signal Communications man was shot by partisans, west of Flers. The cable was bare and wire tapping is suspected.

2150 Commanding General, Seventh Army to Field Marshal von Kluge:
von Kluge: How is the situation in your sector tonight?
Commanding General Army: No essential changes. Terrific fighter-bomber attacks and considerable tank losses. Corps have orders to resume the attack as soon as air activity slackens. Schwerin's new attack has not shown progress lately. I have just told General Funck that Colonel Reinhard will take over the division.
von Kluge: Has the plan for employment of the division been completed, or are there corrections to be made on it? Is it adequate for the job?
Commanding General: That plan should still work.
von Kluge: There is really no doubt about it, inasmuch as every commanding officer is aware of the importance of this operation. Each man must give his very best. If we have not advanced considerably by this evening or tomorrow morning, the operation will have been a failure. Alençon must be held if the troops are to be fed. Defences there must be such that the enemy cannot advance further. I'm putting the remnants of the SS *Leibstandarte* at your disposal. Will you issue the necessary orders immediately. I'll call you again concerning the matter.

2200 Commanding General, Seventh Army to General Funck XLVII Panzer Corps:
The remnants of the *Leibstandarte* are still available for Employment in the push. Where do you want them?
General Funck: At St. Clement.
Commanding General Seventh: There are still 25 assault guns with them.
General Funck: I will have my assistant adjutant order the regiment to move at once. I must report again that I suspect the communication cables of being tapped and there is danger of our conversation being overheard.
Commanding General Seventh: We must take advantage of the situation, no matter what risk. We must break through. This situation demands all exceptions ... personnel question (Schwerin-Reinhard), is only a temporary one.

---

35. *Oberstleutnant* Fritz Ziegelmann, assistant chief of staff, 352nd Infantry Division.

2205 G-3, Colonel Helmdach to Chief of Staff:
G-3 reports that the enemy has penetrated into Laval. Our own troops showed symptoms of routs, after strong fighter-bomber attacks. They retreated far to the east, in spite of the fact that Commanders had orders to build a new line of resistance along the east bank of the Mayenne. The Commanding Officer, General Kuntzen, has been relieved of his command and a court martial investigation ordered. The assault guns of the SS also parked themselves, far to the east, without specific orders. They estimated their fuel to be insufficient for an attack. We were able to blow up the bridges at Laval before the enemy occupied the area.

2215 Field Marshal von Kluge to Commanding General Seventh Army:
von Kluge: In accordance with the situation and in accordance with an order from the Führer, I order the following:
1. 10 SS Panzer has been ordered to break through to you.
2. 12 SS Panzer (whatever is left of it), has been ordered to push southwest to reach . . . SS General Dietrich[36] cannot be employed due to illness. Kruger[37] will take over the Corps. 9 Panzer Division cannot be used for this task because it is employed in combat near Le Mans. The Battalion of 331st Infantry Division must be brought into the area where the remnants of the *LEIBSTANDARTE* were.

von Kluge: I request a situation report and wish to know how you propose to act.

Commanding General Seventh: We were unsuccessful, mainly, because of the sizeable fighter-bomber activity and also that 116 Panzer Division 'muffed' their job. Resistance was stronger than expected, but probably not more than one or two divisions, which by the way, were being continually reinforced.

2230 Chief of Staff to G-3, Colonel Helmdach:
Chief of Staff: Dingler[38] and his entire staff must be brought to us. See to it that this order is transmitted to him. He should report here early, if possible. It must be insured that the staff be ready for action by tomorrow morning.

2235 Chief of Staff to Colonel Wiese:
Chief of Staff: I have relieved Colonel Helmdach from his duties as G-3,

---

36. *Oberstgruppenführer* Josef Dietrich (1892–1966), commanding I SS Panzer Corps.
37. *Obergruppenführer* Walter Krüger (1890–1945).
38. *Oberst* Hans-Jürgen Dingler was the chief of staff of the LVIII Panzer Corps and the context is that the staff of that corps must be brought into the battle.

Army and have appointed Colonel Klosterkemper,[39] who is subordinate to you. I have told Colonel Helmdach that those units must make contact to the north.

Colonel Wiese: 9th Panzer Division has been ordered to group itself in such a way near Fresnay, as to be able to be committed at 0700.

Chief of Staff: This depends entirely on whether Mayenne holds out or not. An operational order and an order from the Führer will be sent to you by officer-courier.

Colonel Wiese: The left combat team of 708th Infantry Division may be surrounded.

Chief of Staff: Helmdach has orders to hand everything over to Colonel Klosterkemper. The duties of Klosterkemper will be taken over by Souche.[40]

2250 Commanding General 2 Parachute Corps to Chief of Staff:
Chief of Staff: Has the G-3, 6 Parachute Division reported to you?
Commanding General 2 Parachute Corps: Not yet.
Chief of Staff: These units will be under you for administration, however, they will be in Army reserve. It is intended that they be committed on your left, pending the requirements of the situation.

2300 Colonel Wolf, QM to Chief of Staff:[41]
We are getting two more 'Black Men' (10 and 12 SS Panzer Divs). Administration must, for the time being, be handled by Eberhard.[42] However, he cannot handle it indefinitely. It must be taken over by us later on.

8 August 1944

1000 Chief of Staff to Major Gemmerich:[43]
Chief of Staff: A radiogram to be sent to 'Achilles':[44] Fighter protection over zone of attack is urgently required.

---

39. Probably *Oberst* Bernhard Klosterkemper (1897–1962), of the 91st Air Landing Division.
40. Possibly *Generalmajor* Stephan Souchay, commandant of Le Mans.
41. *Oberst* Werner Wolff was the quartermaster of Seventh Army.
42. This officer cannot be further identified from the information given.
43. This officer cannot be further identified from the information given. He may have served either with the 91st Air Landing Division or the 363rd Infantry Division.
44. A codename but no further identification is given. From the context, however, it is clearly a Luftwaffe command.

1120 <u>Chief of Staff to Colonel von Criegern/CO LXXXIV Corps</u>:
von Criegern: Enemy penetration from the north towards St. Germain,
depth unknown. Regiment has left. Division intends to hold the enemy
on roadfork southwest of St. Germain.

1135 <u>Colonel Blauensteiner to Chief of Staff</u>:[45]
Blauensteiner: On the front nothing exceptional. Penetration on the left
flank near St. Germain.
Chief of Staff: Division Headquarters of 352 and Panzer Lehr Divs are
detached and attached to LXXXI Corps.

1155 <u>Colonel Helmdach/G-3 (Ops) to Chief of Staff</u>:
Chief of Staff: No substantial change of situation on all fronts. Attack
proceeds only slowly on account of fighter-bomber activity. Division
Headquarters 352 and Panzer Lehr are attached to LXXXI Corps.
Colonel Helmdach: I have the impression that enemy intends to break
through southeast and eastward near Le Mans. Enemy has crossed
river. Strength at least one combat team. Battle Headquarters moved
to Belleme.

1215 <u>G-3/LXXXI Corps to Chief of Staff</u>:
G-3: Estimate of enemy situation: Enemy tries outflanking movement
direction northeast with point of main effort south of Le Mans. Strength
at least one armoured division. Battle noise seemingly northwest of Le
Mans. Since enemy does not appear strong, the following units have
been committed:

One security battalion near Sable. This has apparently withdrawn
in the direction of Le Mans. No communication with Le Mans. One
German Air Force security battalion committed on the western fringe
of Le Mans.

One assault battalion committed east of Le Mans to secure road Le
Mans–Paris–Blois.

Straggler companies committed to guard Le Mans.

CO in Le Mans is Lieutenant-Colonel Tapport. Staff Helmdach is at
the time at a point northeast of Le Mans and will withdraw further to
Belleme.

1230 <u>Colonel Kleinschmidt to Chief of Staff</u>:
Kleinschmidt: Situation east of Juvigny and Mortain generally unchanged.
Chief of Staff: Do you believe that it is possible to continue operations?

---

45. *Oberst* Ernst Blauensteiner (1911–95), chief of staff, II Parachute Corps.

Kleinschmidt: Not at all, not with the forces at hand.

Chief of Staff: What do you believe the enemy has in front of you?

Kleinschmidt: About three infantry divisions (30, 9 and one presently not yet identified) and one armoured division.

Chief of Staff: The main body of the ninth is opposing 84th Infantry Division.

Kleinschmidt: Under protection of his air superiority, the enemy has been able to reinforce himself considerably yesterday. Our combat strengths have been greatly reduced.

1250 Chief of Staff to Colonel Wiese/CO LXXXI Corps:

Wiese: The enemy has penetrated into Le Mans itself with infantry and tanks. Out of touch with CO of Le Mans. Enemy has continued his outflanking move and has bypassed Le Mans to the east. Suggestion for further operations: Attack enemy with mobile units of 9 Panzer Division either south or north of Le Mans.

Chief of Staff: With the first suggestion (south of Le Mans) the loss of time is too great and we run the danger of missing the enemy. Therefore I propose to advance north of Le Mans immediately and to try to throw the enemy out of Le Mans.

1310 Chief of Staff informs Colonel Tempelhoff/CG:

Agree about the situation and about Colonel Wiese's decision on the conduct of operations near Le Mans with the intent to prevent a further enemy advance to the north.

1730 Field Marshal von Kluge to CG:

Field Marshal: I have the intention of placing under your command: The main body of 9 Panzer Division (only day after tomorrow), one Mortar Brigade, one additional Mortar Brigade, when the situation permits (or later), exchange of 331st Infantry Division with 9 SS Panzer Division. All units with the exception of the Mortar Brigade can admittedly arrive only early on the day after tomorrow. The Mortar Brigade should, if possible, be in position by tomorrow morning. In spite of the failures the attack is to be continued under all circumstances. On that point there is to exist no doubt whatsoever.

1745 CG to General Kuntzen/CG LXXXI Corps:

General Kuntzen: If 9 Panzer Division is pulled out, a gap is created which I am unable to close. I would have for the entire front only four battalions and three batteries left. With these units I cannot hope to accomplish my mission.

1845 <u>Field Marshal von Kluge to CG</u>:

CG: Orientation on situation. Enemy has been reinforced on front of attack. Attacks have occurred west of Mortain and from Juvigny towards the east and northeast. On LXXXIV Corps front wide attack which has led to breakthrough not only near St. Germain but also near Vire. The corps tries to seal off the penetrations but has run out of reserves. The shifting of 9 Panzer Division would make very difficult General Kuntzen's mission.

Field Marshal: We have to risk everything. Besides, a breakthrough has occurred near Caen the like of which we have never seen. I draw the following conclusion:

Preparations to reorganize the attack will have to be made first thing tomorrow. Therefore, we shall not continue the attack tomorrow but make preparations to attack on the following day.

8 August 1944

1900 <u>Gen Funck/XXXVI Panzer Corps to C of S</u>:

C of S: CG will visit the General in his Headquarters. I can predict that nothing will happen tonight.

2030 <u>C of S – G-3/Colonel Helmdach</u>:

C of S: The situation on the front demands that the battalions be brought up on trucks.

2050 <u>Colonel von Criegern/CG LXXXIV Corps to C of S</u>:

von Criegern: It has been reported that enemy tanks are advancing from Lonlay to Blancherie. Information is unconfirmed. Right flank is very weak. I am afraid that we will have a hell of a mess on our hands tomorrow. We need replacements.

2100 <u>Gen Elfeldt[46]/CG LXXXIV Corps to C of S</u>:

C of S: Colonel Raum[47] left at 2130 hours to fetch the battalion for you and should be in Truttemer le Grand in about six hours. We shall make further efforts to bring up further troops to the General. The day after tomorrow the Parachute [Illegible] will be committed on the left flank near 'Meindl'. The battalion that was brought up today should be provided with rations.

---

46. *Generalleutnant* Otto Elfeldt (1895–1982), commander, LXXXIV Corps. Taken prisoner, 20 August 1944.
47. This officer cannot be further identified from the information given.

2345 C of S to G-3/Colonel Helmdach:

G-3: General [Hausser] has taken over. Information about the enemy situation unclear.

C of S: Against right flank of Elfeldt heavy attacks which have led to a penetration. On the attack front strong counter attacks are proceeding. No new basic decision has been made upstairs yet. For the time being, the old policy will govern our decisions.

G-3: We shift to M.

9 August 1944

0915 C of S to Colonel Wiese/CG LXXXI Corps:

Colonel Wiese: Estimate of the situation. Tendency of the enemy shows strong movements toward the east. I cannot say where leading units are.

0920 C of S to Lieutenant-Colonel Blauensteiner/CG II Parachute Corps:

Blauensteiner: Left flank has been withdrawn to hill 233. There is weak contact with left neighbour. From 0510–1830 the enemy bombarded the old position. We expect an attack. Up to now nothing special.

0945 C of S to Lieutenant-Colonel von Criegern/CG LXXXIV Corps:

von Criegern: Informs that March Battalion has still not arrived.

0950 General Elfeldt/CG LXXXIV Corps to C of S:

Gen Elfeldt: Generally speaking, the operation on the right flank has succeeded. I have checked on it and found that the right flank is all right. The March Battalion which has still not arrived is being looked for.

1030 Field Marshal to C of S:

C of S: The left flank of LXXXIV Corps has been established. We have succeeded in reorganizing the 363rd Infantry Division along a line from the road bend two kilometres east of Vire in a generally western direction. The regimental groups are lined up alongside of each other and have loose contact with each other. The regiment on the right counts 130 men. The CG announces that as opposed to their right neighbour's observation, the division has fought well. The battalion of 331st Infantry Division has still not reached the front lines. We hope to get it up there still today. Units of the 6 Parachute Division are unfortunately still in the Paris area. We have ordered that they should be brought up as soon as possible. They can, however, hardly be expected here before tomorrow morning. On the rest of the front, no changes. On the left flank of the newly committed LVIII Panzer Corps the enemy is probing with armoured reconnaissance and has penetrated the area of Ger and east of it with individual tanks. All preparations are being made and the Army has already been given the order to continue the attack.

FM: The decision on the execution of the attack will fall today. All preparations for it to be made, however.

C of S: On the left flank of the Army the enemy is advancing from the area of Le Mans in a general easterly direction. The positions of the spearheads are unknown to me. The combat team of the Panzer Lehr Division has been attached to LXXXI Corps commitment on the right flank. Up to now it has held the left flank of II Parachute Corps. But because the enemy's point of main effort is south of Vire this change in position has been made.

1145 Field Marshal to C of S:

FM: How do you judge the continuation of the known operation?

C of S: The enemy has been reinforced. The hitherto known factors would have to be considered. Then the attack would have to succeed. The favourable 'fighter bomber weather' makes the task especially difficult. The steadily lengthening southern flank especially worries us. Therefore the LXXXI Corps was ordered to assemble the main body of its 9th Panzer Reconnaissance Battalion in the area west of Domfront and to attach it to the LVIII Panzer Corps. Whether this will amount to anything, since strong units of 9th Panzer Reconnaissance Battalion are engaged, remains to be seen. Near Ambrieuse enemy exerts strong pressure towards the east. The tank situation has hardly changed since yesterday and is therefore still bad.

1200 C of S to Colonel Wiese/CG LXXXI Corps:

Tonight, the 9th Panzer Reconnaissance Battalion which was committed west of Domfront, was thrown in NE of Ambrieuse without order and knowledge of Corps.

C of S: The gap near Domfront is to be closed under all circumstances. Report is to be made on the units employed on that spot.

1250 Colonel Tempelhoff/CG Army Group to C of S:

C of S: The Field Marshal wants to know how Army judges the chances of success for the continuation of the attack. I answered that the chances cannot be judged positively. They can be judged positively, however, if the Panthers and 2 Motor Brigade are also committed. The

LXXXI Corps reports that the Commanding Officer of 9th Panzer Reconnaissance Battalion which up to now stood west of Domfront has withdrawn his unit without the knowledge of Corps and has committed it near Ambrieuse where enemy pressure is admittedly strong. Now we have nothing but 600 men left to secure Domfront. I therefore gave LXXXI Corps the order to put without fail some troops into that sector and to make a report on them. Report on situation. Left flank near General Elfeldt has been re-established. Strong attacks have not yet been reported, but are expected in the afternoon. Enemy has infiltrated on the front of attack near Barthelemy but infiltration was sealed off. 2 SS Panzer Division has recaptured hill 226 west of Mortain. 15 enemy tanks were observed NW of Barenton. May I ask for an early decision on continuation of the operation today or tomorrow night.

1520 Field Marshal to C of S:

I just had a decisive conference with the Supreme Command. The situation south of Caen having been reestablished and not having had the much feared effects I propose to retain the idea of an attack. Now, however, the attack must be prepared and executed to plan and must not be rushed. The Panzer units are led by General Eberbach[48] under your command. The attacking forces must be reshuffled and switched further south. General Eberbach will arrive at your place with an improvised staff tonight. Whatever we can do will still be done tonight. A part, not too weak, of the 9th Panzer Division must be brought up. Whatever we can get a hold of will be thrown in. I consider it improbable that the operation can be initiated before the day after tomorrow. To launch an attack is out of the question.

1550 C of S to Colonel Kleinschmidt/CG XLVII Panzer Corps:

C of S: Today's order is cancelled. General Eberbach is attached to us with his staff, the whole thing is reshuffled and reorganized.

1700 Colonel Wiese/CG LXXXI Corps to C of S:

C of S: The new situation demands that no new southward movement take place. Once more, I have pointed out the dangers of the situation which might arise on the southern flank of the army sector. But that would be taken care of by somebody else.

1950 C of S to Colonel Tempelhoff/CG Army Group:

The situation at LXXXIV Corps has considerably deteriorated. The enemy

---

48. *General der Panzertruppe* Heinz Eberbach (1895–1992), just appointed to command Panzer Group West, later V Panzer Army. Taken prisoner 31 August 1944.

has advanced with massed forces supported by tanks and has taken the locality of Lalande Vaumont. Counter-measures:

(a) of Corps: 1 combat team of local reserves is being formed NE of . . . Another combat team of 331st Infantry Division is being assembled in the area of Truttemer. North of it are parts of Panzer Lehr Division.

(b) Since these forces might not suffice to seal off the penetration, it has been ordered to commit 1 combat team of the neighbouring Corps which should counter attack in a south-to-north direction, owing to the changed situation. Army intends to leave this combat team there until tomorrow noon only and to pull it back at that time. II Parachute Corps has set up a combat team on its left flank to protect the left wing.

I ask you to emphasize that the combat team of the neighbouring corps is employed only because of the changed situation and only for a short period.

2115 C of S to Colonel Tempelhoff/CG Army Group:

C of S: We would like to know whether a directive on the conduct of operations is still to be expected from Army Group.

Colonel Tempelhoff: Said directive will be issued.

C of S: In this case we ask you to hurry up.

Colonel Tempelhoff: The objective remains the same. The Führer's order is still the basis.

C of S: We expect more detailed instructions soon.

Wartime Intelligence Officer's Comments

The attempt to reach Avranches by the armoured attack towards Mortain had failed, and here we see Field Marshal von Kluge taking the necessary steps for the withdrawal of the forces already committed. The orders by which the attack was originally made and the order permitting the withdrawal both stemmed from the Führer himself. von Kluge seems only to have done what he was told.

10 August 1944

0900 Gen Eberbach to Ops Army Group:

Gen E: I request a fresh division to keep the attack going after the initial thrust, for by the time the attack has been completed and the objective has been reached, a large number of our trucks will be out of action and will have to be left on the road. Above all we lack anti-aircraft ammunition which is of great importance because of the enemy's air superiority. The same holds true for mortar ammunition. I would appreciate it if you could do something about it.

0915 Gen Kuntzen, GOC LXXXI Corps to C of S:

Gen K: I want to report that with my forces (four battalions), I cannot even stop an enemy attack. We are expecting Alençon to be in enemy hands tomorrow.

C of S: Does the General think that the enemy is pushing north and northeast?

Gen K: Yes, there is no doubt about it. I wish you would pass this information on. If any more elements are taken from me I will be unable to complete my mission.

1035 Field Marshal von Kluge to C of S:

Field Marshal: According to instructions from Higher Headquarters, preparations for an attack do not have to be rushed. It is impossible to set a date now as further reinforcements are to be brought up. Our forces should and must be employed as ordered. A commitment north of the present area is out of the question. Further details will be given by the Field Marshal when he visits you tomorrow noon. It is doubtful whether operations on the Northern front will leave us time. It depends, of course, on whether the northern front will hold and I want to emphasize again that in order to save our own strength no counter attacks be launched if a withdrawal can clear up the situation. But even these tactics are affected by the limited area at our disposal. The decision to commit combat group LSAH[49] cannot be approved under these circumstances. It would mean that this force would attack in a direction not in accordance with our plans. I request that in the future no unit shall be pulled out of the Panzer Group without special permission from Army Group. Army has to see to it that it gets along with the forces allotted to it. This seems absolutely necessary. We shall again receive tanks from the pool from which we can draw to a limited extent. The date is not yet set. Enemy pushes from Le Mans towards Alençon must be stopped.

1230 C of S to Colonel Tempelhoff/Army Group:

C of S: I am reporting that it is impossible to pull troops out of the sector on the south wing of the Army.

---

49. LSAH or Leibstandarte Adolf Hitler, the 1st SS Panzer Division.

1600 <u>Gen Elfeldt, GOC LXXXIV Corps to C of S</u>:
Gen Elfeldt asks permission to keep battle group SCHILLER in view of the situation.

1800 <u>Field Marshal von Kluge to Colonel von Gersdorff</u>:
The Field Marshal requests a situation report on LXXXI Corps before anything else.

Colonel von Gersdorff: The enemy is located along the left wing of LXXXI Corps. It is established without any doubt that 5 US Armoured Division is pushing forward from Le Mans in a general direction to the north. According to captured documents its right wing is pushing toward Belleme, its left wing in direction of Alençon. 9th Panzer Division is in contact with these forces in the general area southwest of Mammers. General Kuntzen however, calls attention to the fact that there is a gap near Bonnetable between 9th Panzer Division and those elements of 352nd Infantry Division which are under the command of General von Schuckmann[50] and which are located mainly along the road from Le Mans to Nogent, on the high ground of La Ferte-Bernard. He should shift some troops from the right to the left wing in order to protect the supply base which is north of Belleme. However, he could only do that if he can withdraw from his present holding line, which runs from Domfront south via Mayenne–Evron–Sille, to a newly reconnoitred one.

Field Marshal von Kluge: This is out of the question! This is impossible because the foundation of the intended attack would be changed thereby. How you can help yourself, I don't know. We cannot judge that from here.

Colonel von Gersdorff: General Kuntzen reported that the units had been in a relatively close formation but were dispersed by bomb carpets. The armoured group is northwest of Beaumont. He is now attacking the enemy from both sides. He pulled one more battalion out of Alençon for commitment in the southeast. Our entire supply is based on the area between Chartres and Alençon. Supplying the army has been highly endangered by the thrust to the north. If the enemy succeeds in thrusting northward beyond Mammers, then he will sit in the middle of our supply dumps which naturally, cannot defend themselves.

Field Marshal von Kluge: This is entirely clear. I have no units left at the moment. If, however, I take troops from your reserves, then it represents

50. *Generalmajor* Eberhard von Schuckmann (1899–1966), commander of the 352nd Infantry Division.

an act which practically sabotages all preparations. The Parachute Regiment was still in the Paris region last night according to Colonel von Gersdorff. We sent a cable for it to come here in a hurry. There is nothing else to do. I will divert the Parachute Regiment immediately, so Kuntzen can catch it.

Colonel von Gersdorff: It is a reinforced battalion which consists of one battalion, a mortar battalion, one motorized artillery battalion, one platoon of heavy anti-tank guns, one mixed signal company and parts of a field hospital.

Field Marshal von Kluge: This unit is at your disposal for immediate commitment in Kuntzen's sector. Everything else will be taken care of by Army at once. It is essential that this battalion be committed as quickly as possible. A withdrawal of our line is prohibited. It is self-understood that Kuntzen must only try to shift forces from his right wing to the left if he can ascertain that the line will be held.

Colonel von Gersdorff: The following units have been identified in front of the right wing of LXXXI Corps. 1st US Infantry Division near Ambrières, 80 near Mayenne (so far it had been supposed in Great Britain) and 90th US Infantry Division is assumed to be further south, near Evron and Sille. It is not clear whether these are only elements or the entire divisions. We are having difficulty in identifying the various elements. 5 US Armoured Division has now definitely been identified north of Le Mans through signal documents. Field Marshal von Kluge would like to know this evening whether Army Group can count on having its orders actually executed. Colonel von Gersdorff now brings up the subject of taking the line back to the high ground north of Mortain.

Field Marshal von Kluge: This means giving up terrain to the east which will have to be retaken later on. For the present, everything will remain as is.

[von Gersdorff] The counter attack near La Lande made good progress. Battle Group SCHILLER attacked from the southeast, 353rd Infantry Division from southwest, a battle group of Panzer Lehr and 331st Infantry Divisions attacked from the east. The penetration was sealed off tightly. However, the enemy was able to penetrate near Maisoncelles and to occupy Hill 332. The battalion south thereof was forced to withdraw its right wing and presumably withdrew altogether further south, so that the enemy now again dominates the region north and west of Maisoncelles. Field Marshal von Kluge orders that the attack is not to be continued any longer. All units must be pulled out again as soon as possible. The C of S asks to consider if it will then be necessary to fall back tonight to a line which runs from the right point of contact, Vengeons to Maisoncelles.

Field Marshal von Kluge: I agree to that – and to La Lande-Vaumont where it connects north of La Lande-Vaumont–Beaufiel–northwest Sourdeval–Hill 191 and runs in a generally northeasterly direction.

Field Marshal von Kluge: The order by the Führer states clearly that counter attacks will no longer be carried out and that one has to disengage wherever there are possibilities for disengaging moves. The possibilities are limited. Therefore, every disengaging move must be checked for the least necessary withdrawal which would force the enemy to keep moving his artillery forward and to employ new methods. Withdrawal of so many kilometres at a time must be stopped radically. Because then you have no room left for operations.

Colonel von Gersdorff: We would not have been able to pull out 116 Panzer Division otherwise.

Colonel von Gersdorff: In order to pull out *LEIBSTANDARTE*, which is scheduled for tonight, the right wing of LUTTWITZ must be taken back east of Le Mesnil-Tove to the line west of Brouains – west of Barthelemy. The proposed line in connection with the withdrawal of the two divisions but which has not yet been occupied, runs as follows: Beaufiel to south-southwest–Hill 191–then southwest to Brouains–Hill 180–Hill 280–along the main road west of Barthelemy–linking up with right wing of 2 SS REICH–Hill 183.

Field Marshal von Kluge: That would mean the withdrawal of a front which we had so much trouble in holding. Two enemy infantry divisions have been identified in front of the line: 4 and 30 aside from 2 Armoured Division. I request that the line of 2 Panzer Division and 2 SS Division remain unchanged.

Withdrawal from Hill 191. The bulge of Gathemo may be given up. (116 Panzer Division can then be pulled back). Beginning at Hill 191 the line will no longer be changed. Everything else will depend upon the conference of the Field Marshal with SS General Hausser and General Eberbach tomorrow.

The Field Marshal wishes to know tonight when he can expect the arrival of the parachutists.

2150 <u>C of S to Colonel Kessel, Army Group:</u>[51]

C of S points out that there are large storage dumps in the forest east of Alençon which cannot be moved so quickly. He (probably referring to the enemy) can be there today. At this moment Army would have to draw all its supplies from the neighbouring unit.

2310 <u>C of S to Colonel Wolff/Quartermaster General:</u>

C of S: We hope that the left Corps will be reinforced by the parachute unit tomorrow. It is doubtful whether this unit will be sufficient to protect that area. The question arises whether we will be able to move the supplies before the enemy gets there.

Colonel Wolff: I hope to be able to move the fuel and bring it up to the front. There is probably no hope for the ammunition.

Wartime Intelligence Officer's Comments

The Seventh Army Telephone Journal, captured by the Polish Armoured Division in August, has provided a lengthy and interesting account of high level reactions to the progress of the campaign in the west. Following is a further translated instalment full of the worries and fears which beset the enemy commanders as the Allied drive gathered momentum. The most striking feature of the conversations recorded below is the continued absence of any reaction to the breakthrough at Falaise which by the time referred to in this instalment of the Journal, was already well under way. Whether its importance was not fully appreciated or why no reference to it is made, is not clear. At any rate, the high ranking officers quoted below were greatly concerned about the situation further west. Moreover, it may well be that this Journal is not complete, a possibility which is enhanced by the fact that only three conversations are recorded for 10 August, four for 12 August and three for 16 August.

Editor's Comments

In point of fact, the conversations relating to Operation TOTALIZE were found in the records of Fifth Panzer Army, the formation responsible for the sector of the front in which that operation took place. See Document 2/4 below

---

51. This officer cannot be further identified from the information given.

11 August 1944

1045 Colonel Kessel/Army Group to C of S:

C of S: The enemy attacked at 0930 along the entire front of the 9th Panzer Division. He is also attacking at present with 25 tanks east of Mortain, he occupies Hill 317 and there is a gap of 1 km. Our forces are too weak and the enemy is infiltrating. Counter-measures are in progress.

1100 C of S to Captain Jung/Army Group:

C of S: All is quiet on our right front. The enemy has attacked along the road that runs south from Vire. Nothing new in the XLVII Panzer Corps area. East of Mortain the enemy has penetrated into LVIII Reserve Panzer Corps sector and has occupied Hill 317. He is receiving continuous air support.

1110 Colonel Kessel/Army Group to C of S:

C of S: The enemy has penetrated in force into the LXXXIV Corps sector west of Lalande-Vaumont. He has taken Hill 243 and Les Beaugards and is proceeding south on road Vire-Sourdeval. There is a second break-through near Gathemo where he has reached Point 305, La Charterie. He is turning north and south from there.

1500 C of S to Colonel Tempelhoff/CG, Army Group:

C of S: The enemy has broken through and is advancing from the NE of, and along the road Vire–Sourdeval. A second breakthrough occurred in the Gathemo area in an easterly direction on Hill 305. From there the enemy has turned south and north. Counter-measures with small local reserves are in progress. In the south the enemy has broken through near Mortain and has reached Hill 305. He has opened a gap of 1 km there. If the 116 Panzer Division and the *LEIBSTANDARTE* are pulled out today as scheduled, we suggest the following line: starting from La Lande–Vaumont–SW to the crossroads, SE of Vengeons west of Sourdeval–road bend 3 km SW of Sourdeval–Point 314–hill east of Mortain.

Colonel Tempelhoff: This line is approved.

1845 Colonel Wiese/CG, LXXXI Corps to C of S:

Colonel Wiese: The thrust towards Alençon appears to be headed by Second French Armoured Division.

1720 Lieutenant-Colonel Blauensteiner/CG II Parachute Corps to C of S:

Lieutenant-Colonel Blauensteiner reports an enemy attack with 26 tanks.

12 August 1944

1400 Lieutenant-Colonel Blauensteiner/CG II Parachute Corps to C of S:
Lieutenant-Colonel Blauensteiner announced that the unit on his
right (Fifth Panzer Army) intends to withdraw to Rully which would
jeopardize his Corps' position.

1410 C of S to General Elfeldt/CG LXXXIV Corps:
At 1000 the enemy launched a strong attack near Vengeons and has
reached La Gillottière.

1630 General Elfeldt/CG, LXXXIV Corps to C of S:
General Elfeldt: On the left wing the line has been restored. Le Tertres is
back in our hands. Les Guernets is held by the enemy.

1650 C of S to Colonel Tempelhoff/CG, Army Group:
C of S: The unit on our right flank (Fifth Panzer Army) announces that
they are going to have their left wing, which links up with our troops,
back to Rully.
Colonel Tempelhoff: Army Group rejects that plan.

13 August 1944

1100 Colonel Dingler/LVIII Panzer Corps to C of S:
Colonel Dingler reports an enemy breakthrough 1 km in width near
Domfront.

1150 C of S to Colonel Dingler:
C of S: I have informed Army Group but I am afraid that they will tell us
to help ourselves. You have to move anti-tank weapons to your left wing
in order to protect Domfront. Possibly the line will have to be taken
back a little to improve the situation.

1450 C of S to Colonel Dingler:
C of S: 708th Infantry Division has been attached to us and we are
putting it at your disposal. Send a liaison officer to contact the forward
HQ of the division and find out where their main HQ is. I believe
that it is SE of Domfront. The troops of 708th Infantry Division are
between Domfront and Mayenne. Will you kindly inform us of: 1. the
location of the Division; 2. the Division's formation; 3. the best way to
commit it.

1500 <u>C of S to Colonel Dingler:</u>

C of S: We will withdraw after all with your right wing at Connecting Point 175 north of Beauchene. The 2nd SS Panzer Division has to be pulled out. After it has been relieved it will move into the area Ranes–Fromentel.

1520 <u>Gen Elfeldt/CG, LXXXIV Corps to C of S:</u>

Gen Elfeldt reports on the situation and announces that the enemy is in Les Masures and Truttemer Le Petit.

1630 <u>Gen Elfeldt to CG, Army Group:</u>

Gen Elfeldt: Due to the inability of the CG, 363 Infantry Division to make decisions I request that he be relieved and replaced by Colonel Klosterkemper and Major Gemmerich.[52]

14 August 1944

0940 <u>C of S to Lieutenant-Colonel Blauensteiner/CG, II Parachute Corps:</u>

Lieutenant-Colonel Blauensteiner: Yesterday's and last night's attacks were considerably stronger than we had thought earlier. The casualties range from 40 to 46 men per battalion. The planned MLR was never reached because of that. It might be possible for our left flank unit to try to link up with us further north.

0950 <u>Gen Elfeldt/CG, LXXXIV Corps to C of S:</u>

Gen Elfeldt: The right wing does not worry me so much; the worst part is the lack of artillery ammunition.

C of S: We can get ammunition from II SS Panzer Corps. For the rest we have to depend entirely on Fifth Panzer Army. The C of S is also giving the general the new MLR.

1150 <u>Colonel Dingler/CG, LVIII Panzer Corps to C of S:</u>

C of S: Will you kindly ask the CG, Army Group to return to his HQ immediately, or if that takes too long to call his HQ as an important decision has to be made. According to information I received from General Eberbach an attack by Panzer Group is impossible. I have completed the draft of our future combat plans but I would like to submit it to the CG, Army Group for approval.

1445 <u>CG, LXXXIV Corps to C of S:</u>

CG, LXXXIV Corps: Several tanks penetrated into Domfront and are

---

52. The commander of the 363rd Infantry Division was *Generalleutnant* August Dettling (1893–1980). Dettling was not removed from command.

now sitting tight. A counter-thrust has been initiated. If we only run up against small forces it might be successful. If we meet strong resistance the situation will be difficult. There is no contact with 708th Infantry Division yet.

1800 Colonel Dingler/CG, LVIII Panzer Corps to C of S:

Colonel Dingler reports a breakthrough near Domfront and the occupation of Hills 214 and 201 north of Domfront. Counter-measures have been initiated.

1930 Lieutenant-Colonel Blauensteiner/CG, II Parachute Corps to C of S:

Lieutenant-Colonel Blauensteiner: The enemy has penetrated into the section of the unit on our right and is in Conde. Counter-measures of 21st Panzer Division are in progress. Consequently, the unit on the right could not hold its line as ordered and we will have to withdraw to re-establish contact with them. That will also entail a withdrawal of the left wing.

1935 C of S to Colonel von Criegern/CG, LXXXIV Corps:

C of S: Due to a breakthrough near Conde on your right flank unit has to seek contact with the unit to his right further back. This will force you to withdraw your right wing. Will you please agree with the Parachutists on a point where your lines will meet.

15 August 1944

1040 Colonel Dingler, C of S LVIII Panzer Corps to C of S:

Colonel Dingler: The situation in the vicinity of Dompierre is under control. Our forward elements are at Point 226, 3 km SW of Dompierre.

1345 General Elfeldt/CG, LXXXIV Corps to C of S:

General Elfeldt informs us that there has been no contact with the enemy after the disengaging movement. There are possibilities that the disengaging movement along the right wing may not be executed according to plan due to the loss of several vehicles. The General asks us to consider whether the II Parachute Corps could help out in this case.

1400 C of S to Lieutenant-Colonel Blauensteiner/CG, II Parachute Corps:

The C of S explains the situation at LXXXIV Corps and requests II Parachute Corps to furnish fuel to the LXXXIV Corps if at all possible so that the vehicles can be pulled out.

1410 <u>Gen Elfeldt, LXXXIV Corps to C of S:</u>

General Elfeldt: Disengagement completed. So far the enemy has not followed. No more contact is reported. The fuel situation is such that the assault guns can not be committed any longer.

C of S: The CG, Seventh Army requests that weapons such as assault guns, tanks, etc. be filled up with fuel regardless of other motor vehicles. We have informed Army Group again that movements which they ordered depend upon the fuel and ammunition situation entirely.

16 August 1944

1000 <u>Lieutenant-Colonel von Criegern, C of S of LXXXIV Corps,</u>
<u>to C of S:</u>

Lieutenant-Colonel von Criegern: Strong enemy forces have penetrated into Menil de Briouze. The Ninth Reconnaissance Battalion has withdrawn to the east. Furthermore, strong enemy units are reported in the vicinity of Bellou. The fuel situation is difficult. We did not receive any fuel last night.

C of S: Prepare to withdraw in the general direction of Bellou as far as the line of the road bridge 800 metres south of Landigou. You will have to bring back your left wing accordingly, in the direction of Hill 228, west of Briouze. The 10th SS Panzer Division has been ordered to attack the enemy near Bellou and to throw him back toward the south. You will have to hold yourself skilfully along the southern wing of 10th SS Panzer Division. Let us hope that we will be successful in driving the enemy out of the area around Bellou. General Eberbach has sent a strong reconnaissance force to the south. You must build up your forces in the south, and, if necessary, eventual movements will have to be carried out during daylight. If the fuel situation requires it, then the supply vehicles will have to stay where they are. At any rate, it must be assured that all the fuel be made available to the armoured vehicles.

1120 <u>C of S to Colonel Dingler, C of S of LVII Panzer Corps:</u>

Colonel Dingler: Le Menil is in the hands of the enemy. We have ordered a reconnaissance of Briouze. The situation is more stable along the right wing. Therefore, there is a possibility of being able to rush more units to the south. Estimated strength of the enemy: approximately one regimental combat team.

1920 <u>Lieutenant-Colonel Blauensteiner, C of S of II Parachute Corps to C of S</u>:

Lieutenant-Colonel Blauensteiner reports:

(a) That vehicles of his unit are being stopped in the Paris region and are simply being confiscated for different tasks.

(b) Because of the lack of fuel, while it is possible for us to effect tonight's movement, the present stock of fuel is insufficient for tomorrow's move.

Document 2/4 [53]

Fifth Panzer Army Defends against Operation TOTALIZE

Editor's Comments

On 8 August 1944, as Field Marshal von Kluge tried desperately to stem the American breakthrough into Brittany, First Canadian Army launched a massive attack on the eastern flank of the Normandy bridgehead. Codenamed Operation TOTALIZE, it was preceded by massive carpet bombing carried out by heavy bombers and featured the employment of hundreds of tanks and infantry carried, for the first time, in fully tracked armoured personnel carriers dubbed 'Kangaroos'. The objective of this attack was the high ground around the town of Falaise and, although it lost much ground, Fifth Panzer Army, the former Panzer Group West, was just barely able to slow down and ultimately stop the onslaught. In three telephone conversations that took place on the evening of the first day of the TOTALIZE attack, General Heinz Eberbach, commander of Fifth Panzer Army, tried to make von Kluge aware of the dangerous situation now developing on the eastern part of the bridgehead, as well as the western part.

---

53. Army Historical Section, Report No. 50, *The Campaign in North-West Europe. Information from German Sources, Part II, 6 June–22 August, Invasion and the Battle of Normandy*, Directorate of History and Heritage, Ottawa.

8 August 1944

2100 <u>Conversation between General Eberbach and</u>
<u>Field Marshal von Kluge</u>

Eberbach: May I orient the Field Marshal on the situation? At the front of LXXXVI Corps the enemy has attacked between Chicheboville–St. Aignan and has pushed forward into the area Conteville, Poussy and Conteville still in our hands. A number of enemy tanks knocked out.

With I SS Panzer Corps: There the enemy has forced his way into the main line of resistance after aerial preparations more intense than 18 July.[54] Starting last evening at 1000 hrs and lasting throughout the whole night. With a very large number of tanks, about 500.

von Kluge: What, 500?

Eberbach: Yes, at Chicheboville alone there were 200 continuously throughout the whole day. The enemy has penetrated the main line of resistance there and pushed forward as far as St. Aignan, retaken in counter-attack. Then renewed area bombings which crushed 12th SS Panzer Division so that only individual tanks came back. The enemy pressed forward further south as far as Gaumesnil and is continuing his advance. I SS Panzer Corps has built up a battle line with anti-tank and flak guns, which has held so far. Whether this line will hold out until tomorrow if the enemy attacks more energetically is questionable. Actually the new Infantry Division[55] as well as the Hitler Youth Division are 50% knocked out. I shall be lucky if by tonight I am able to round up 20 tanks, including Tigers.

The onslaught continued throughout the whole day against 271st Infantry Division.

Detachments of Hitler Youth Division were thrown in there. They had considerable casualties from enemy drum fire.[56] 271st Infantry Division: 2,000 casualties, infantry very weak. No success in ejecting the enemy from Grimbosq. On the contrary, with new tanks which he is continuously bringing across the river, he has taken Brieux. On LXXIV Corps' front the enemy has attacked energetically and so far, broken through the main line of resistance with 40 tanks in the direction of Cauville. Le Plessis was captured by him, but since noon it is back again in our hands.

---

54. A reference to the heavy bombing used during the start of the British and Canadian Operation GOODWOOD, which began on 18 July.
55. A reference to the 89th Infantry Division, which had just arrived in Normandy.
56. *Trommelfeuer* or 'drum fire', meaning heavy bombardment.

Located opposite LXXIV Corps: 7th British Armoured Division, 8th British Armoured Brigade, 27th British Armoured Brigade, 50th and 53rd British Infantry Divisions. The opponent will, with good weather, again continue his attacks tomorrow and endeavour to push through in the direction of Falaise. I will commit, as second line, two Grenadier Battalions, one Artillery Battalion and one 8.8 cm Anti-Tank Company. I must confess quite frankly that I am looking forward to tomorrow with anxiety.

von Kluge: I can understand that.

Eberbach: I cannot take out the two mortars brigades before nightfall.

von Kluge: You are not giving up a whole brigade but only a regiment; arrange this with the Seventh Army yourself. Likewise the Russian Artillery Battalion 15.5 cm. remains with you. We must be clear thereon, tomorrow or the day after, there will be a decision here. I am unfortunately not in a position to send you anything. Whatever can be brought across the Seine will be sent to you under all circumstances.

That this would all go so quickly, we too did not expect. But I can imagine that it did not happen quite so unexpectedly.

I have always anticipated this and have always looked forward to the coming day with a very heavy heart.

2135 Continuation of Conversation between General Eberbach and Field Marshal von Kluge

Eberbach: Reporting that the enemy has pushed through with 40 tanks to the South and has attained Langannerie north of Grainville. I have nothing left, as 85th Infantry Division only arrives tomorrow morning. I have spoken to the Flak to the effect that they take the 8.8 cm up front and that they be committed south of Grainville in order to intercept this tank thrust, for I have trepidations that the enemy will push further to the South as there is moonlight. The situation is, that the Hitler Youth Division has been exhausted so much by area bombings that I SS Panzer Corps was not able even by means of roving staff officers to get together a combat team again. Telecommunications, wireless included, are knocked out.

2½ Battalions of 89th Infantry Division are between Hautmesnil and Bretteville.

von Kluge: How about the artillery?

Eberbach: 89th Infantry Division and 12th SS Panzer Division: 50% casualties.

von Kluge: As a last measure, I have set into march this night 20 tanks of 9th SS Panzer Division but I fear that, with the long approach march, only half of them will arrive tomorrow morning.

2220 Continuation of Conversation between General Eberbach and Field Marshal von Kluge

von Kluge: If you get back one panzer division which I had taken away from you, what will you then be short of most?

Eberbach: Most of all, tanks are lacking.

von Kluge: Have you a Commander who understands how to handle tanks? Where is the Commander of the Hitler Youth?

Eberbach: The Hitler Youth Commander telephoned me this afternoon from St. Aignan; he was there to organize the resistance.

von Kluge: That is 'Rapid Meyer' (*der schnelle Meyer*). Have you had news of him since then?

Eberbach: No news. That was before the area bombing.

von Kluge: Early, or during the night?

Eberbach: I mean the bomb carpet which was laid down anew towards noonday. Since then, I have no further news from him.

von Kluge: If I send you a tank formation, would that help you?

Eberbach: Yes.

von Kluge: Have you then a man who could lead them?

Eberbach: Yes, that man Wünsche.

von Kluge: He is still there? Aha! I am considering whether I could still send you a panzer battalion.

Eberbach: If it were possible.

von Kluge: Perhaps also another one from Alençon. During the night, naturally.

Eberbach: If we are lucky with the fog. If they could come to Falaise? I would spot [supply] fuel there.

von Kluge: Yes, I will call you up shortly.

2230 Continuation of Conversation between General Eberbach and Field Marshal von Kluge

von Kluge: Has the situation deteriorated or improved?

Eberbach: One cannot say improved, the opponent appears to arrange his formations afresh. All his attack have been conducted with tanks without infantry. Since the Evening Report, I have the impression that everywhere, including LXXIV Corps, he is withdrawing tank forces to engage them too in the main area of penetration on the Caen road in the direction of Falaise. I believe that tomorrow he will attack perhaps even stronger still and on a wider front; from left flank I SS Panzer Corps up to LXXXVI Corps. Enemy has pressed forward from Hautmesnil with very strong elements through to Langannerie. I hope that we succeed in destroying the enemy during this night in Langannerie where he is not supposed to be so strong (12 tanks), and hold the line St. Sylvanin–Bretteville.

von Kluge: With what forces will you do that?

Eberbach: With elements of LXXXVI Corps (battle groups), and elements of Hitler Youth Division. No contact with Meyer so far, only Wünsche is here.

von Kluge: The tanks of 9th Panzer Division will be sent off on the march from Argentan to Falaise, so that early tomorrow they will be half on. That is a very weighty decision for me, a major abandonment of an order that has been given to me [by Hitler]. I know of no other solution – have no further forces. If it goes on like this tomorrow, there will be no more stopping [the Allies] at all.

At 0500 hrs, a capable senior officer of Fifth Panzer Army or 1 SS Panzer Corps is to stand at the railway crossing 800 metres south of Falaise on the road leading from Argentan to Falaise, forked roads south of the railway. I know that, in the long run the forces will be inadequate.

Chapter 3

The German Experience of Battle

Soldiers' Diaries and Memories

Document 3/1[1]

Diary of Private Bucher, 264th Infantry Division, November 1943 to 3 September 1944

Wartime Intelligence Officer's Comments

The following extracts from the diary of Private Andreas Bucher, an Alsatian, aged 24 years and conscripted by the Germans, gives a vivid account of the impressions of a non-German in the Wehrmacht.

Introduction

This diary, intended to be an account of all the horror and paralysing terror called war, should reflect the great events of what was going on in my own little soul. Already once I have kept a diary, in 1939/40, while serving with the French Army in Northern France, Belgium and Dunkerque. I destroyed it when I fell into German captivity. Somehow, the last years of war have broken me. I'm afraid of the future. Will sunshine clear up my life again so that I can feel young and gay once more?

29 Nov 43

Rendered oath of allegiance. The silliest comedy I've ever seen; and they even dared to play the 'Great Lord, we praise Thee' after the ceremony.
　　[Word illegible]

---

1. ISUM 116, 23 October 1944, taken from *First US Army Prisoner of War Report*.

Berlin, Ost-West Axis [word illegible] This really beautiful street hasn't been hit as of April 44. It is covered by a huge camouflage net. How much longer will the street remain undamaged?

25 Apr 44

Today, the strangest thing happened to me. I got my assignment; I am supposed to join the 264th Division, the very same division I fought against at Dunkerque.

26 Apr 44

I pass through Leipzig by train. A big factory on the right side of the tracks in flames. Berlin is damaged even worse this time than before. Frankfurt radically destroyed, looks simply terrible.

29 August 44, Düsseldorf

I took a walk in the woods. There, dugouts can be found in the mountainside at regular intervals, to serve as air raid shelters – but only partly ready; to the bigger part they are under construction. The entire population of Düsseldorf walks there in the early evening hours between 8 and 9 to secure a good place – and since the weather is so nice people are camping in the woods and along the roadside near the shelters. You can find all kinds of people there, from babies to stone-old grandma's. These conditions create immorality – under the cover of darkness, women sleep with young soldiers and often also with foreign workers.

30 May 44, Aachen

Our company has to unload meat from a refrigerator car – 20 tons of rotten meat but good enough for the Wehrmacht. Here you could see an example of a 'United Nation' – political bosses with mountains of sandwiches, white bread, butter, sausage, ham, chocolate; NCOs got cigarettes by packs, we OR receive 2 pieces each. Officers drunk from stolen wine. These gentlemen disappear with big quantities of the best meat. We didn't get lunch, in fact nothing to eat till 1800 hours. A special squad was ordered to clean a cellar. One man from the Party supervised the work. There were piles of meat cans, sardines, wine, rum.

12 July 44

Said a Sergeant: 'You can say what you want but I went yesterday to see the sad bunch of replacements and there you won't find a single soul who still believes in victory. Everybody states that the war is lost for us.'

23 July 44, Düsseldorf

Reitzenstein Kaserne. 16 years old 3-week-soldiers arrive here to be shipped to Trondheim, Norway. There are many among them who are nothing but children, others are cripples. Will they ever be any good – I doubt it. Today arrived the first 2000 Home Guard soldiers, between 45 and 60 years old. They weren't even issued uniforms, they just wore the armband. They complain a lot, in fact all the time. The other soldiers shake their heads. 'V-5'[2] they remark bitterly.

1 September 1944

Received a letter from Heidelberg according to which all boys 14 years of age were ordered to dig trenches in Alsace. Today I was transferred to the 42 MG Fortress Battalion, as a messenger. Destination West Wall. This battalion is composed of Home Guard soldiers, half crippled – I found many among them quite obviously off mentally. Some had their arms amputated, others had one leg short, etc., – a sad view. 'V-31' they joke. A bunch of fools!

30 September 1944

Our soldiers behave as if they were in enemy territory. They break into houses and pillage in the good old custom. Troops which are employed against them prove to be good masters in this art of war themselves. People are enraged. They are united in an ardent desire to see Tommy arrive; in spite of the heavy propaganda they are not afraid of him.

3 September 1944 Düsseldorf

Today the craziest rumours are floating around. Cologne is overrun by refugees from Metz, Saarbrücken and Trier. In the entire neighbourhood, boys and girls are called upon to dig entrenchments and build bunkers. American armoured columns are near Trier; street fighting in Brussels. Vehicles of all kinds coming from the front move through the street in

---

2. This is a joke, there was no V-5 weapon.

never-ending columns. At the Railroad station paratroopers, ragged and dirty. The garrison is alerted. It's hard to distinguish between rumours and truth.

Document 3/2[3]

Extracts from Diary of a *Panzerschütze* of 4th Company, I Battalion, Panzer Regiment 100, 21st Panzer Division, 7 June to 13 July 1944

7 June

<u>0330 hrs</u> We drive to our company. Roads of the advance very congested.

<u>1000 hrs</u> Arrival at the supply transport of our company. Have to stay there until noon. We are told that our company had their first engagement on 6 June. *Oberschütze* K. hit by a shell in the assembly area.

<u>1200 hrs</u> We take the kitchen to the company. Company already fighting near St. Honorine 093713. My tank does not take part in the engagement but I listen in on the radio to the progress of the fight.

<u>1800 hrs</u> Company returns. Tanks got 25 anti-tank hits. Loading number[4] Patsch dead. Buried at St. Honorine. My tank is not taking part in the battle. Number 55 direct anti-tank hit is blown up with crew. Corporal Aderl, Lance-Corporal Libonski, Galle, Gent and Reckin. Lieutenant Neumann is wounded but stays with the company. Lieutenant Neumann shot down an enemy fighter with an MG and Cpl Eichler hit a Matilda[5] tank. We go into assembly area at Herouvillette 120722.

---

3. ISUM 30, 29 July 1944
4. The loading number was the member of the crew who loaded the main gun and operated the radio.
5. As the Matilda was obsolescent by 1944, this was another type of tank or possibly a Matilda or Valentine Scorpion used for mine clearing.

9 June

Assembly area under enemy artillery fire. Stay there until 1800 hrs.

<u>1800 hrs</u> 21st Reconnaissance Unit attack Escoville 123711. Attack bogged down in close country as every 110 yards there is a new hedge held by the enemy with anti-tank guns. Company must go back as it is a real witch's cauldron apart from artillery fire. Tank 01 receives a direct hit with an anti-tank gun and is set on fire. Crew escape but a lance-corporal is killed on his way back. Lieutenant Hoffmann is wounded. Corporal Köritzer and Lance-Corporal Martin return to the assembly area. Cpl Behrendt is missing. Tank 23 damaged by anti-tank gun and is on fire. Cpl Rohsack returns to our lines. Panzer Grenadier Sturm comes back wounded. Wiezens, Leyendecker and Vogel are missing. Tank 33 damaged tracks, crew escape. Sergeant Korflur blows up the tank. Crew returns to our lines. It is impossible for us tank people to achieve any success whatever in hedge country. Lieutenant Neumann takes over administrative command of the company. We return to old assembly area. 14 HE [rounds] used up.

16 June

Still with J section [unit vehicles repair section]. Hans Liebich buried in part of chateau Frenouville 116627. Our battalion excluding four companies with lorried infantry, artillery, engineers and rocket projectors are attacking. First Lieutenant Osteroh is killed. Lieutenant Horne takes over company. Lieutenant Thoner [takes over] four company.

23 June

<u>0600 hrs</u> Alarm. We drive to Demouville 102675 assembly area, which is shelled and mortared by the enemy. Enemy artillery fire mauve light signals as warning of tanks to their aircraft whereupon enemy air attack follows.

<u>0800 hrs</u> Our whole battalion in attack on St. Honorine. During battle we have to change clutch. Company is under heavy fire from anti-tank guns in St. Honorine. Line of attack under artillery and mortar fire. Tank 02 is hit by anti-tank and set on fire. Crew except drive escape. On our return Lieutenant Fetibach is wounded. Cpl Reinhart as well. Tank 12 hit but crew escape. Tank 34 hit on front place and gun but is able to return to J section. We must go to J section for oil change then proceed to assembly area Banville 135674.

28 June

Expected enemy does not appear after our trip of two days.

<u>0900 hrs</u> We attack ourselves 2 km west of Verson 965655. Contact enemy and throw them back. While continuing the advance we meet about 60 German tanks and 60 SP guns. Tank against tank attack develops. My leader who looked out of the turret is killed. We withdraw seeking cover. Heavy enemy artillery fire during the engagement. We withdraw on the order of our commander. We destroy one tank. On our journey back our tank suffers damage and is taken in tow by 13, but we cannot move due to front sprocket having been shot off. 2 Company Tank takes us in tow. Are approached by enemy scout cars which have been reported by the lorried infantry as enemy tanks so we retire, as not being able to move ourselves.

<u>2400 hrs</u> Arrived at J section. Tanks 11 and 32 did not take part in this engagement by day due to damage by anti-tank hits. 32 is blown up by own crew. Lieutenant Thoner and Corporal Pfeifer wounded. We had 2 Battalion of the *Leibstandarte Adolf Hitler* in support. 7 tanks shot up.

13 July

Lie in reserve area of Emieville. Quiet. Occasional artillery fire. Tigers have been put under command of our battalion.

Document 3/3[6]

Extracts from the Diary of *Obergefreiter* Norbert Ohe, 9 Troop, 276 Artillery Regiment, 276th Infantry Division, 15 August to 19 August 1944

15 August 1944

We had to retreat again. All roads are choked with MT. It looks as if they are trying to pull the motorised columns out of the pocket first.

---

6. ISUM 55, 23 August 1944.

16 August 1944

Our troop has been dissolved. I have been put into 9 Troop. The British have landed near Toulon. They say that our new *Düsenjäger* (turbine operated fighter planes)[7] have brought down 400 enemy aircraft the very first day.

18 August 1944

Nothing to eat for two days. Two of our vehicles were only 500 metres from a V-1 site today and we saw it explode.

19 August 1944

Today we moved East under fire. A lot of equipment had been left behind everywhere. The roads are still choked with transport. Only one road out of the pocket is left. The Allies are less than 50 km from Paris. Orleans has been taken.

Document 3/4 [8]

Extracts from the Diary of a Medical Sergeant, 17 August to 22 August 1944

17 August 1944

We have not seen a German fighter for weeks . . . I am wondering how the war will end, nobody believes in a turn for the better. No rest or sleep by day or night, only much work.

20 August 1944

For several days now we have been inside the pocket. We are supposed to fight our way out. Two divisions make an attempt, but 3 km in front of our objective we find ourselves between British tanks. Our comrades of

---

7. A reference to the Me 262 jet fighter, which was introduced into service in late July 1944 but was not nearly as successful as the diarist states.
8. ISUM 55, 23 August 1944.

the infantry fall like flies. There is no leadership left. I don't want to fight anymore, it is so useless. God grant that we may get out of this alive. I wonder what my wife is doing now.

22 August 1944

It is all over. I am in a PW camp near Caen. We receive rations but very little water. I am longing for home.

Document 3/5[9]

Diary of Sergeant W. Krey of 732 Grenadier Regiment, 712th Infantry Division, 31 August to 30 September 1944

31 August 1944

<u>10 p.m.</u> I am sitting in the Quartermaster's office with De Haan with Second Lieutenant Vollmuller when Chelius comes running into the room and calls out –'Operation Bruges' (*Fall Brugge*). The dice have fallen, our division is to be thrown into the line. We are to fight the tanks with rifles . . .

<u>3 a.m.</u> Without being given a zero hour we are suddenly told that everything must be ready to move off at 6.45 a.m. Now there is a general hustle and bustle. There is a shortage of vehicles – half our equipment has to be left behind. I am ordered to hand it over to the relieving division.

2 September 1944

I have finished my jobs by about 10 a.m. The commander asks about plans of minefields, demolitions, inundations, etc. – I haven't the foggiest. I was not briefed sufficiently before leaving. The situation must have got worse, for the officers are standing in front of maps and looking grave . . . At

---

9. ISUM 108, 16 October 1944. Taken from *Second British Army Intelligence Summary,* No. 128, 10 October 1944.

noon I leave HQ with Schneller and Cpl Georg. My orders are 'to join up with the main body.' It would seem impossible for three men alone to get through for southwest Flanders is the worst part of the area occupied by terrorists. I must carry out the order however . . . There appears no possibility of getting out of the pocket. North is the sea, east the Schelde, and south and west are the British . . . The squadron strikes south – deeper into the pocket. We form the advance guard . . . We march all night.

3–5 September 1944

(These entries describe the difficulties encountered on the march, dodging terrorists, getting indefinite orders from Captain Goldbeck, with whose leadership they become dissatisfied, their apparent desertion by their officers who, they think, must have crossed by car over one of the still functioning ferries in the north.)

6 September 1944

Just before reaching the cross-roads Bergen op Zoom–Antwerp–Flushing a convoy comes toward me. As it passes I recognise the OC, 2/Lt Hertel. I call out to him, overjoyed at having found one of our officers . . . He will remember my words as long as he lives . . . 2/Lt Hertel promises to fetch Captain Goldbeck at once . . . Hours later he returns without the captain and the veterinary surgeon.

Document 3/6[10]

Extracts from the Diary of an Unidentified Corporal, 4th Company, Grenadier Regiment, 719th Infantry Division, 25 August to 17 September 1944

Wartime Intelligence Officer's Comments

The extracts start when the Division was stationed in the Dutch islands, and this battalion on the island of Schouwen. As the unit goes into action, the

---

10. ISUM 99, 25 August 1944.

tale of cowardice, desertion, plunder and destruction is hardly reminiscent of the well-trained disciplined German Army that goose-stepped into France in 1940. The diary is no doubt coloured by the writer's personal resentment against certain of his officers, but it nevertheless confirms a great deal of what has already been told by Belgian and French civilians who witnessed the sight of the Wehrmacht in retreat.

25 August 1944

A propaganda officer from Corps and propaganda officer Keller of our Division are on the Isle. The cattle dealer, our company commander, has to give a political lesson under supervision. He spoke before officers and NCOs – Two attacks of fighter-bombers on ships near strongpoint 46. Some killed and some wounded. Observed dive bombing from out of the sun with rockets.

25 August 1944

At 0700 hours again fighter bomber attacks. We were in great danger. The Americans and troops of De Gaulle in Paris?

27 August 1944

Hauling ammunition for fighters. At 0300 hours we were allotted hotel rooms at Bergen Op Zoom. Our railway AA guns shot down two four-engined bombers with 8 rounds. Six secret wireless agents were marched through town. Anti-German feeling has grown considerably.

28 August 1944

Rosendaal D73 has been badly hit. Many attacks by fighter bombers on the Dutch railway system. The population considers us the losing side already. Baroness von Ketteler (a staff helper from Munster), a typical officer's mistress, is with a pilot officer at Zeist.

29 August 1944

The base wallahs[11] in the big towns live more opulently and lasciviously than before. Amsterdam is now a diseased and whoring town. Forced

---

11. Here, the translator has been rather generous with his use of British army slang. It should be remembered, however, that this material was being translated for an audience familiar with British army terminology, doctrine, tactics and slang, and translators sometimes stretched things a bit.

march from Rosendaal to Kruisland D63. A tank company with aged Renault type tanks in Kruisland. The four officers of our unit have their mess in the catholic priest's house!

30 and 31 August 1944

The chicanery of the company continues against me after my return. For the time we will remain in Burgh D25. The Battalion Commander justifies this at a parade of NCOs. Major-General Sievers[12] spoke to the officers at Steenbergen D63. He lost his third division in France. His 16 Luftwaffe Field Division went to Normandy with many vehicles (easy chairs, canaries, rugs, chicken hutches, etc.) All that was missing was ammunition and weapons. That is the typical way in which Luftwaffe units are run.

1 September 1944

The whole battalion is leaving the Isle. In pouring rain I drive to Zierikzee D34 as the last man to leave. On the ferry, of course, the company favourites have the best places.

2 September 1944

Stay for the night in a boiler room. 1000 hours at Schiedam D67. At night quartered in civilian houses. Start of chaotic circumstances. The Commander puts me in charge of the anti-tank section. Good news! We are supposed to go to Luxembourg. During the night we are told of our new field of action. Alas, it is the Albert Canal.

3 and 4 September 1944

Receive my bazookas in very bad condition at the harbour of Schiedam. Proceed to the station. Held up by enemy air activity. To Rosendaal by train. From there further progress by rail is impossible. Wild flight along the rails and roads. Luftwaffe and Marine! Thousands of officers are trying to save their lives. March to Antwerp. Complete disorder. We have to protect the retreat of these cowardly bastards. 719 Division stops the enemy advance for the time being. Many casualties in 12 Company.

---

12. *Generalleutnant* Karl Sievers, former commander of the 16th Luftwaffe Field Division and then the 719th Infantry Division.

5 September 1944

Since Monday afternoon we've been at the demolished bridge over the Albert Canal. Terrorists take part in the battle. Alone I go back to Merxem J79. The whole way I didn't meet one German soldier.

6 September 1944

Strong enemy artillery fire in our sector, Americans or Britons only 300 metres from us. Assault guns of the SS are supposed to come to our assistance. Communication path is under fire. The Company pets are not runners any more now. The General is with us.

7 September 1944

Soldiers trying to escape were caught at Breda and some sent back to the front. Our Company got some reinforcements in this way. Still strong artillery fire.

8 September 1944

Great activity by the enemy on the other side of the canal. It is rumoured that on our side 'terrorists' are active.

9 September 1944

4 Company sends one platoon to Merxem to reinforce 12 Company. One dead, four missing. In spite of heavy counter attacks the enemy held his bridge head over the canal. The stealing in empty houses is terrific. Isecke, one of the most cowardly in 4 Company, wins laurels plundering!

10 September 1944

Martin makes a report on the cowardice of Zeisler at Merxem. Shubert takes my pistol away with a very flimsy excuse. I ignore the cattle dealer and all the sods around him. The old Company pets are now with the transport.

11 September 1944

A patrol of 3 Company went to the other side of the canal during the night. An enemy patrol was on our side at the same time. Callenberg has been a deserter since 6 September. Rumour of von Kluge's suicide.[13] Model (55) his successor. The Regimental Commander very dissatisfied with 3 Company's sector.

12 September 1944

Enemy patrol breaks in in our sector! Smoke bombs and mortar fire. They take a sentry from 3 Company with them. This causes a hunt for partisans through all the houses in the village. The wanton destruction and plundering is indescribable. There are no more decent or respectable men left around me.

14 September 1944

The Anglo-Americans are at Hasselt, Eupen and Metz. Daily, enemy artillery fire. Enemy patrol breaks into 4 Company sector. Enemy air activity increases daily. Saw an interesting example of a newspaper from liberated Antwerp.

15 September 1944

Had a set-to with the Officer Commanding. He takes the bicycles away from my section because he thinks we may retreat. 'Position will be held to the last man' he shouts at me. The badly mauled 3 Battalion is in our sector as reinforcements. Americans cross the border of the Reich!

16 September 1944

Model's appeal to the troops is made known to us. Anti-aircraft platoon is very busy plundering the chateau. The cattle dealer goes to the hospital because he fell from his bicycle. On purpose? A 21-year-old lieutenant from the *Hitlerjugend* battle school is his successor. He needs four batmen!!

17 September 1944

Officer Commanding 2 Company is also in hospital. Same 'sickness' as the cattle dealer. There are deserters from all companies now. Strong activity of enemy airforce. I have not seen a single German aircraft.

---

13. Suspected of complicity in the bomb plot against Hitler, *Feldmarschall* Günther von Kluge was recalled to Germany but committed suicide on 17 August 1944.

Document 3/7 [14]

Extracts from the Diary of an Officer, Boulogne Garrison, 7 September to 19 September 1944

Wartime Intelligence Officer's Comments

A captured diary gives the thoughts of a German officer during the siege of Boulogne. The picture of despondence and resigned acceptance of whatever fate has in store is one that has become increasingly evident in German letters and PW interrogations. It is significant that in this last testimonial of a fairly intelligent man, no reference is made to a belief or faith in either Naziism or Hitler. Defiance or hate of the Allies is also markedly absent. Only a dull and stolid hope that the Fatherland will not suffer at the hands of the enemy remains of the original ambitious nationalism of Nazi Germany.

7 September 1944

Encircled in Boulogne. For days I knew that there was no getting out of it for us. It is very hard to get used to the thought of having one's span of life nearly finished, and not to see one's wife and children again. If fate is favourable I may become a PW . . .

Last night Boulogne lay under heavy artillery fire. I wonder what tonight will bring. The assault preparations of the enemy must be nearly completed and we expect the attack any time.

8 September 1944

We have still not seen the enemy. During the night there was heavy artillery fire again. Some of the shells came quite close and so we moved from our billets into shelters. If only something would start – this waiting is the worst. One is so terribly alone in strange surroundings with one's thoughts which always go back home to wife and children. Poor Louise, now it will be your lot to wait in uncertainty, to hope and to despair. I wonder if my children will have to grow up without the help of their father? . . .

---

14. ISUM 83, 21 September 1944.

9 September 1944

Last night was comparatively quiet. Yesterday late in the afternoon enemy bombers attacked the forward defensive positions of Boulogne. My God, how long will it be until the town itself will be the target. Can anyone survive after a carpet of bombs has fallen? Sometimes one can despair of everything if one is at the mercy of the RAF without any protection. It seems as if all fighting is useless and all sacrifices in vain.

Always the worry about the family, and added to it the worry about the Fatherland. What will become of Germany if things should not go alright? Dismal and grey is the outlook for our future. God in heaven have mercy on our people.

10 September 1944

Today is Sunday but what is the difference. Yesterday afternoon enemy bombers again attacked Mont Lambert. As long as this fort holds out we will be alright. Once it falls the town is finished as well ...

11 September 1944

The night was very quiet again. I would have liked to have slept longer and dreamt of home, but with the awakening all the thoughts and worries of yesterday returned. Sometimes I wonder if I have always done my duty towards my family ...

We have lovely weather again today with a brilliant sun in a cloudless sky. How wonderful life could be for humanity if there wasn't a war. Will there ever be peace again?

All day long artillery fire on our outlying strong points and in between attacks by fighter-bombers. The outskirts are being evacuated by the French. I wonder if that means that the real show will start tonight? The morale of the troops is bad, and no wonder. They are mostly old married men and the situation is quite hopeless.

12 September 1944

Again lovely weather after a quiet night. The civilians have orders to evacuate the town by tomorrow night, and then I imagine it will be our turn to do our bit. I wonder how much longer I will live. Last night I played cards with two of my comrades, but even that couldn't banish our troubled thoughts. Dear diary, I am glad I have you. It quietens me to put down my thoughts which usually go out to family and country.

Generalfeldmarschall Gerd von Rundstedt, the German commander in the west, arrives to inspect a German unit in the spring of 1944. The Wehrmacht was waiting for an invasion that they knew was going to happen.

Generalfeldmarschall Rommel inspects converted French equipment of the 21st Panzer Division with the divisional commander, *Generalleutnant* Edgar Feuchtinger.

German ingenuity led to the creation of hybrid vehicles with German weapons mounted on the chassis of captured Allied vehicles. This example is a leFH18 105mm howitzer mated with a French Lorraine fully-tracked armoured ammunition vehicle.

Another hybrid was this French Somua half-track armed with multiple 80mm mortars.

A most improbable marriage was this mounting of a le FH16 105mm howitzer on the chassis of a British Mk VI light tank captured in 1940.

A complete regiment of self-propelled 105mm guns mounted on captured British Mk VI tank chassis, on parade at Versailles.

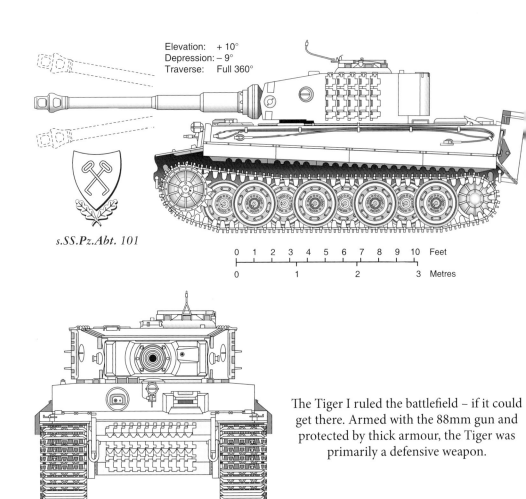

Elevation: + 10°
Depression: − 9°
Traverse: Full 360°

s.SS.Pz.Abt. 101

| 0 | 1 | 2 | 3 | 4 | 5 | 6 | 7 | 8 | 9 | 10 | Feet |

| 0 | | | 1 | | | 2 | | | 3 | Metres |

The Tiger I ruled the battlefield – if it could get there. Armed with the 88mm gun and protected by thick armour, the Tiger was primarily a defensive weapon.

Protection in the Frontal Arc – A Comparison

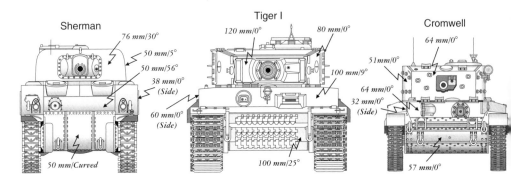

Sherman
76 mm/30°
50 mm/5°
50 mm/56°
38 mm/0° (Side)
60 mm/0° (Side)
50 mm/Curved

Tiger I
120 mm/0°
80 mm/0°
100 mm/9°
100 mm/25°

Cromwell
64 mm/0°
51mm/0°
64 mm/0°
32 mm/0° (Side)
57 mm/0°

A knocked-out gun position on the Normandy coast.
Although these positions mounted heavy weapons they were
no match for Allied air and naval might.

The Tiger II was an improved model with thicker armour that was sloped to provide
additional protection. Only twenty-five of these vehicles served in Normandy.

The Panther was one of the best medium tanks of the war and far superior to its Allied counterparts. However, it burned fuel at a furious rate and required considerable maintenance. This example, which belonged to I/12th SS Panzer Regiment, was knocked out by Canadian infantry at Bretteville on 8 June 1944. More than 600 Panthers were deployed in Normandy.

The Jagdpanther was a very effective combination of the deadly 88mm gun on the chassis of the Panther. Fortunately, only one anti-tank battalion deployed twenty-five of these vehicles in Normandy.

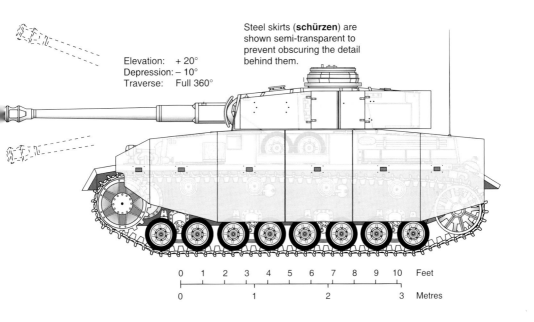

Elevation: + 20°
Depression: – 10°
Traverse: Full 360°

Steel skirts (**schürzen**) are shown semi-transparent to prevent obscuring the detail behind them.

| 0 | 1 | 2 | 3 | 4 | 5 | 6 | 7 | 8 | 9 | 10 | Feet |

| 0 | | | 1 | | | 2 | | | 3 | Metres |

The Mk IV medium tank was the work horse of the panzer divisions and more than 800 were deployed in Normandy. Inferior to the Sherman in mobility and armour, it had a superior main gun.

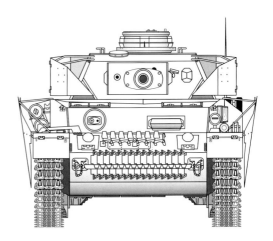

Protection in the Frontal Arc – A Comparison

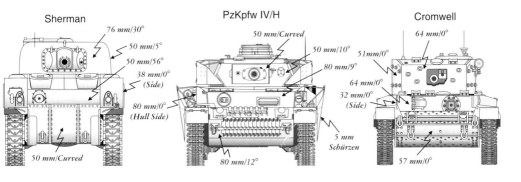

Sherman

76 mm/30°
50 mm/5°
50 mm/56°
38 mm/0°
(Side)
80 mm/0°
(Hull Side)
50 mm/Curved

PzKpfw IV/H

50 mm/Curved
50 mm/10°
80 mm/9°
5 mm
Schürzen
80 mm/12°

Cromwell

64 mm/0°
51mm/0°
64 mm/0°
32 mm/0°
(Side)
57 mm/0°

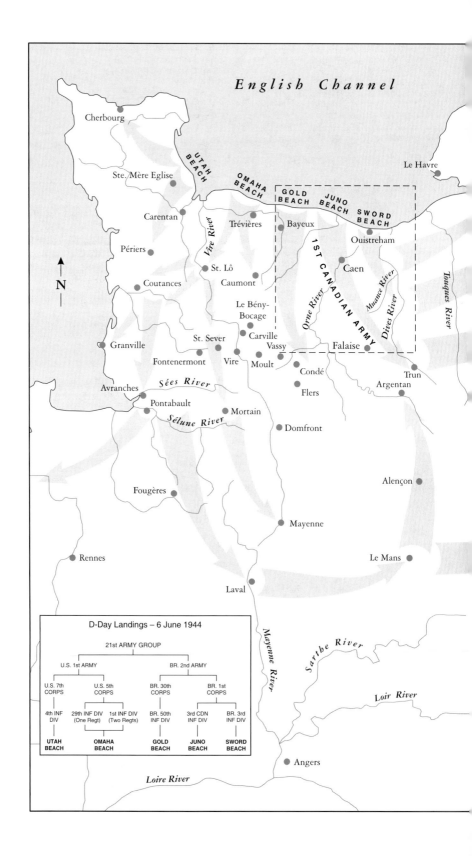

English Channel

Cherbourg

UTAH BEACH

Ste. Mère Eglise

OMAHA BEACH

Le Havre

GOLD BEACH

JUNO BEACH

SWORD BEACH

Carentan

Trévières

Bayeux

Ouistreham

N

Vire River

Périers

St. Lô

Caen

Coutances

Caumont

1ST CANADIAN ARMY

Orne River

Muance River

Dives River

Touques River

Le Bény-Bocage

Granville

St. Sever

Carville

Vassy

Falaise

Fontenermont

Vire

Moult

Condé

Trun

Sées River

Avranches

Flers

Argentan

Pontabault

Sélune River

Mortain

Domfront

Alençon

Fougères

Mayenne

Rennes

Le Mans

Laval

Mayenne River

Sarthe River

Loir River

D-Day Landings – 6 June 1944

21st ARMY GROUP

U.S. 1st ARMY		BR. 2nd ARMY	
U.S. 7th CORPS	U.S. 5th CORPS	BR. 30th CORPS	BR. 1st CORPS
4th INF DIV	29th INF DIV (One Regt) · 1st INF DIV (Two Regts)	BR. 50th INF DIV	3rd CDN INF DIV · BR. 3rd INF DIV
UTAH BEACH	**OMAHA BEACH**	**GOLD BEACH**	**JUNO BEACH** · **SWORD BEACH**

Angers

Loire River

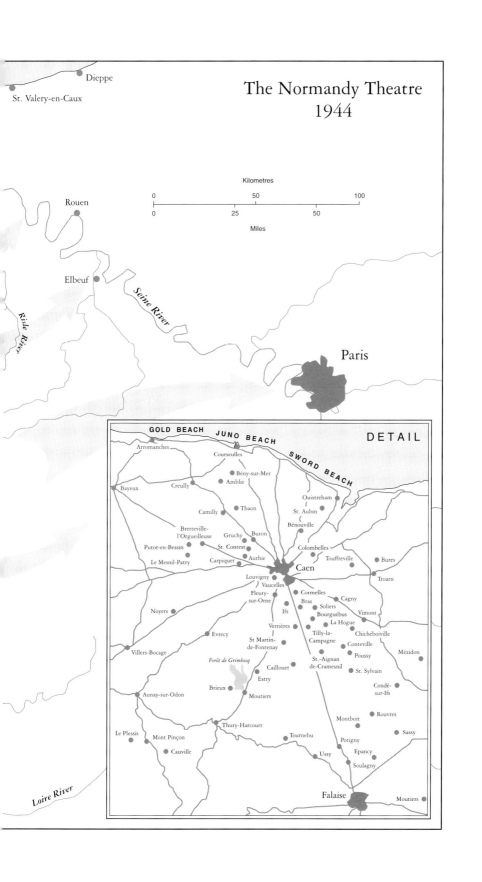

The Normandy Theatre
1944

Kilometres

0   50   100

0   25   50

Miles

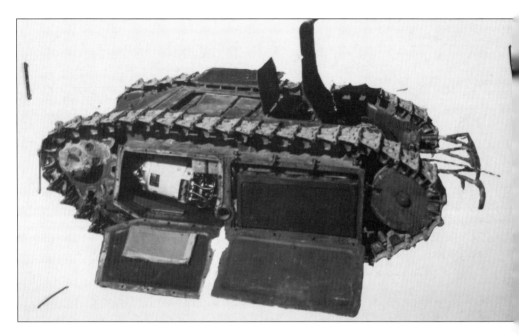

Goliath tracked mine. Controlled by cables and carrying up to 200lbs of explosives, this was a remote-controlled miniature armoured vehicle used to demolish buildings and vehicles.

Allied tanks like this Sherman of the 1st Hussars of the Canadian army, which has been penetrated by at least six projectiles, suffered from superior German tanks and anti-tank guns during the campaign.

Panzer grenadiers of the Panzer Lehr Division in their SPW 251 half-track.
This formation was the strongest German armoured division in Normandy being
equipped with more than 200 AFVs and over 600 SPW 251 half-tracks.

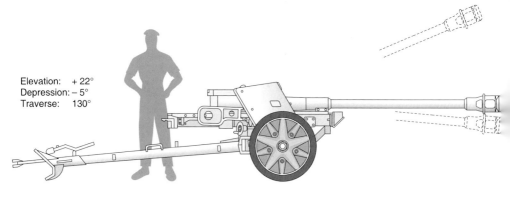

Elevation: + 22°
Depression: – 5°
Traverse: 130°

Tank killer. Although most Allied armoured crews feared the powerful 88mm gun, it was the humbler PAK 40 75mm, the standard German divisional anti-tank gun, that accounted for more Allied tanks.

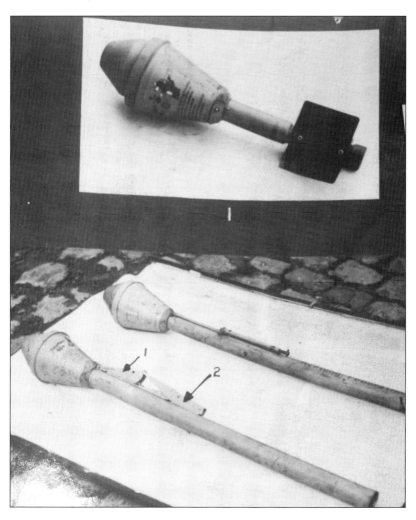

Above: A photograph from the Intelligence Summaries shows a *Panzerfaust* 30 launcher and projectiles. The *Panzerfaust* ('armoured fist') was a cheap, disposable, recoilless anti-tank weapon firing a hollow-charge projectile that could penetrate up to 5in of armour.

Left: American soldiers examine an 88mm *Panzerschreck* ('Tank frightener'). Based on the American bazooka, the *Panzerschreck* fired a shaped charge that could penetrate up to 4in of armour.

A photograph of a German 150mm howitzer from the Canadian Army Intelligence Summaries. In Normandy the German artillery was completely outgunned by their Allied counterparts, both in numbers and quality of weapons. The 150mm howitzer was one of the standard weapons of the Wehrmacht but it was an outdated design.

German vehicle columns under air attack during the battle for the Falaise Gap, August 1944. Allied tactical aircraft pounded the retreating Wehrmacht relentlessly during its withdrawal from France.

The 2nd French Armoured Division prepares to move forward in Normandy, August 1944. With complete control of the air, the Allied armies could assemble in such mass formations without fear.

American troops fighting in the hedgerows, July 1944. The Wehrmacht did not have a high opinion of Allied infantry in Normandy – one report described the Allied infantryman as 'a hard fighter only as long as he has good support from artillery and mortar units'.

A German column surrenders to Canadian troops, St. Lambert-sur-Dives, 19 August 1944. The little village of St. Lambert was in the middle of the best escape route out of the Falaise pocket and was the scene of heavy fighting.

Nearly 200,000 German soldiers were listed as missing in the fighting in northern and southern France in the summer of 1944. Many were actually prisoners of war such as these men, 'HIWIs' or 'volunteers' from the Asiatic states of the Soviet Union. By 1944 Germany was running out of men and began to conscript these troops of very dubious quality.

The inexorable enemy stands on the borders of the Fatherland. Will it be possible to hold him there? Woe my country should we lose this war. Life will not be worth living then. What will become of our children?

13 September 1944

Last night Lieutenant Lotzin of the engineers came to us for a three day attachment to advise us on fortifying positions. We passed the time until midnight with a bottle of Cognac. Alcohol is the only thing which can comfort anyone in our position. I am glad my parents are not alive anymore. They will not have to witness the terrible fate of our homeland. They rest in peace. Soon I shall join them.

This afternoon more heavy air attacks on Mont Lambert and the outer defences of Boulogne. Most of the civilians have wandered off with bits of their belongings. What a tragic spectacle. When will tormented humanity have peace again? Artillery activity is increasing. Soon the show will start.

14 September 1944

Still bright and sunny weather. I may move to 6 section today. At the harbour command everyone is desperately gay and tries to drown all worries in alcohol. And those filthy jokes which aren't even funny! I'll be glad to get away from there. I wonder what is happening at home with the enemy on German soil.

15 September 1944

Friday, and another week has nearly gone by and still no assault, but it will surely come soon. Le Havre fell two days ago and consequently more enemy troops will be available now. Right now the enemy is bombarding us with leaflets asking us to desert. With the situation as hopeless as it is this is quite a temptation for some of the soldiers.

16 September 1944

Saturday – the day on which I always write the long weekly letter home. But that was in the past. Now we can neither send nor receive mail any more . . . I still desire to see my destroyed homeland once more.

Last night I visited Lieutenant Arnold Hauptmann with whom I had bunked for so long. He is in the same state of mind as I am, very depressed. He told me that Captain von Nostitz was taken PW and also most likely our friend Heinz Hochmeister. I wonder if I shall see them again.

The night was quiet but all day we had fighter-bomber attacks on the outlying strong points. If only the weather wasn't so favourable to the enemy air force. Battles are being fought now in the outer defences of the Siegfried line and also on German soil. Will we be able to hold the overwhelming force of the enemy?

This afternoon we had some fighter-bomber attacks on our positions. Fortunately nobody was hurt. Two houses in the neighbourhood were destroyed. God help anyone who hasn't got a shelter or a slit trench handy when they come.

17 September 1944

It is nine months today since I last went on leave. What a good time I had. And today what a contrast. I was just ready to go to breakfast when we had to run for shelter and we have been there ever since. The bombardment by bombers and artillery was terrific. It is 1600 hrs now. I am looking at your pictures, my loved ones. I am quiet now and resigned to my fate whatever it may be. Farewell my little ones I pray to God that he may protect and guide you.

2000 hrs. All afternoon a heavy artillery barrage fell on our position. We could not move. Then we heard tanks approaching and had to surrender. It is a wonder that we are still alive. One shell hit our MG position, but the man on duty had just gone to relieve himself. We were treated very decently and are now waiting in our basement for evacuation tomorrow morning. I am now a PW of the Canadians. It may be a long time before I see my family again, but some day I shall.

18 September 1944

We are still waiting for evacuation. Street fighting is still going on but it cannot last much longer. It is a hard fate to be a PW. Dull and grey like the sky above stretches the future ahead of me.

19 September 1944

We spent the second night in our old shelter. I think today we will be taken to the citadel where the other PW are. Our guard, a young Canadian, is a very decent sort of soldier. Over there they would say (here he writes in English) 'He is a good fellow.' He let us gather some of our belongings so that we might have our necessaries with us. How glad I will be when I am able to send word home to my family that I am still alive and well.

Document 3/8[15]

To the Bitter End: The Last Hours in the Falaise Pocket

Wartime Intelligence Officer's Comments

The following information was obtained from interrogation of an Officer PW captured on 21st August 1944 at St. Lambert-sur-Dives.

At 2 o'clock we received a report that the gap had been forced. We were accordingly to move and drove off with three cars. We drove two or three kilometres and then came onto roads which were completely blocked. There were four or five columns of traffic which had run into each other with dead and wounded in between. We put our vehicles into one column and got stuck in it. Then we went on foot from 3 o'clock in the morning until six. Eventually we arrived forward at the place where the gap was supposed to be, and met about two to three hundred men. They were composed of a paratroop 'Battalion', to which SS and Army and German Air Force and Navy personnel had attached themselves. Two tanks joined us – a Mark IV and a 'Panther'; they were put in the vanguard with scouts ahead and one platoon behind them, and then the troops. Suddenly there was heavy firing into the sunken road. At first it sounded like fire from Anti-Tank guns and mortars and MGs, interspersed with rifle fire. The tank immediately reversed and ran over some of our men, whereupon all the infantry streamed back. I took up the position at the rear to hold up the retreat and I shot the first one who came along. An RSM stood beside me and brought them to a halt. Then the tank drove up and I ordered it to drive ahead again. Soon however the tank was hit and set on fire. We

---

15. Information from an officer prisoner captured on 21 August 1944 by Canadian troops at St. Lambert-sur-Dives, Appendix E in Report No. 15, 'Enemy Casualties in Vehicles and Equipment during the Retreat from Normandy to the Seine,' in *Operational Research in North West Europe: The Work of No. 2 Operational Research Section with 21 Army Group – June 1944–July 1945* (London, 1945).

lay down flat and then came heavy firing along the sunken road from ahead. We had a great many dead and wounded. We lay for 10 minutes and then the fire eased off a bit. I heard the sound of tanks, so I made two men come forward with 'Faustpatronen'[16] which we still had with us. It slowly became light and then we saw Americans in the opposite hedge. We fired at them with MG and tommy-gun fire. Then the enemy started firing again. There was suddenly heavy fire out of the whole hedge with cannon and MGs. Then someone at the rear started to wave a white flag on a stick. We shot him at a distance of 100m. After a second attempt with a white flag had also proved unsuccessful, we heard the noise of an enemy tank ahead again. In the meantime we had brought up our second tank, the 'Panther'. This was given orders to take up a position behind the shot-up Mark IV tank and to shoot up the advancing tank with its guns. The 'Panther' made a mistake in not taking up a position diagonally behind the Mark IV but driving past it. It was hit and burst into flames. Later, another white flag appeared, and again we fired at the troops surrendering. We were occupied with trying to get up to the enemy tank with the 'Faustpatrone' when American troops captured us.

---

16. The early name for the anti-tank weapon later called the *Panzerfaust*.

Chapter 4

The Individual Soldier's Experience

Letters to and from Home

Document 4/1[1]

Letters Home, July 1944

From *SS Mann* H. Graul of 5th Company, 21st SS Panzer Grenadier Regiment, to his uncle, 21 July 1944

One has to endure quite a lot here. I don't know what will happen if we are not relieved soon. So far we have had 20 killed and 60 wounded in this company ... There is a great difference between Tommy and the Russians. Here one must have good nerves to stand being shelled for hours on end, and whoever manages to get out of it alive is pretty lucky. No doubt you will have seen in the Army Communique some mention of the SS Division Frundsberg. I'm in that Division. Most of the men begin to lose their hair at 19.

From unknown soldier (probably of 21st Panzer Division) to his wife, 17 July 1944

I must write to you at night otherwise there is no time for letter writing. It is only midnight and now exactly the same as last night our aeroplanes are humming above us. We plainly hear the explosions of our bombs and even the house in which we are sitting, trembles. We can see Tommy's flak firing quite madly.

---

1. ISUM 30, 29 July 1944.

The war here is a very unequal struggle. We are too weak compared with our opponents If we had as much support as our enemies, things would have been different long ago. We have to be too careful with our ammunition but we think it important to hit something with the few shots we fire. As opposed to this, Tommy, the same as ever, shoots all over the place indiscriminately . . . but where is our support? I mean the much talked-of Retaliation Weapon (*Vergeltungswaffe*).[2] There have been rumours for some time that something of the sort is in action against London. But if they don't do something about it here soon, things will look pretty black for us. If Tommy was a bit more of a soldier, he could push us anywhere he wanted to.

You can tell that to those fellows who strut about in their pretty uniforms at home, with their pistols strapped round their bellies. Let them come and see for themselves sometime the unequal fight that is going on here.

From *Gefreiter* Heinz Koch of I Battalion, 982 Grenadier Regiment, 272nd Infantry Division to his mother, 20 July 1944

I'm sitting in my little shrapnel-proof dugout and am writing you this letter. I haven't much time, as I may be thrown to the ground with my face in the dirt at any moment. Dear Mother, hell is let loose here. The dirty dog is firing all the time: this morning he has again put up a continuous barrage lasting six hours. The only good thing is that we have a good position, which the enemy can't overlook . . . I'd like to know how much longer this is going to last. They keep talking such a lot about V.2, but I shan't believe it until it actually happens . . .

---

2. *Vergeltungswaffen* or retaliation weapons included the V-1 flying bomb and the V-2 missile.

Document 4/2[3]

From a Letter of *Obergefreiter* W. Doehla, FPN 43769B, Dated 18 August 1944

... We had to retreat in a great hurry. All the other units pulled out without firing a shot and we were left to cover them. The Tommy must have got wind that there were only a few of us left and he attacked with tanks and infantry. At the same time the enemy artillery opened a barrage and it is a miracle that we got away without casualties. The engineers did a very good job demolishing everything as they went back, but in spite of it the enemy is right on our heels. I wonder what will become of us. The pocket is nearly closed, and besides that the enemy is already at Rouen. If he succeeds in breaking through to the sea we might as well make our last will. I don't think I shall ever see my home again. However we are fighting for Germany and our children and what happens to us matters. I close with the hope that soon a miracle will happen and that I shall see my home again.

Document 4/3[4]

Letter to Private Alfred Nikolaus, FPN 23289, From his Brother in Strasburg

... August 1944

Dear Alfred,

Just received your letter of 11 August; and your letter of 6 August still lies unanswered before me; so I can answer them both today ...

Yes, dear Alfred, there really are times in Germany when everything in the homeland is at the mercy of the enemy bombers and fighters and without protection. All the still available planes are used largely at the front – it seems they don't expect a breakdown at home as much as they do at the front. No wonder as at home we are still too well 'protected' by

3. ISUM 85, 3 October 1944.
4. ISUM 85, 23 September, from *First US Army G-2 Periodic Report 85.*

thousands of Gestapo and SS men, who are 'unavailable' for the front lines during the war, while others are forced to give their lives just for those 'people', and their relatives are being 'murdered' at home. That is where we have come to in Germany and that is why the word must be: Make an end as quickly as possible, and end at any price!!

Any further loss is senseless, the end is unavoidable. Many high officers realized that and wanted to make an end to this senseless shedding of blood, wanted to save what there is to save – they had to pay with their lives and were hanged as 'traitors'. They 'hang' frontline soldiers, men with the highest decorations, those scoundrels! They do what they want with human lives, they are the biggest criminals of all times, and one must see it as a deliverance when they receive their just rewards. That day is not far off now; all it needs is for one sector of the front to crumble today or tomorrow, and the end has come. A catastrophe cannot be avoided – only perhaps prolonged or delayed.

Here all is still the same; I wanted to bring the parents here for a spell, perhaps I can do it later. Hoping that our fondest wish may soon be fulfilled, we send our love, your brother,

Philip and Marie

Hope to see you soon! Better to be a prisoner of war of the British or Americans than to die a hero's death for the Führer or the Party.

Document 4/4[5]

Letters from German Soldiers to Their People at Home

A Corporal from 12th SS Panzer Division writes:

I am leader of a section, fine brave chaps. It is a pleasure to lead such fellows against the Tommy. Got the iron cross and have 18 days of close combat fighting behind me. Don't think I shall get leave, as I had 14 days in June. There have been some changes in the Reich, however leave it to Himmler, he will make a clean sweep. We notice it here out front.

---
5. ISUM 45, 13 August 1944

A Private from 12th SS Panzer Division Reconnaissance Battalion, 18 years of age, writes to his parents:

I just read that all 18 year olds had their first baptism of fire. I am included since I was in it since 7 June. Mail is really bad. No railways are functioning in France. Don't worry about food, we have more than you at home, so don't send me any. All my best friends have been killed only myself and my gunner are alive (writer is in charge of an armed semi-track vehicle). If at all possible could you send me some cigarettes, but don't delay – you know the proverb 'Red today, dead tomorrow'. (*Note: The proverb is right, this soldier was killed the following day*).

A Sergeant from 1056 Grenadier Regiment to his wife:

Just a few lines. You know what we front soldiers must feel like, with artillery fire and bombs day after day, night after night. There we are eight men in five funk holes, waiting until we are hit. But the incomprehensible [*sic*] German infantry man has nevertheless mastered the situation and will continue to do so. All of us are hoping and waiting for the secret weapons which have so often been discussed.

The same Sergeant writes to his parents:

The RAF rules the skies. I have not yet seen a single plane with a 'swastika' and yet in spite of the material superiority of the enemy we Germans hold firm. The front at Caen holds. Every soldier on this front is hoping for a miracle and waits for what has been spoken of so much (*the secret weapons*).

A German soldier to his mother:

It is now two days that I am in the front line. Opposite us are the Canadians. Mostly young lads who are in action for the first time. We have no trench system. The ground is too hard and full of stones.

A letter from a loving husband:

My darling little Mimi. Hope you are well and that your toothache is gone. Over us shells are humming through the air in the direction of the enemy, but we get thrown back at us ten times their number. The Tommy has a vast quantity of artillery to send over to us 1,000 rounds is for him a matter of minutes. I am lying here in the very front with Eko (*a friend*). His funk hole is some 50 yards away from mine. We spend the nights together as we are not allowed to sleep at night. Some of our friends were attacked by 14 Tommies last night. Immediately 3 of our chaps got wounded, but the remainder stayed in the hole and fired with all we had. The Tommy left 2 men killed and one wounded. All three were Canadians. We took the wounded man to Company HQ where he was attended to. A *Volksdeutscher*[6] (Slovak of German extraction) deserted in the first few hours we were in the line.

Document 4/5[7]

Letters Home, Late August 1944

Lance Corporal Klippel to his wife, 21 August

In 4 days it will be 5 years that we have been separated except for short intervals, I wonder how much longer it is going to last . . . But although there are some heavy battles going on here I am sure we will come through alright and that we will bring the war to a victorious end. Please God that I may be united with you again after that . . .

Lance Corporal Wiek to his wife, 21 August

Here in the west the battles are very heavy, but with the help of the new weapons which the Führer has promised us we will come out victorious . . .

A Medical Officer (name and unit unknown) to his wife, 22 August

The superiority of the enemy air force is really astonishing. We can be thankful that we have so much territory to retreat in without endangering our own country. There are many things I cannot understand at all. I would do many things differently, especially the way in which we wage this war, which should be much more radical. I would not leave one stone

---

6. *Volksdeutsch* were 'racial Germans', persons of German descent living in the occupied nations. As the war went on, they were liable for conscription into the Wehrmacht.
7. ISUM 66. 3 September 1944.

on top of another. I would leave a complete desert behind wherever we retreat. The fruit of our four years of occupation of France is very poor indeed. I cannot help but feel that too many became soft during their stay in France and got away from severity and hardness of thinking. Maybe I shouldn't write things like that to you because the home front has not that unconditional faith in our final victory as the soldiers. Don't worry about me. We can hear the rumble of guns at the front once in a while but the front will never catch up with us, and so I feel quite safe . . .

Corporal H. Schreiner to his mother, 22 August

We soldiers are mostly of the opinion that the war will be over soon. At least the way it is going at present it cannot go on much longer. We only hope that we will come out of it alive and will be able to join our loved ones again . . .

Corporal F. H. Hoffman to his wife, 23 August

Today I have the first chance to write a letter home after some terrible days of being encircled and cut off. Nobody who hasn't been there can imagine what it was like. All we saved was just our life. We were hunted like rabbits . . . I haven't had mail now for 16 days and am worried very much whether you are safe after the recent aerial attacks. I am waiting for mail but when will it arrive? . . .

H. Ahrens (rank unknown) to his wife, 23 August

Worse than anything are the enemy aircraft. Like hawks they come out of the sky upon their prey to leave a burning vehicle behind. They say that soon a new German Luftwaffe will appear, and everyone will breathe a sigh of relief when that happens . . . Of course you know that I cannot write about military matters, but we certainly do not agree with things as we have seen them here. Today they said that the Führer was here and made Model Commander in Chief in the west. If this is right it is not hard to guess that some of our higher ups were in sympathy with the 20 July [plot], because what we have seen here was anything but strategy . . .

Lieutenant K. Huppke FPN 08589T to his wife, 23 August

I am thinking of you, all my dear ones today. I have a lot of time for thinking to-day as enemy aircraft have kept us in our bunkers for the last 12 hrs. Who would have ever thought that they would turn up in such numbers? I think it is just about time that they were utterly destroyed. The announcement that this will take place shortly has given us all new courage. We have never lost faith that we have been forgotten by our leaders. No – our faith has won through, day after day, night after night we have struggled in the depth of our souls. Sometimes we get very down even if it costs the extreme in individual sacrifices . . . If we can hold out a few more weeks we will be advancing again. We were getting too used to having nothing but victories in this war, but we had to learn to take reverses as well. That is a hard and painful lesson to learn.

Lance Corporal G. Mückelberg, FPN 48527, to his wife, 23 August

We have been encircled twice now and just managed to get out of the 'Kessel'. We lost most of our vehicles including mine. With the vehicle I lost all my belongings except what I had on, everything also was burned. After that one of my comrades and I started out on foot. We walked for 5 days and just before we reached the Seine we ran into our Artillery Troop again. That was our tough luck, because we hadn't intended to get back to our unit again. Now we had to keep going back with our troop and keep on going back, but it was slower than walking because the roads were so jammed with transport that we were hardly moving most of the time. This was not a 'disengagement according to plan', but one hell of a wild confusion with everybody looking out for himself and trying to get away. So far I have got away intact, but who knows for how long, because I rather expect that the enemy has completed his next encircling move by now. You cannot imagine the stuff Tommy has got and we have nothing to put against it. It is hopeless anyway, the enemy strikes so hard that we lose our pants trying to get away and it won't be very long before we are back at the Westwall again. At least we have still enough to eat. The worst of it is that we don't get any mail. Yesterday I finally got two letters from you, the first after a long time, but they were a month old. Well, I am still living in hopes that some day we may meet again.

Corporal Ignaz Schwegmann to his parents, 25 August

Twice I have been very lucky not to have been taken prisoner like most of my comrades. American reconnaissance elements had caught up to us. We had to use the small side roads in our retreat because American tanks and English aircraft command all the main roads, and of course during the day we stay holed up and dare not move at all. When I talk to the boys who have been in every one of our campaigns all I hear is that there was never anything like this . . .

Able Seaman W. Lier to his wife, 25 August

The last two days we had clouds and rain. It wasn't very comfortable to be wet all the time but at least we had peace from enemy aircraft. Today they were all around us again like hornets, chasing every vehicle which dares to move. In spite of all we look with confidence into the future. One day, maybe not very far away, will come the great change of fortune. Don't lose courage or the faith in the final victory even if it looks very black at present . . .

Document 4/6[8]

Letters from Home, April to June 1944

To SS *Obersturmführer* Fächer, 12 SS Reconnaissance Battalion from his wife at Budrich, 21 April 1944

I was very anxious about you when you had to go out in all that AA fire (*when Fächer's leave was finished and he went out of the house*). The whole horizon over the factory district looked terrible. Last night we sat from 11 till 4 down in the shelter. I always bring our little boy down first and then get the other two children ready. The girls will not help us at all. It is impossible to get them out of bed . . . You would be surprised to know that our telephone is still out of action . . . last Wednesday bombs fell over the whole area Hamm, Lippstadt, Paderborn . . . If you have missed your night's rest you feel rotten all the next day. Are you being bothered by raids? . . . Dear Hans, could you possibly spare me a little coffee. We are very short.

---

8. ISUM 23, 18 July 1944.

To *SS Mann* Heinz Steffen from Leni, 3 May 1944

In your last letter you say that after the war every SS man will have as many women as fingers on his hands; don't be quite so conceited, because I don't think you will be able to create harems for yourselves as many of you seem to think.

Girls are not better [behaved] than yourselves, but there is no need for you to accept everything that people write as being true. I know six or seven girls who write to anything from five to twelve soldiers, but I, for instance, correspond with only a few of these . . . I will have you know that respectable girls are rationed – only frumps are free . . . After five years of war, one gets rather weary, but never mind, all will be well when you return victorious.

To *Oberschütze* Emil Gehm from his family in Olsbrücken

6 June 1944

We have heard the latest news on the radio . . . now the worst is before us. Things are in a bad way – what will happen to us now at home? From what one hears, they must already have sent over whole armies . . . We can no longer sleep and we don't want to work any more; we are always thinking of you and how you are getting on.

16 June 1944:

You often used to write to us that Tommy would be chary of coming. Now it has all happened quicker than you or we dreamt of. When we read the paper and listen to the wireless, Oh! it's dreadful to think what is happening where you are . . . Write when you have a little time, so that we shall know that you are still alive.

Document 4/7[9]

Letters from Home, September 1944

To *Obergefreiter* Rudolf Schlote, FPN 16997, from his wife at Bielefeld

Here at work we have got the 60 hour week. From 7 in the morning till 7 at night with a half hour break at midday and on top of it this wonderful atmosphere at home. Sometimes it becomes insupportable. One no longer dares to think and plan. Herr Elges was just saying that life will soon no longer be tolerable in a sober condition. And the general situation is, at the moment, so strained that something will probably snap in the near future. Let's hope that an explosion will then come and that it will turn out according to your wishes and lead to a happy ending.

That you have in the meantime been from France into Belgium and now into Holland is simply terrific. So that's how quickly it can go when one is chased. It was nice that you were able to get hold of a nice concertina and also a sleeping bag, but I hope it will be possible for you to bring them home. Otherwise it will be a pity about all your trouble and also about the other things if you were not able to keep them. In the present circumstances I suppose it cannot be counted upon. Should you be sent further back, say back into Germany, and you are able to use the postal service, then it would be best for you to send me by post all your things, which are only dead weight for you anyway. Pack it as well as you can and send it to me by express as articles of value. Then I might get it d.v. [*deo volente*, 'God willing']. . .

And now you are so near to me and yet it is not possible for us to meet. We are only allowed to travel 25 km now by ordinary passenger service, express and through trains may not be used at all. Holiday and leave journeys are also banned at present. Here in the works all leave has been stopped, as is the case everywhere. Decent people now have to wait while others have already had their leave. Well even this will not get me down for if you come home I shall take leave of absence whether they like it or not. Yes, the Americans and English are now walking around in Paris. Yes it is a funny feeling even for me, although I have never been

9. ISUM 92, 30 September 1944, from *Second British Army Intelligence Summary*, No. 116, 28 September 1944.

there myself, when I read the names in the papers. You were lucky again to get away in good time. You have no doubt seen Paris again, what it was like, and it is probably questionable whether you will ever get there again; it will be a nice recollection for you ... Perhaps you will already be somewhere else when this letter reaches you and then you will still be without mail from me. For in the last few weeks it has always happened that every time I wrote to you, you had moved again. My letters to you appear to be chasing right through the west. But I won't lose heart, others don't, everything will come right in time ...

To *Obergefreiter* E. Schreiber, FPN L24827, from his wife at Oberwiesenthal, 10 September 1944

I received your letter of the 3rd September today, I was awaiting it with great anxiety. You have no idea how I have been worrying about you ever since I have heard from the Army Communique that heavy fighting is already taking place in Antwerp. But it seems as though things had not got that far on the 3rd September when you wrote me this letter. Also the Allies were brought to a slight halt there. What are the people in Holland doing? (Perhaps they are now feeling the current going against you). I was so nervous and upset last week about the Allied advance and my thoughts were constantly with you. I await your next letter with the greatest anxiety. Oh, when one thinks over this war, now all our boundaries are threatened from all sides, and look where we were once! But it is said that we shall get it all back again by the means of <u>our new weapons</u>! Do you believe it too?

Chapter 5

Tactics

General Directions

Document 5/1[1]

Panzer Group West, Directions for Conducting Battles

CONFIDENTIAL
85th Infantry Division Operations Branch
Division Battle HQ 9 August 1944

Subject: Experiences from the fighting of the last few days

(1) In attached appendices are given extracts from the orders of Panzer Group West for your Information. Care must be taken that all junior officers and NCOs are well informed on the matters contained therein even before the division goes into action. All training will be conducted accordingly.

(2) Since many of the men of the division have not been under fire before, it is to be expected that casualties will occur through unnecessary gathering of troops. All officers and other ranks who have had battle experience must see to it that the troops are well dispersed.

This order will be destroyed directly brigade HQs have taken notice of it.

---

1. ISUM 49, 17 August 1944.

Appendix 'A'

Panzer Group West Operations Branch   HQ 6 July 1944

Subject: Directions for Conducting Battles

(1) Counter thrusts with tanks against the British will yield inexpensive success only if they are made at once. Otherwise the enemy will have put out mines and heavy casualties will be inflicted by artillery and low flying aircraft before reaching the starting point of the attack. The whole division must be on the alert as soon as an artillery barrage starts and observers must be sent forward. Action may be taken if necessary without orders and artillery must be placed in a position from where it can give best support for the defence as well as for immediate counter thrusts.

(2) The material superiority of the enemy air force makes ground reconnaissance especially necessary.
   Observation by every outpost
   Observation by artillery OPs
   Constant patrol activity
   Fighting patrols (PW interrogation and captured documents)

(3) Strict wireless discipline must be enforced. Offences must be punished, otherwise unnecessary casualties will occur.

(4) Single anti-tank guns are useless. Only anti-tank positions in depth make sense. They should be in open ground. The best defences against tanks near hedges are *Panzerfaust* and *Panzerschreck*; on roads, mines.

Appendix 'B'

The Commander-in-Chief   Operational HQ 13 July 1944
Panzer Group West
Operations Branch

Observations during my recent visit to the divisions give me cause to issue the following order:

(1) The HKL[2] is still too closely manned. In it should be only about one third of each company, the other two thirds should be in two lines 600 and 1200 metres behind the HKL. Reinforce the HKL at night

---

2. HKL or *Hauptkampflinie*, main line of resistance, the defensive line that must be defended at all costs.

if necessary. Whoever puts most of his men into the HKL will have high casualties without being able to prevent a break-in of the enemy.

(2) It is reported that the British use dummy shells just before the infantry breaks into our positions. These shells have the same sound as real ones but no blast effect. Through this and the use of smoke the enemy has been able to break into our positions on several occasions before our men came out of their trenches.

Deductions:

Observation must never cease. To prevent casualties use mirrors from unoccupied houses. Fire with all weapons as soon as the enemy start laying smoke screens.

(3) At one of our panzer divisions the enemy sent up scout cars under the protection of smoke. These cars had stovepipes arranged on them out of which they fired on our tanks.

Counter measures:

Observe and aim quickly. The thin armour of the scout cars is easily penetrated.

(4) Use mines mainly by laying them indiscriminately. Only at important points will mine panels be laid. Panels are too easily taken up. Mines strewn about make the enemy step warily everywhere and it is nearly impossible to take them up completely. Dummy minefields and minefield signs are also useful.

(5) Often much equipment and ammunition is left behind at focal points of battle. On account of our supply shortage everything must be taken along, which will also be better for the morale of our troops.

Appendix 'C'
The Commander-in-Chief   HQ 2 August 1944
Panzer Group West

Subject: Conduct during enemy attack

(1) Counter battery fire is generally impossible due to supply difficulties. But our artillery must always fire on:
  (a) enemy guns which can be seen
  (b) enemy guns which are especially disagreeable in their effect, if their positions can be seen by OPs
  (c) enemy heavy guns

(2) To each position belongs a dummy position. Build position on reverse slope, dummy position on forward slope. Dummy positions are only good if out of them fire is opened periodically.

(3) Due to the difficulties of supply economizing with men and materials becomes very necessary. Newly arriving divisions will put into reserve the following:
   (a) Men, especially experienced officers and NCOs
       Company strength should never be more than 70 all ranks
   (b) Weapons and ammunition
   (c) OP personnel
   (d) Wireless apparatus

(4) Our anti-tank guns are still firing too soon. Enemy tanks try to draw their fire and any gun which does fire is soon put out of action.

Anti-tank guns are still scattered all over the front. Main points of anti-tank effort must be established, which consist of several anti-tank guns arranged in two rows [*i.e. ranks*]. These points may be reinforced by dug-in tanks or assault guns.

An anti-tank gun reserve must be established for action against enemy flanks. Avoid heights. Saddles and reverse slopes are ideal for positions.

Anti-tank guns which are not at least 100 metres behind the HKL are soon put out of action by enemy artillery. In the HKL belong the close combat anti-tank weapons.

Too little use is made of lone forward anti-tank guns. These must fire on their target and then immediately change position.

Chapter 6

Infantry Weapons and Tactics

Document 6/1[1]

Defensive Tactics, 38th SS Panzer Grenadier Regiment, 17th SS Panzer Grenadier Division, July 1944

Wartime Intelligence Officer's Comments

The following directive was found on the body of a German officer.

Since up to now the enemy has in all cases attacked the foremost line with heavy artillery barrage and air support, the foremost line of resistance shall be protected from now on as thinly as possible. Strong reserves should be provided so that a penetration of our lines can be neutralized by immediate counterattack. By this method also losses through artillery barrage and air bombardment shall be kept to a minimum.

In the attack on our foremost lines of resistance, anti-tank grenades and mines are to be used against the tanks which are followed by enemy infantry. Deployment in depth is to be stressed and all approach routes to our position carefully determined.

---

1. ISUM 23, 18 July 1944.

Document 6/2[2]

Orders of 22nd SS Panzer Grenadier Regiment, 10th SS Panzer Division, July 1944, Regarding the Manning of a Defence Line

Wartime Intelligence Officer's Comments

The following extracts from regimental orders of 22nd SS Panzer Grenadier Regiment dated 5 July 1944 illustrate a typical method of manning a main defence line and sub-allotting heavy weapons.

(i)   Occupation of main defence line

II and III Battalions, each two companies up and one company in reserve. I Battalion as decided verbally, pending arrival of battalion reinforcements.

During daytime the two men at each defence post will rest in alternate shifts. Both to keep watch throughout the night.

Each fox-hole will be occupied by two men during the night, in order to prevent recurrence of an incident when the sole occupant was surprised by the enemy and taken prisoner.

(ii)   Reconnaissance

As from tonight each battalion will send out a reconnaissance party forward in its area. Object of reconnaissance: to find out how the enemy's main defence line runs and in what strength it is held.

I Battalion will send sufficient covering parties well in front of the main defence line until it is possible to put out stronger reconnaissance patrols.

Information required: Condition of approaches leading to enemy obstacles, etc.

(iii)   Heavy Weapons (Orders given verbally 4 July 44)

Two platoons of 13 Company will take up positions enabling them to operate as a whole in front of II and III Battalions, with one platoon so

---

2. ISUM 30, 29 July 1944, from *Second British Army Intelligence Summary*, No. 54, 28 July 1944.

placed that it can operate principally on right in front of I Battalion, and overlapping beyond the right boundary of the regiment.

14 Company will take up positions enabling it to beat off low-level air attacks and to operate in a counter-attack role when ordered by the regiment, with two platoons behind I Battalion and one platoon on the south east slope of feature 112.

15 Company will remain in reserve at the disposal of the regiment in the area immediately north west of Maltot and will reconnaissance, as per verbal orders, the existing prepared positions in the rear of I and II Battalions with a view to incorporating these in the extension of the switch-line (*Riegelstellung*[3]).

(iv)   Alarm Units

All remaining elements of the regiment not committed in the front line will be collected into alarm-units. Complete nominal rolls will be kept of personnel available daily. Alarm practices will be carried out by order of the commander.

(*Obersturmführer* Fleischer is hereby appointed CO for Avenay. State of alarm only by my order).

(v)   Respirators [gas masks]

Will be worn, without exception, when [the] enemy fire smoke.

(vi)   Regimental Battle HQ.

Location unchanged.

Wartime Intelligence Officer's Comment:

Regimental HQ then believed to be at Avenay 9559. From the context, I Battalion appears to have been on the right of the regimental sector. This agrees with a PW report that HQ I Battalion was in the Chateau at Eterville on 10 July 44. From identifications of 9 Company and 6 Company on 4/5 July 1944 at 9562 and 9664 respectively; the latter again at 9763 on 8 July 44, it is likely that III Battalion was left and II Battalion centre.

---

3. *Riegelstellung* are switch-line positions, defensive positions oblique to the front which are intended to prevent enemy penetrations from being exploited to either flank.

Document 6/3[4]

General Principles for the Officer Commanding a Panzer Grenadier Company (Motorized), Extracted from a Pamphlet Issued by the Inspector-General of Panzer Troops, 12 June 1944[5]

(i) The operational task must always be held sacred to you. You must not, without urgent cause, deviate from it nor forget any details of the task. Speed of execution is essential. Therefore, do not lose any unnecessary time through briefing. Do not forget to inform your NCOs and leaders of your support weapons as to your operational intentions. Let them know how you intend to carry out your orders. Let nothing divert you from the fulfilment of the task. Do not engage an enemy who has nothing to do with your task, unless directly threatened.

(ii) Only a continuous battle reconnaissance can protect you against any surprises. Therefore always: EYES TOWARDS THE ENEMY! Remember that scouting troops must be composed of sufficient strength to carry out a successful mission. In all circumstances think of cover, reconnaissance and communications, bearing in mind how important it is to liaise with artillery OPs and neighbouring units.

(iii) During battle one of your activities will consist of a constant review of the situation. Only by keeping abreast of minute to minute developments can you form a correct decision at the decisive moment and give your orders without hesitation. If you are not in the picture you will be found wanting at the critical moment. Overhasty and uncertain decisions and orders are made and given, as a result of which losses are incurred.

(iv) Even in most urgent circumstances your orders must not only be concise but also singularly clear. Think of the words of Moltke, who stated that orders which may be misunderstood are fundamentally always misunderstood. The same applies to intelligence. Along these lines instruct your NCOs to report frequently, and you yourself constantly report to battalion.

---

4. ISUM 31, 30 July 1944.
5. The original article was 'Kampfgrundsätze für den Führen einer Panzer-Grenadier-Kompanie (mot.)', in Nachrichten blatt der Panzertruppen (June 1944), pp 4–8.

(v) You can only lead your company efficiently if your operational system is running smoothly. Enforce strict wireless discipline from your platoon commanders and wireless operators, otherwise the costly equipment which has proved itself with well trained and disciplined companies under the greatest strain, will not produce results.

(vi) Slackness of your NCOs and men, who say 'it is not worth it, we shall manage, nothing will happen' are not an excuse for you, should losses be incurred.

(vii) Each Grenadier of the battalion transport should know that running away from a tank means suicide.

Document 6/4[6]

Battalion Orders for Defence,
II Battalion, 980 Grenadier Regiment,
272nd Infantry Division, 15 July 1944

Wartime Intelligence Officer's Comments

The following extracts are from an order issued by II/980 Grenadier Regiment on 15 July and illustrate the thoroughness with which the enemy prepares a defence position, and show particularly his concern with our artillery fire.

Battalion Order

(i) As from today all personnel of the battalion are forbidden to enter houses. All houses in the locality have been partly mined. No warning notices or other signs indicating mining, have been affixed. The companies will be instructed on this subject.

(ii) The companies will clear up immediately all roads in their area and other important roads required for dispatch rider traffic. Special care

---

6. ISUM 31, 31 July 1944, from *Second British Army Intelligence Summary*, No. 55, 29 July 1944.

will be taken to remove all trailing wires. Telephone lines not in use will be wound up. Lines in use will be dug in and relaid for protection along walls at road edges.

(iii) Enemy artillery HF[7] is directed principally on prominent landmarks. The concentrations brought down on these landmarks are carried out on the basis of a predicted shoot. This is not done with the aid of a map, but with the aid of aerial photographs. If enemy air photographic reconnaissance reveals groups of soldiers standing about in front of houses or positions, on badly camouflaged positions, this is used as the basis for the next HF. Instruction on this subject will be issued generally, so that everyone may realise that the reason for most enemy shelling is his own indifference to observation from the air.

(iv) Every company will dig slit trenches at 20 metres intervals along the runner and communication trenches, to provide immediately cover for runners and maintenance personnel against sudden concentrations. The slit trenches will be marked by poles with small bundles of straw or a small white cloth strap attached to them. These slit trenches, etc., will be well camouflaged against observation from the air. 5 and 8 Companies will build slit trenches from the battalion telephone exchange (former battalion battle HQ) to left of the SMG[8] position of 8 Company: from there to new battalion HQ the slit trenches will be dug by 6 Company. Direction of track south of feature along the telegraph poles. Special attention will be paid to camouflages in this sector.

(v) Mines with trip wires have been fixed to road obstacles in company areas. No alterations whatever will be made to these obstacles, and passage through the obstructed points is strictly forbidden.

(Signed)
Werner
Captain, commanding II Battalion

---

7. HF is Harassing Fire, artillery fire brought down at varied intervals intended to hamper enemy movement and lower morale.
8. SMG, submachine-gun.

Document 6/5[9]

Tactical Handling of Volksgrenadier Divisions, September 1944

Wartime Intelligence Officer's Comments

The following are extracts translated from a captured document originated by the OKH[10] on 23 September 1944 on the tactical handling of the Volksgrenadier Division. It deals almost exclusively with the means of making the best use of the limited equipment and reduced number of men available.

(1) The economies, especially in MT,[11] are a handicap to the swift employment of the Volksgrenadier Division in a war of movement and in raids.

(2) The Volksgrenadier Division only has a Fusilier Company: this makes reconnaissance and the formation of reserves within the division difficult.

(3) The mobility of one battalion of the division is increased by its additional equipment with bicycles and horse transport for A and B echelons (Bicycle Battalion).

(4) The Infantry Company is greatly strengthened in assault and fire power in the attack and defence by its two machine pistol platoons. It no longer has any MMGs.

(5) Care must be taken that each infantry company only attacks with a strength of 60–80 men, the rest being collected in the FEB[12] or the Regimental Training Company.

(6) All heavy weapons of the battalion are contained in the heavy company.

(7) 13 Company: Greater fire power with eight heavy mortars (12 cm) and four light infantry guns . . . concentrate the fire.

(8) 14 Company: Equipped solely with *Panzerschreck*.

---

9. ISUM 132, 9 November 1944, from *12 British Corps Intelligence Summary*.
10. *Oberkommando des Heeres* (OKH), the army high command.
11. MT is Motor Transport.
12. FEB, is *Feld Ersatz Bataillon*, the replacement and training unit of a division or corps.

(9) Regimental Training Company: is to be set up by each Grenadier Regiment during the formation of the division ... If the Division can form a FEB, the Regimental Training Companies will be dissolved.

(10) Artillery: The organisation of troops of 6 guns effects an economy of men and equipment. Gun positions of 6 guns are increasingly open to air attack and counter-battery, therefore good camouflage and construction of positions.

(11) Limited means of towing guns demands the use of RSO[13] and horses at the point of main effort. If fully mobile employment of the whole artillery is necessary, recourse must be had to towing vehicles and horses from other parts of the division and from local resources.

(12) The 7.5 cm field gun is well suited by reason of its great range and low trajectory as an artillery or anti-tank weapon.

(13) <u>Use in an anti-tank role</u>: There are the following possibilities:
    (a) Parts of the battery (3 guns per troop)
    (b) The whole battery ... (as an exception).

(14) <u>Anti-tank</u>: The following are to be employed to establish an anti-tank zone in depth:
    (a) The anti-tank weapons of the Volksgrenadier Regiments in the infantry zone of the main defence position.
    (b) The anti-tank company in the Divisional *Schwerpunkt*.
The Assault Gun Battery is the mobile anti-tank reserve of the division.

(15) <u>Engineer Battalions</u>: The great demand on engineers can only be fulfilled in view of the modest establishment of engineer personnel if both Engineer Companies are:
    (a) Fully available for engineer duties.
    (b) Employed concentrated at the point of main effort.

---

13. RSO, *Raupenschlepper Ost*, a fully-tracked transport vehicle.

Chapter 7

Anti-Tank and Artillery Weapons and Tactics

Document 7/1[1]

Achtung! Panzerfaust

Amendments to the official instructions for the *Panzerfaust* weapons, previously known as *Faustpatronen*, stress the following points, which have emerged as the result of fatal accidents in the course of live practice with these weapons:

(i) The propellant charge is permanently situated in the discharger tube. Even without a loaded grenade, it is therefore highly dangerous to fire the weapon, since the propellant gases emerging from both ends of the tube may cause fatal accidents.

(ii) With the grenade head removed and the tail unit remaining in the tube, safety zones must still be observed, since the latter may prove lethal up to 55 yds.

(iii) Beware of the propellant blast from the rear of the discharger tube.

Wartime Intelligence Officer's Comments

In view of the dangerous nature of the Panzerfaust *weapons, Allied troops will be well advised NOT to handle them, unless they are familiar with their design.*

---

1. ISUM 19, 7 July 1944.

Document 7/2[2]

Care in Firing *Panzerfaust* and *Panzerschreck*

Wartime Intelligence Officer's Comments

The following translation of an order warns personnel to observe safety regulations strictly when using Panzerfaust *and* Panzerschreck *weapons, and describes in vivid detail what happened to one unfortunate German who failed to do so:*

(a) *Panzerfaust*

(i) The necessary care in handling this weapon is emphasized again. A member of this division lost his life due to great carelessness. It happened as follows:

> F. unscrewed the head of the *Panzerfaust* in order to arm it. He explained the operation to men standing round him. During this operation he pressed the back end of the tube against his groin. In spite of his knowledge of safety instructions, he pushed the release button. The flame of the propelling charge, shooting out the rear part, tore off his right leg and opened his belly. He died from his injuries.

(ii) The fuze is constructed in such a manner that it is set off only through impact with a hard object. In most cases the hollow charge grenade therefore does not explode if falling on soft ground.

(iii) <u>Destruction of Duds</u>. Search for cover, deposit a hand grenade 1 cm in front of the grenade, press against the ground, pull out the pin, take cover!

(b) *Panzerschreck*

(i) Protection provided by the glove for the left hand is not sufficient. Powder particles will pierce it. The issue of heavier gloves is awaited. In the meantime leather gloves (if necessary also knitted gloves) will be worn underneath. The space between both gloves over the back of the hand will be stuffed with a heavy layer of newspaper.

---

2. ISUM 19, 7 July 1944.

(ii) <u>Forehead Protection</u>: Field cap with visor will be worn, turned around (visor backward) and pulled down as far as possible, with vision still possible. Protection hood over it! Improvise accordingly with field caps without visor!

Document 7/3[3]

How to Use the *Panzerfaust (Klein)*

The following notes on the use of the *Panzerfaust (klein)*, formerly *Faust-patrone* 1 (Gretchen), are based on examination of specimens captured in France and of documents:

(a)   Description:

The weapon is used for the attack of armour from a range of about 100 ft. It consists of a hollow charge projectile fired from a tube containing propellant charge.

There is no recoil. The *Panzerfaust (klein)* can be fired with the body in any position so long as the rear end of the tube has a free exit.

(b)   Preparation for action:

(i)   Unscrew the head
(ii)   Take the wooden ring out of the tube
(iii)   Hold the tube vertical with the sight outwards
(iv)   Set in the fuze with the percussion cap upwards
(v)   Insert the wooden ring with the rubber disc so that the rubber disc covers the fuze
(vi)   Set in primer 34 so that the paper cover points to the fuze
(vii)   Screw the head on to the tube

(c)   Coming into action:

(i)   Withdraw the safety pin
(ii)   Open the sight so that it stands at right angles to the tube

---

3. ISUM 15, 11 July 1944, from *GSI (Tech) 21st Army Group.*

(iii)   Cock the striker by pushing the bolt forward until the pin is at rest and the release button is seen. The bolt will then return to its original position. The *Panzerfaust* is now ready for action; i.e. cocked and set at safe.

(d)   Firing:

(i)   Take the weapon under the right arm with the left hand supporting it about 2' behind the front end of the tube.

(ii)   <u>To release safety catch</u> – Press the bolt to the left.

(iii)   <u>To aim</u>: The following must all be in one straight line – the eye – red line in the vision slot – the top edge of the projectile – the target. The sighting arrangement is set for 30m. AFVs travelling at right angles to the direction of the projectile are sighted on their leading edge.

(iv)   <u>To fire</u>: Press the release button downwards with the thumb of the right hand.

(v)   After firing take cover immediately in order to avoid being hit by flying splinters.

(e)   Safety Precautions:

(i)   Only set to fire immediately before use. It can, if the projectile is not launched, be set at safe again.

(ii)   To reset to safe, place the bolt with the knob vertical; then push it forward until it reaches an obstruction and hold it there. Press the launching knob and let the bolt slide slowly backwards. This will release the firing pin.

Document 7/4[4]

Tactics of 277th Anti-Tank Battalion, 277th Infantry Division

1st Company Battle HQ
12 July 1944

To: HQ Platoon
1, 2, 3 and 4 Platoons
Supply Column

1. The line held at present will be maintained at all costs until the impending employment of further weapons of a new type produces a decision in our favour.

2. All units employed in the main defence zone in depth, including the Anti-tank Company will expedite the digging of positions with all means at their disposal. Uncamouflaged positions are both senseless and useless, attract enemy fire and do more harm than good.

3. Emphatic instructions on strict economy in the use of ammunition will be given by the NCOs. The standard to aim at is that fire be withheld, especially against attacking tanks, up to the very close range at which success can be assured. *Panzerschreck* and *Panzerfaust* have been particularly successful in country where there are hedges which obstruct visibility. 25 of the tanks knocked out so far on the invasion front have been accounted for with these weapons. Enemy infantry should be allowed to approach as near as possible, so that they can be destroyed at closest possible range.

4. Knocked out enemy tanks will either be salvaged immediately (to be used as tractors) or blown up or otherwise destroyed (set on fire).

5. Supply column will start preparation of quartering area for all round defence immediately. NCO i/c: Corporal Knoch.

6. Each platoon will supply alarm units immediately, 1 NCO, 3 men. The section leader need not necessarily be an NCO.

---

4. ISUM 29, 13 July 1944, from *Second British Army Intelligence Summary*, No. 53, 27 July 1944.

7. To prevent enemy interception of our W/T, division will monitor all W/T traffic. Disciplinary action will be taken against all infringements of wireless security, as these cause unnecessary casualties.

8. Low flying aircraft will be engaged by every man and every MG. Siting of MGs in close proximity to the guns and the use of tracer ammunition during the day for AA defence is not recommended.

Signed . . .
Oberleutnant & Commander 1 Company

Document 7/5[5]

Tactics of 326 Artillery Regiment, 326th Infantry Division

The interrogation of four PW from III Battalion 326 Artillery Regiment of 326th Infantry Division has revealed that:

(i) Firing was not stopped on appearance of British air observer posts.

(ii) Troops did not change position immediately on being engaged by counter battery fire but if the nature of fire made it obvious that a position had been identified the change of position would take place as soon as darkness fell.

(iii) Vacated positions were often camouflaged as if occupied but no use was made of dummy flashes.

(iv) The troop gun line was normally 200 metres long with roving gun 200–500 metres to a flank. (It should be remembered that this battalion was entirely equipped with 12.2 cm Russian howitzers).

(v) Detachments were trained in anti-tank shooting but had no armour-piercing ammunition.

(vi) British counter battery fire was invariably brought down before troops could fire more than 4–5 rounds.

---

5. ISUM 38, 6 August 1944.

Document 7/6[6]

German 8.1 cm Mortar Tactics, II Battalion, 979 Grenadier Regiment, 271st Infantry Division

The following account of the use of 8.1 cm mortar was given by an NCO of II/979 Infantry Regiment of 271st Infantry Division.

The tactical unit was stated to be a platoon of three sections, each of two 8.1 cm mortars. PW stated that in Russia, they had nearly always fired as a section not as a platoon.

Their positions were usually approximately 1000 yards behind the forward infantry. The mortars were always dug in around holes 2 metres in diameter. If the ground was rocky, turf and rocks were used to build up a wall. There were always one or more alternative positions. The positions were usually laid out roughly in a line parallel to the front with approximately 100 metres between mortars of different sections.

On arriving in position, ranging was usually carried out. A forward OP[7] was set up with a range finder ('E-Messer'), and a telephone line was run back to the NCO in charge of the centre section. Orders were given from the OP for one mortar to fire on a certain compass bearing, and corrections were given.

The following shells were kept by each mortar: HE: 132. Smoke: 9. The ammunition was dug in holes around the mortar position and at least 30 rounds had to be readily accessible to the mortar crew. The remainder was handled by the ammunition number from the holes which were between the main and alternative positions.

The NCO received the orders from the OP and passed them on to the next ammunition number who in turn passed it on. This method apparently worked satisfactorily.

Positions were only changed when for good reason it was thought their position was being registered. The system was:

(i) go to ground shelters, usually at least 100 metres from the mortars.
(ii) wait for fire to stop.
(iii) change positions.

PW stated positions could be changed completely in ten minutes.

---

6. ISUM 58. 28 August 1944.
7. OP, Observation Post.

The most usual type of shoot PW had carried out was fire for effect ('*Wirkungsfeuer*') when one of the six mortars in the platoon fired ten shells as rapidly as possible.

Chapter 8

Armoured Vehicles and Tactics

Document 8/1[1]

A German View of the Hornet

Wartime Intelligence Officer's Comments

The following extracts from a semi-official German publication dealing with the strong and weak facets of the 8.8cm Pak 43/1 on Panzer Jag. III/ IV chassis (Hornet) may be of interest to units who come up against this 'insect'. It will be recalled that the Hornet has recently been renamed Rhinoceros (Nashorn).

(1)   Weak Points of the Hornet

(i) High Silhouette

Height 8 ft 10 in – width 9 ft 6 in. Therefore presents a big target, difficult to cam[ouflage], particularly in open country.

(ii) Weak Armour

Front and side superstructure shields are only 100mm (.4 in) thick. Therefore not to be used as if it were an assault gun. Anti-Tank rifle liable to cause casualties to crew and often to the vehicle itself.

(iii) Fighting Compartment Open at Top

Therefore susceptible to artillery, mortar and SA fire.

---

1. *21st Army Group Intelligence Summary*, No. 129, 11 July 1944.

(iv) No Turret

Gun only traverses 15 degrees left and right. Therefore at a disadvantage in close fighting as the whole vehicle may have to be traversed.

(v) Limited Ammunition Supply

Normally only 16 rounds are carried. Maximum 40 rounds (AP[2] and HE). Therefore Hornets must retire frequently in order to replenish with ammunition. Ammunition should be brought up as close as possible on Maultier lorries.

(vi) Frequent Engine Breakdowns

The Hornet is constructed from parts of Mk III and IV tanks. The engine is weak and has a life of approx. 940 miles. Therefore get the most out of every mile.

(vii) Specialist Crew

Apart from the leader, the crew are all highly trained specialists. Therefore risk no unnecessary losses through incorrect use of the vehicle. Such losses can never be made good.

(2)   Strong Points of the Hornet

(i) Excellent Gun

Lethal up to 2200 yards. Therefore protection of FDLs[3] is possible from positions well in the rear.

(ii) Effective Ammunition

Every hit with an AP [Armour Piercing] shot is lethal. The HE ammunition has a good splintering effect and should be used with the fuze set at delayed action. Indirect firing with the Auxiliary Sight 38 is also possible up to a range of about 11,000 yards.

(iii) Great Firepower

45 Hornets per Battalion. 14 per Company. Therefore complete superiority over enemy tanks if whole battalions or companies are employed. This will be all the more so if good observation of the enemy tanks is available.

---

2. AP, Armour-piercing.
3. FDL, Forward Defence Localities, sometimes battle outposts. Small positions located forward of the main line of resistance of HKL for the purposes of observation and warning.

(iv) Good Signal Communications

'Intercom' facilities for crew and R/T between vehicles. 30 watt R/T communication between company and battalion. The battalion signals section has four pack and two 30 watt wireless detachments.

Document 8/2[4]

Use of the Panther

Wartime Intelligence Officer's Comments

Some interesting observations on the Panther are contained in a captured German document issued to tank crews by the Inspector of Armoured Troops.

(a) Panther is not invulnerable. Sides and rear can be perforated by 7.62 cm anti tank guns. Therefore flank protection is always important (use of smoke). When Panthers are used together with Mark IIIs and IVs, for instance in the break-through of an enemy position, it is recommended that the Panthers lead the attack and that the IIIs and IVs follow up behind so as to be available for flank protection or pursuit after the successful break-through.

(b) Panther cannot cross minefields with immunity. Mines can immobilise a Panther, if only for a short time.

(c) The large fuel consumption of Panthers makes it necessary to consider whether the eventual success of a particular operation makes the undertaking worthwhile. Panthers use up twice as much petrol as Mark IIIs and IVs.

(d) Economic use of ammunition is particularly important with Panthers. Well-trained gunners are therefore essential.

(e) Panthers should only be used in conjunction with Panzer grenadiers, trained in cooperation with tanks.

---

4. ISUM 30, 29 July 1944.

(f) No attack will ever be carried out without preliminary reconnaissance. This will often have to be done by tank crews on foot.

(g) Panthers are not as suitable as Mark IIIs and IVs for fighting in wooded country. For fighting in built-up areas, they are best employed from dominating positions.

(h) Arrangements must always be made for Panthers to be protected by other troops at night.

(i) Immobilised Panthers must never be recovered by other Panthers unless the ground is under enemy fire. The 18-ton semi-tracked tractor should normally be used – five per Panther for cross-country going, and two to three per Panther on roads

(j) Even Panthers must seek alternative positions after firing, but the new positions must not be so far away that the unit becomes separated.

(k) Owing to its superior range, Panther is less suitable than Mark IIIs, IVs or Assault Guns for the role of supporting Panzer grenadiers in mopping up an overrun enemy.

(l) The great firepower of the Panther must not lead to increased spacing within troops as this makes the provision of mutual support more difficult.

(m) The high performance of the Panther gun makes it possible to engage enemy tanks at long ranges. The Russian KV 1 tank can be shot up at a range of 3718 yards and the T 34 at between 1640 and 2187 yards.

Document 8/3[5]

German Heavy Tank Battalion Tactics

Wartime Intelligence Officer's Comments

A PW from 508th Heavy Tank Battalion in Italy has given some interesting details of the tactics employed by this battalion. These tactics are to a large extent borne out by our experiences with 503rd Heavy Tank Battalion operating with 21st Panzer Division and 101st and 102nd SS Heavy Tank Battalion. The following notes are therefore well worth a study from the point of view of their application to the fighting in Normandy.

Formations

The smallest tactical unit employed is the platoon. The battalion is seldom used as a whole. PW has never taken part in any action in which more than one company was involved but he had heard that in Russia heavy tank battalions had been employed in 'pure tank battles'.

According to PW only two standard formations were used in Russia for the employment of heavy tank squadrons in the attack.

(a) Arrowhead formation (*Keil*)

```
                        1 Platoon
                            x
                        x       x
                                    x
    2 Platoon               x Company         3 Platoon
        x                   Commander             x
    x       x                               x       x
            x                                           x
                        X Spare
```

(b) Broad Arrowhead Formation (*Breitkeil*)

```
                        1 Platoon
                          x   x
                        x       x
    2 Platoon               x Company         3 Platoon
      x   x                 Commander           x   x
    x       x                                 x       x
```

---

5. ISUM 48, 16 August 1944, taken from *Allied Forces Headquarters Notes*, No. 47.

According to the PW the second formation is adopted more often than the first and is thought to afford better protection especially against enfilading fire from anti-tank guns. The distance between individual tanks naturally depends on the terrain. As a general rule, in open country, the distance between the two leading tanks in each platoon is about 100 metres, the distance between them about 50 metres. In close country, intervals are of course smaller, on an average about half of the intervals adopted in open country.

Each tank has an allotted arc of fire and the clock method is used for this purpose. In the broad arrowhead formation the responsibility of each tank in a platoon is as follows:

Both leading tanks	– from 11 o'clock to 1 o'clock
	Gun travelling position at 12 o'clock
Right rear tank	– from 1 o'clock to 3 o'clock.
	Gun in travelling position at 2 o'clock
Left rear tank	– from 9 o'clock to 11 o'clock.
	Gun in travelling position at 10 o'clock

Thus a total of 180 degrees is covered by the whole platoon. As a rule each tank endeavours to deal by itself with enemy weapons engaging it. If this is impossible the help of another tank is sought and this tank is called up by WT. The principle employed here is:

> Rear tanks help front tanks to engage frontal targets
> Front tanks help rear tanks against enfilading targets

The application of this principle, however, necessitates the breaking up of the formation as the supporting tank must wheel into position. During this movement it is bound to expose at least part of the flank, the most vulnerable point. Tank crews are taught to avoid this move, moreover the mutual protection which tanks can give each other while in formation is lost.

Battalion Attack

PW has never taken part in a battalion attack. He stated, however, that the formation usually adopted was thus:

1 Company		2 Company	
1 Platoon		1 Platoon	
2 Platoon	3 Platoon	2 Platoon	3 Platoon

3 Company

x x x x x x x x x x x x x x x x x x x

(all tanks in line)

Platoons in this formation can be in arrowhead or in broad arrowhead formation. The battalion commander usually travels in his tank with one of the leading companies.

Cooperation with Infantry

PW could not recall an action in which he had taken part without infantry support. On some occasions infantry rode on the tanks (up to 30 men on one Mk VI) into action and dismounted as soon as engaged. As a rule the tanks then slowed down or stopped and covered the advance of the infantry until the latter was held up. Defended positions, heavy weapons, strongpoints or pillboxes, were then indicated by the infantry by WT over Pack sets, for the tanks to deal with. This was invariably done in clear except for the cover name of the platoon or company. PW had never seen targets indicated by fire, tracer or smoke.

In Russia the protection of the tanks against enemy close combat anti-tank weapons was the responsibility of the supporting infantry. In Italy, however, the anti-tank platoon has this task in addition to its primary role of destroying enemy armour with close combat weapons.

Cooperation with Armoured Troop Carriers

PW has been in action where the supporting infantry was carried in armoured troop carriers. This method was only employed in completely open and flat country and 2–3 carriers were placed between 2 tanks. The infantry did not dismount but fired from the vehicles. PW stated that this method of attack increased the difficulties of protection against enemy infantry.

Cooperation with Other Tanks

508 Heavy Tank Battalion had a light platoon equipped with Mk III and Mk IV tanks. It appears that the purpose of the inclusion of these tanks into a heavy tank battalion was to provide the heavier and slower tanks with a more mobile flank protection and to use the lighter tanks to engage lesser targets. According to PW this proved unsatisfactory because the Mk III and Mk IV tanks could not engage targets from the same range as the Mk VI tanks and had to leave the formation to assume firing positions. It was generally found that the best use for them was a heavy infantry tank.

Methods of Firing

PW stated that firing was only done when the tank was stationary. It was strictly forbidden to fire on the move (except the MGs) and while in motion the gun was always fixed. He had never heard of a 'gyro stabilizer' or similar devices being used in German tanks. He stated that targets were engaged at the following ranges:

Heavy Anti-tank guns (7.62 cm or similar calibre)
                                     1800 m. maximum
Sherman tanks   2000 m. maximum
HE targets (infantry concentrations, etc)
                                     600–1000 m. maximum

When used as artillery, tanks only used direct fire. For ranges under four kms the gun sights were considered sufficient, for greater ranges a scissors telescope was used by the tank commander and the fire controlled by him. By this method accurate firing could of course only be done by day, but PW stated that targets which had been registered visually during the day were sometimes shelled at night.

He had never heard of indirect firing being done by tanks. He considered the ammunition expenditure to be too great for the limited supply of a tank and that indirect fire was a task for artillery or SP guns.

Attack on Artillery Positions

PW stated that it has always endeavoured to outflank artillery positions which had to be attacked and to engage them from the flank or the rear. If, however, such a manoeuvre would expose the flank of the tank and the ground afforded little chance for hull-down positions, it was preferred to engage the guns frontally at the earliest possible moment.

Attacks against Inhabited Localities

Tanks never attacked built-up areas without infantry support. If heavy weapons concealed in such an area could be shelled by tanks from outside the area this was invariably done. Otherwise infantry had to cover the entry of armoured vehicles into the built-up area and to draw fire from points of resistance. It was also thought desirable that platoons or sections, depending on the size of the locality, should move in simultaneously from several sides.

Intercommunication

PW could supply little information on this subject. He stated that if more than one company was employed, all companies and platoons had the same frequency. Intercommunication with aircraft was done only from the battalion commander's tank, but PW could give no details. Flag signals were usually provided for the possibility of a breakdown of the WT set and the colours used were Red, Green, Yellow and Blue. (This method is, however, thought to be completely unsatisfactory and PW has never seen it used in action.)

Handling of the Mk VI Tanks

The broad track was always used in action, the narrow track on the march. PW stated that the outer row (of the three rows) of disc wheels on the suspension was found unnecessary, and that even when the broad track was used, the outer wheels were sometimes removed. The manoeuvrability of the tank is said not to be affected by this.

According to PW the track can be changed in 40 minutes.

In all actions in Russia the turret was kept closed and locked.

PW mentioned that when ascending a slope (which is under cover from enemy observation) the gun of the tank is always depressed as far as possible so as to be in the most favourable firing position when moving over the crest.

Reconnaissance for Attack or Counter Attack

Usually a platoon commander is detailed to reconnoitre the ground for an impending action. He proceeds in his tank as far as possible and then continues on foot. As a rule either the loader or WT operator, or both, accompany him and the turret MG is taken out for the protection of the reconnaissance party. The driver and gunner invariably remain in the tank.

PW mentioned that as a result of a reconnaissance the speed of the tanks in the advance is usually determined before hand and given out to tank commanders before the action. Good hull-down positions (*Hinterhangstellungen*) are noted by the party and pointed out on the map to the tank commanders. They are, however, not allotted to individual tanks beforehand.

Methods of Maintenance

Responsibility for routine maintenance between the tank crew is divided in the following manner:

Driver: Engine, tracks, suspension, chassis
Gunner: Sights, turret gear, gun breech and firing mechanism, MG breeches
Loader: Ammunition, barrels of gun and MGs
Wireless Operator: WT set
Commander: Supervises the maintenance and stands by to help out

The Workshop Platoon in HQ Company is equipped to carry out first line repairs. The next stage in the line of maintenance for Mk VI tanks is usually the Army Motor Transport Park (*Heereskraftfahrpark*). If a heavy tank battalion is attached to an armoured division which possesses Mk VI tanks, the divisional workshops are usually competent to carry out second line repairs. For bigger repairs the tank has to be evacuated to Germany.

Camouflage

PW stated that at all times camouflage received the highest priority when tanks leaguered[6] after a move. Nets were never used for this purpose. Whenever possible the tanks were parked in barns, sheds or ruins of houses or under trees. If no cover was available, four poles were erected and a roof constructed with planks, corrugated iron sheets or odd materials found in the area. Tanks were always well spaced even at the expense of spreading troops out over a wide area. No effort was made to conceal tracks.

---

6. Leaguer or lager is a Commonwealth armoured corps term that means a position to which tank units withdraw at night to re-fuel and re-ammunition.

Recovery

The recovery of damaged tanks is the responsibility of the Engineer Platoon. If tanks are abandoned on the battlefield a party is always sent out to determine whether recovery is possible. If this party considers recovery impossible every effort is made to demolish the tank. For the recovery itself, which is invariably done at night half tracked towing machines from the workshop platoon are used.

Influence of Wind on Tactics

Wind in the direction of the attack is apt to betray the movement of tanks much earlier than desired. This is particularly so in the case of Mk VI tanks, which make considerable noise. PW stated that to overcome this a strong artillery barrage was laid down in front of the tanks to conceal the noise.

Wind coming from the direction of the enemy has an adverse effect if smoke is used against the armour. PW stated that crews put on respirators as soon as smoke was employed (irrespective whether on friends or enemy). Once smoke got into the tank it remained until the tank could be properly ventilated and the vision and work of the crew were seriously hampered.

Interchangeability of the Crew

Neither in training nor in practice were arrangements made to provide for interchangeability of the various members of a tank crew. Theoretically the tank commander is supposed to be able to take over every function in the tank. PW stated, however, that in practice this is seldom the case. He mentioned an incident in Russia when his tank had received a hit which had wounded the driver and where the tank commander succeeded only with the greatest difficulty in turning the tank and driving it back.

Ammunition

In Russia, PW's tank carried 120 rounds for the gun (90 HE and 30 AP). The normal allotment of MG ammunition was 4500 rounds but on all occasions this figure was exceeded. Each tank carried a certain number of hand grenades to be used if the crew had to abandon the tank.

Document 8/4[7]

Panthers and Tigers (A German View)

Wartime Intelligence Officer's Comments

A lot has been written in recent months in praise of these two heavyweight German beasts.

The following extracts from German official documents throw another light on the subject, and may excite interest, if not encouragement.

(a) Tiger

'When Tigers first appeared on the battlefield, they were in every respect proof against enemy weapons. They quickly won for themselves the title of "unbeatable" and "undamageable".

But in the meantime, the enemy had not been asleep. Anti-tank guns, tanks, and mines have been developed, which can hit the Tiger hard and even knock it out. Now the Tiger, for a long time regarded as a "Life Insurance Policy", is relegated to the ranks of simply a "heavy tank" ... No longer can the Tiger prance around oblivious of the laws of tank tactics. They must obey these laws, just as every other German tank must.'

(b) Panther

(i) 'It is particularly important to ensure flank protection for the "sensitive" sides of the Panther tanks. The Panzer Regiment command must always keep a reserve of tanks up his sleeve, which he can use at a moment's notice to block any threat from the flank ... This reserve should normally be about 1100 yards in the rear. It has been found advisable to let the available Mark IV tanks in the Panzer Regiment take over the task of protection from the flanks, while the Panthers quickly press on and drive a wedge into the enemy position.'

(ii) 'Both the track of a Panther and a Tiger sometimes slips or becomes disengaged from the teeth of the driving sprocket and jams, owing to the assemblage of undesirable matter. The consequent tensioning of the track is so great that it is generally not possible to free the track by knocking out a track pin.'

---

7. ISUM 12, 7 July 1944.

The German report adds that a certain Tiger Battalion solved this problem by cutting the over-tensioned track with hand grenades exploded under it, but adds that the practice should not be resorted to unless the tank would otherwise have to be written off.

Document 8/5[8]

8.8 cm Pak 43 on Panther Chassis (Jagdpanther)

Wartime Intelligence Officer's Comments

An official German manual on the 8.8 Pak 43 on a Panther chassis (Jagdpanther), Sd Kfz 173,[9] gives some fresh facts on the performance and handling of the vehicle in battle.

Jagdpanther is evidently designed to fulfil the dual role of 'Assault' gun and mobile anti-tank gun. The manual recommends that targets should be engaged from 2,700 yards.

(a) 'Jagdpanther' is heavy anti-tank equipment. It is designed for use by the high command as a '*Schwerpunkt*' weapon for the destruction of enemy tank attacks. 'Jagdpanthers' are organized in Army Troops heavy anti-tank battalions. A battalion consists of 3 companies of 14 'Jagdpanthers' each and there are 3 'Jagdpanthers' at Battalion HQ. Each company has 3 troops each with 4 'Jagdpanthers', and there are 2 Jagdpanthers' at company HQ.

(b) With its 8.8 cm anti-tank gun (L/71) 'Jagdpanther' can destroy all known types of enemy tanks at long ranges. Its cross country performance and armour protection enable it actually to attack enemy tanks and to assist friendly tanks in frontal attacks.

---

8. ISUM 76, 14 September 1944, from *21st Army Group Technical Intelligence Summary*, No. 3, 11 September 1944.
9. *Sonderkraftfahrzeuge*. Every vehicle in active use in the Wehrmacht, armoured and unarmoured, was given a *Sd. Kfz.* number, by which it was designated.

(c) The limited traverse, vision, and available means of defence at close quarters, do not permit 'Jagdpanthers' to be used in the role of tanks and make it necessary for them to be protected by infantry or tanks.

(d) The employment of the complete battalion is the primary consideration toward obtaining a decisive success. If it is found necessary to employ single companies, they may be placed under command of formations down to and inclusive [of] divisions but not lower. They may be placed in support of brigades and battalions. The 'Jagdpanther' unit commander will be consulted before tasks are allotted. In all circumstances he remains responsible for the execution of his task.

The battalion is responsible for the repair of vehicles in sub-allotted companies.

The employment of individual section (4 'Jagdpanthers') is only permissible against fortified positions and in close country.

The use of individual 'Jagdpanthers' is forbidden.

(e) 'Jagdpanthers' should be located where the enemy *Schwerpunkt* and thrust line is known to be in order to strengthen up existing Anti-tank weapons. Here they should be committed to battle as complete units.

(f) 'Jagdpanther' is not a static anti-tank gun. It is not designed for the role of protection.

(g) 'Jagdpanther' is not an artillery piece on an SP carriage. The engagement with HE ammunition on unarmoured targets is only permissible – if there are no enemy tanks about; if there are no other heavy guns available or if they have been knocked out; if the ammunition supply allows.

(h) After completing their mission at the front 'Jagdpanthers' should be withdrawn for repair and maintenance. The readiness for action of a 'Jagdpanther' depends on the amount of regular maintenance that it is possible to do.

(i) Full use must be made of the range of the gun when attacking enemy tanks, particularly when the enemy has a large superiority in numbers of tanks. Targets should be engaged in good time from 2700 yards.

(j) When 'Jagdpanthers' are in concealed positions unknown to the enemy, it is best to let enemy tanks ride into the field of fire. The tanks can then be engaged at short range with the effect of surprise. Concentration of fire is desirable.

(k) When engaging targets, full use should be made of manoeuvrability. Firing positions should be changed frequently and it is possible to increase the effect of 'Jagdpanthers' by opening up from unexpected directions.

(l) An enemy tank attack can be pinned down by a proportion of 'Jagdpanthers', while the rest attack the enemy tanks from the flank or rear and destroy them.

(m) The tasks of a 'Jagdpanther' unit during an attack by tanks are:
support of the first wave by engaging enemy cruiser and heavy tanks;
pinning down the enemy tanks from the front while the enemy flanks or rear are being attacked;
protection of either or both flanks of the attacking tanks.

(n) In the case of an attack by infantry, 'Jagdpanthers' should follow immediately behind the leading rifleman. Their main task is then the engagement of enemy tanks to the front and to the flanks. If no enemy tanks put in an appearance, targets, the engagement of which would assist the infantry attack, can be taken on by machine gun fire and HE.

(o) In attacking fortified positions 'Jagdpanthers' can effectively support the advance of the assaulting troops by firing at vision and weapon slits.

(p) In the pursuit, 'Jagdpanthers,' together with other mobile units, follow up the enemy ruthlessly. Petrol and ammunition supplies must be ensured in good time.

(q) In the defence, 'Jagdpanthers' should be concentrated and held in readiness in the rear of sectors particularly threatened by tank attacks. Approach routes, assembly areas and fire positions should be reconnoitred and prepared beforehand. Dispersal over a wide front lessens the effect of fire and increases the difficulties of command and supply. 'Jagdpanthers' must never be dug in on main defensive lines. Enemy tanks, which have broken through, must be destroyed in the manner described in paras (i) to (l).

(r) After disengaging and retiring from the battle, 'Jagdpanthers' should be used for mobile fighting in the intervening terrain between defensive positions.

(s) When fighting in built-up and wooded areas, 'Jagdpanthers' can give fire support to the attacking forces until the enemy position has been penetrated.

Their employment within such areas has a limited value only as their tactical mobility cannot be exploited and the length of the gun often prevents the vehicle from being traversed. Complete protection by infantry must always be provided.

(t) 'Jagdpanthers' can be used at night in close cooperation with other weapons provided the attack is limited in range and complete facilities for reconnaissance and guidance are available.

Chapter 9

Allied Evaluations of German Armoured Vehicles, Weapons and Tactics

Document 9/1[1]

Experience with Tiger Tanks in Italy

Wartime Intelligence Officer's Comments

In the battle for Florence contact was made by 2nd New Zealand Division for the first time with Tiger tanks in any number. The following are from preliminary points which emerged during those encounters, regarding the characteristics and use of this enemy AFV. Several of them confirm views previously expressed in official papers.

(i)   Employment

Tiger tanks were employed, usually well sited and well camouflaged with foliage so as to be difficult to pick up, as follows:

In hull-down positions to delay infantry and to pick off our tanks.

From pre-selected positions which were reached via covered routes. From these positions the enemy would fire a few harassing rounds, withdraw, and occupy an alternative position.

As close support for enemy infantry, to thicken up artillery concentrations, and to engage buildings occupied by our troops.

1. ISUM 92, 30 September 1944, from *2nd New Zealand Division Intelligence Summary*.

With, almost invariably, the support of at least one other tank or SP gun, which remained silent until or unless needed.

Sometimes with infantry accompanying it. These troops who might be only six to twelve in number, deployed on the flanks up to fifty yards from the tank.

(ii)   Vulnerability

The heavy front and rear armour of the tank make the likelihood of it being knocked out by hits on these parts remote. Frontal attack and flank attack together are therefore desirable. The side armour is definitely vulnerable to 17-pdr. fire. The back of the tank, over the engines, is also a weak spot and a large exhaust hole just over the left of the centre of the back provides another weak point. HE is considered by some to be the most effective ammunition to use against these rear parts.

The Tiger was usually well enough sited to make the deployment of a sniping anti-tank gun, M-10 or towed gun for stalking purposes, difficult. Unless very careful reconnaissance is carried out to site the gun to the best advantage, and to locate supporting tanks or SP guns, the effort may be fruitless. The maximum time for reconnaissance, and the maximum information, appear therefore essential for a[n armoured] troop commander who is called upon to engage a Tiger.

The gun and tank seem to be slow to manoeuvre and fire. It can also be effectively blinded by 7.5 cm American smoke ammunition. On one occasion two smoke rounds, followed by AP, were enough to force a Tiger to withdraw. This is a method of attack strongly recommended by our own tank commanders.

(iii)   Aggressive Use of Tigers

Tigers were sometimes used almost recklessly, their crews taking risks to a degree which indicates that they have the utmost confidence in the vehicle. This can render them vulnerable to anti-tank hunting squads armed with the PIAT[2] or other close range anti-tank weapon. The Tiger when closed down and attacking on its own at some distance from its supporting gun is definitely vulnerable to such weapons.

---

2. PIAT, Projector, Infantry, Anti-Tank. This was the Commonwealth equivalent of the bazooka and was a spring-loaded weapon with a hollow-charge projectile. It was surprisingly effective but its range was short.

(iv)　Use of Artillery to Counter Tigers

The concentration of field artillery to counter Tigers is effective. Even if a 'brew-up' does not result, the tank has invariably withdrawn. It appears obvious that tank crews do not like shellfire, as the possibility of damage to vital parts (track, suspension, bogies, wireless aerials, outside fixtures, electrical equipment, etc.) is always present.

Medium artillery has been incorporated in several of our artillery concentrations. Medium artillery is ideal if a sufficiently large concentration is brought to bear, but owing to dispersion of rounds it is preferable to include a good concentration of field guns to thicken up.

We have no actual experience of heavy artillery engaging Tigers, although it is known that they have done so.

It is hard for our tanks to locate a well-camouflaged Tiger sited in a defensive role, and stationary. Artillery OP's, if given a suspected area, can be used to advantage. A case did occur when a suspicious object was located in an area reported by our tanks to contain a Tiger, and the OP commenced to range. A round falling in the vicinity of the suspect completely blasted away all camouflage and the Tiger beat a hasty retreat.

(v)　[Anti-Tank Gunners' Experience with Tigers]

The following are some experiences of anti-tank gunners in contact with Tigers:

A Tiger was observed 3,000 yards away engaging three Shermans. It brewed-up one Sherman while the other two withdrew over a crest. A 17-pdr. was brought up within 2,400 yards and engaged the Tiger side on. When the Tiger realized that it was being engaged by a heavy gun it swung round 90 degrees so that its heavy frontal armour was towards the gun. In the ensuing duel one shot hit the turret, another the suspension, while the two near misses probably ricocheted into the tank. The tank was not put out of action. The range was too long to expect a kill but our tactics were to make the Tiger expose its flank to the Shermans at a range of about 500 yards by swinging round onto the anti-tank gun. This he did, and on being engaged by the Shermans it withdrew. The infantry protection of some 6–12 men was engaged by our machine guns.

One Tiger [was] just off the road at a road and a track junction engaging our forward troops in buildings, another Tiger about 50 yards up the side and supporting the firing tank. A field artillery concentration which appeared to be from one battery was called for and although no hits were observed both tanks withdrew.

A Tiger on a ridge was engaged by what appeared to be a battery of mediums. After the first rounds had fallen, the crew baled out (it is not known why) and shortly afterwards while still being shelled one man returned to the tank and drove it off. The remainder of the crew made off in the direction of their tank some ten minutes later.

A tank was located in the garage of a two-storey building, from which it was driven twenty yards, fired a few harassing rounds and returned to its hide-out. Many hits were recorded on the building by our 4.2 inch mortars, but little damage was visible. The tank was withdrawn from the area each night even although it was in an excellent concealed position and protected by infantry. The house was examined later and although it was considerably damaged and there were several dead Germans about, there was nothing to indicate that damage had been done to the tank.

Document 9/2[3]

Analysis of 75 mm Sherman Tank Casualties Suffered, 6 June to 10 July 1944

Editor's Comment

Allied armoured crews had a very difficult time in Normandy as they faced an opponent who was not only a master of camouflage but also possessed superior weapons with longer range. It is no surprise that many Allied soldiers became convinced that every German tank they encountered was Tiger and every anti-tank gun the dreaded 88mm, in one of its various forms. The operational research section of 21st Army Group studied Sherman tank casualties in the first month of fighting and came up with some interesting results.

---

3. Report No. 12, 'Analysis of 75mm Sherman Tank Casualties Suffered between 6th June and 10th July 1944', in *Operational Research in North West Europe: The Work of No. 2 Operational Research Section with 21 Army Group – June 1944–July 1945* (London, 1945).

1. Introduction

The following survey of 75mm Sherman tank casualties suffered in Normandy between 6th June and 10th July deals only with casualties and not with terrain, extent of enemy opposition, etc.

General information on tank casualties is collected by REME[4] on such subjects as total number of tanks damaged, total brew-ups and the seriousness of the damage inflicted, but at the suggestion of DSD[5] Second Army, more data was collected; in particular the number of hits to knock out a tank, the number of hits which have failed to penetrate, the proportion on front, sides and rear and their angles of penetration.

In order to obtain this information a representative sample of tank casualties was taken from those fronts where 75mm Sherman tanks fought between 6th June and 10th July, data being collected both from recovered and unrecovered vehicles. To test that the evidence was, as far as possible, representative, the proportion within the sample of brew-ups, mined tanks and AP casualties was also found and this proportion compared with that given by AFV (Tech)[6] and REME, Second Army, who had access on these points to all 75mm Sherman tank casualties. Agreement was good so that further evidence given in this report on angles of penetration, etc., can justifiably be assumed typical till proved otherwise.

2. Data Collected

The data collected is given in the following table:

Analysis of Sherman Casualties

		Proportion of total tanks
(i) Total tank casualties analysed:	45	
(a) Number penetrated by German AP shot	40	89%
(b) Number mined	4	9%
(c) Number damaged, unidentified but 'brewed up'	1	2%
(ii) Total 'brewed up'	37	82%
(a) Number penetrated by shot and 'brewed up'	33	73%
(b) Number mined and 'brewed up'	3	7%
(c) Number 'brewed up' by unknown causes	1	2%

---

4. REME, Royal Electrical and Mechanical Engineers, the organization for the repair and salvage of vehicles, armoured or not.
5. DSD, Director, Staff Duties.
6. AFV (Tech), Armoured Fighting Vehicles (Technical) branch of REME.

(Note: In several cases it is difficult to distinguish between penetrations of 75mm and 88mm particularly after the tank had 'brewed up.' Too much reliance must not be placed on the proportion of such penetrations though the proportion given agrees well with the estimated occurrence of such guns given by GSI (A)[7] Second Army Main HQ.

Estimates by fighting soldiers were found to be unreliable since many reported they had been knocked out by 88mm, when in fact it had been 75mm shot, while the reverse mistake has not yet been discovered.

(iii) Tanks penetrated by German AP shot

	Number of hits	Proportion of total hits
A.		
(a) Total hits recorded	65	
(i) 75mm	53	82%
(ii) 88mm	12	18%
(b) Number of penetrations	62	95%
(i) 75mm	50	77%
(ii) 88mm penetrations	12	18%
(c) Number of failures to penetrate	3	5%
(i) 75mm failures	3	5%
(ii) 88mm failures	Nil	0%
(d) Average number of hits to knock out a Sherman tank	1.63	
(e) Proportion of hits which knock out a tank	62%	

B. Distribution of Hits

	Front	Sides	Rear	Total
Hull	7	24	6	37
Turret	12	12	4	28
Total	19	36	10	65

C. Distribution of Failures

	Front	Sides	Rear	Total
Hull	0	0	0	0
Turret	1	1	1	3
Total	1	1	1	3

---

7. GS I (A), General Staff Officer I (Armour).

D. Distribution of hits required to knock out each tank

Number of hits	1	2	3	4	5	6	7	8
Tanks knocked out	21	11	21	–	–	–	1	

E. Distribution of angles of penetration

	0–5°	5–30°	30–90°	Total
Hull	20	12	5	37
Turret	12	11	2	25
Total	32	23	7	62

% Distribution

Hull	32	19	8	59
Turret	19	18	3	40
Total	51	37	11	99

F. Further study of tanks that had fought but had not been penetrated was also made

Total tanks inspected	124
Hits failing to penetrate	8

3. Discussion

1. The proportion of brewed up tanks is high and it is therefore important to know whether or not this must always be the case. A more recent examination of later battles, which is not yet complete, has shown that the 1st Battalion Coldstream Guards (5 Guards Armoured Division) have suffered fewer brew ups than other units, e.g. during Operation BLUECOAT only 1 in 20 casualties, of which casualties at least 12 were due to penetration. The unit concerned attributes this to the fact that they carry no extra ammunition outside the armoured bins. It should be recognized that in no recorded case in our sample has the extra outside applique armour resisted any hit, and therefore the protection afforded by keeping all ammunition in the bins is almost certainly due solely to the internal flying fragments failing to penetrate the ammunition.

2. The small number of AP hits failing to penetrate is noticeable. This small number has been confirmed by the opinions of technical adjutants, etc., who agree that the proportion was probably not above 5%. This opinion is in keeping with the calculated expectations of failures based upon penetration figures for 75mm and 88mm guns at the ranges of engagement estimated by tank crews. There have also been complaints

at the apparently low resisting power of the present Sherman armour. REME, 5 Gds Armoured Division state that an AP300 and an AP500 Browning, both fired at 100 yds range, penetrated ½ and 1½ inches respectively into the turret armour.[8] Added to this, it is at present the practice to recondition for service partially brewed-up tanks whose quality of armour might often be low.

3. From the data collected, it will be seen that the proportion of hits on the sides and front of the 75mm Sherman tank is more or less equal and therefore, for up-armouring to be effective, a large area would need to be strengthened. For instance, up-armouring the front of the tank so that in the cases considered it would have given 50% protection on this face, would only have decreased penetrations by 15%. In consequence, if changes are required, it would appear wiser to use the extra weight-carrying of the 75mm Sherman to take a better gun; i.e., to make German tanks more vulnerable rather than to attempt to decrease our own vulnerability. This suggestion would appear to be in keeping with present policy.

4. Requests have been made by DTD[9] for any additional battlefield data to assist decide on the optimum thickness of individual armour plates and on their optimum distribution. On the evidence of this report, where tanks are expected to attack in country as, or more, enclosed than Normandy, it is recommended that almost homogeneous defence be assumed (a homogeneous defence being defined as a defence where the enemy are able to hold their fire so long, they are as likely to hit from the side or rear as from the front: for the use of this convenient term see DTD armour reports). Therefore, for optimum armour distribution etc., a 'pdv' (probability directional value) for an almost homogeneous defence should also be used.

It is considered that present homogeneous German defence is due to ease of concealment and that, until better methods of spotting tanks and A/T are found, such a form of defence will continue and can safely be assumed for similar terrain. It should be carefully noted, however, that the present sample of tanks has been taken from a series of battles where our forces

---

8. Translated, this means that the Royal Electrical and Mechanical Engineer element of the Guards Armoured Division tested .30 and .50 calibre Browning machine-gun rounds on a Sherman with the results noted. These results were not very impressive in terms of protection.
9. DTD, Directorate of Technical Development.

were nearly always attacking, and it may well be that, in defence, more frontal hits will be recorded.

Document 9/3[10]

Effect of German Anti-Tank Mines on Vehicles

Wartime Intelligence Officer's Comments

The following notes are compiled from recent information received from AFHQ. It is difficult to generalise on the effects of mines on vehicles; such variables as type of ground, position of striking and speed of the vehicle, are all important factors.

(a) B Vehicles[11]

A single Tellermine will wreck the wheel and axle assembly on the side which hits the mine. The spring will be destroyed in the heavier vehicles, the chassis is not necessarily damaged. Personnel travelling over the wheel box of a 3-ton lorry or 15 cwt truck normally receive injuries if that wheel hits a single anti-tank mine. Protection is afforded by the use of sandbags on the floor of the vehicle. Experiments have also been made with Jeeps and other B vehicles by addition of armour plate to the underside; this affords good protection.

A double Tellermine is sufficient to wreck the vehicle.

Damage to carriers depends on the position of the mine when struck and may be:

(i) Broken track only (exceptional)
(ii) As above and the bogie wheel torn off
(iii) As for (ii) and floor plate burst on same side as mine.

The damage as a rule is extensive.

---

10. ISUM 17, 2 July 1944, from *War Office Technical Intelligence Summary*, No. 31.
11. Category B Vehicles in the Commonwealth armies were unarmoured load and personnel carrying vehicles that were not fighting vehicles. Category A Vehicles were fighting vehicles.

(b)   Tanks

A single Tellermine breaks the track of Sherman and other American tanks of similar suspension and often damages the bogie. A double Tellermine may result in the bogie assembly being totally destroyed.

On the Crusader, one Tellermine will break the track and buckle the bogie wheel. Two or more will bend or break the axle shaft. The damage in the case of the Sherman, Grant and similar AFVs usually necessitates repair in 2nd echelon or even base workshops.

Document 9/4[12]

Notes on German Defensive Tactics in Normandy

Our troops are operating in undulating country containing a number of small villages, most of which are surrounded by woods and orchards. The edge of the woods generally have deep ditches; the lanes are narrow and frequently are sunken or have high banks. Most of them have high hedges or trees. The ground in between the woods is covered with crops about 3 ft high. The hedges are of a similar or greater height. Visibility is considerably restricted and there appear to be many more woods on the ground than are shown on the map.

The enemy makes great use of snipers and small parties with LMGs. They lie out for days, sometimes within our Company locations and try to pick off officers and patrols. Some have been found using wooden bullets which are said to have an effective range of 100 yds. They also concentrate on any head that may be sticking out of tanks or Armoured Cars. In yet another instance the snipers were most skilfully sited and concealed. Their standard of shooting varied however. They also appeared incapable of learning any lesson from the fate of their comrades. They persistently sniped from church towers although one man after another was killed in doing so. Subsequently six dead snipers were found in the tower. The most effective way of dealing with this sniping proved to be the 'set a thief to catch a thief' method. Our sniper, by carefully watching located enemy snipers, eliminated them in turn.

---

12. ISUM 23, 18 July 1944.

They make full use of incidents of the ground and cover. Some of the more stout hearted formations are prepared to lie very low in the face of our tanks. Two examples have been reported by a Squadron Leader. In the first, he was clearing a wooded village and after the exchange of a few shots, about a company came out with their hands up. In the second and similar circumstances, the enemy was well concealed and dug in. They waited until the tanks were right in among them and then they came out of their dugouts with every type of anti-tank weapon and opened up with grenades and PIATs [sic] at ranges as low as 10 yards. The Squadron Leader lost 6 tanks and 8 tank commanders and had to kill 50 or more before they surrendered.

It has been observed in recent actions that the enemy does not always retire in the way that is expected. In one instance some of our troops were ordered to clear one orchard which they succeeded in doing. However, some of the enemy managed to get away and instead of retiring toward their main body to the west, they moved to the north and southeast. Though small in numbers they came around behind the attackers, and were such a nuisance that the orchard previously cleared had to be abandoned.

During the operations on D-Day, companies found considerable difficulty in operating in woods which were occupied by the enemy, a large number of which were sniping from the trees. This method of holding a wood proved very effective and caused a number of casualties to attacking troops who, in one case, had to withdraw.

It is suggested that one method of dealing with these tactics is to support the attacking troops with medium machine-guns firing into the tree tops over the heads of the infantry, light machine-guns giving support on ground level.

Document 9/5[13]

Effective Range of German Tank Guns

Effective ranges of German tank guns firing APCBC,[14] AP 40[15] and Hollow Charge ammunition are given in a semi-official [German] publication dated 1944.

The German definition of effective range is a range at which it is possible to engage the enemy and obtain worthwhile results having regard to the area of burst and the chances of hitting the target.

Gun	Tank on which mounted	Effective Range in Yards		
		APCBC	AP 40	Hollow Charge
8.8 cm KwK 36/L/56	Tiger	2187 in exceptional cases 2734 yards. Troop fire up to 3281 yards		1640
7.5 cm KwK 42 L/70	Panther	ditto	2187	
7.5 cm KwK 40 L/48	Mark IV	1640 (in exceptional circumstances up to 1968 yds)	1094	1312
5 cm KwK 39 L/60	Mark III	1312	875	

---

13. ISUM 29, 13 July 1944, from GS I (Technical), 21st Army Group.
14. APCBC, Armoured-Piercing, Capped Ballistic Cap, an improved type of anti-tank round, more effective than the solid AP round.
15. AP 40 was a special German anti-tank round available for most calibres of weapons which had improved penetration capability at short range.

Document 9/6[16]

Rates of Fire of German Tanks and Assault Guns

A captured document gives the following maximum rates of fire for German tanks and SP assault guns:

Tank Guns	Rate of Fire (rounds per minute)
7.5 cm KwK 40 (Mark IV)	8–10
7.5 cm KwK 42 (Panther)	8–10
8.8 cm KwK 36 (Tiger)	8–10
8.8 cm KwK 43 (Tiger II)	8
Assault Guns	
7.5 cm StuG 40 (Assault Gun)	8–10
15 cm StuHaub 43 (Grizzly Bear)	5

16. ISUM 29, 13 July 1944, from *GS I (Technical), 21st Army Group.*

Chapter 10

The Training of Senior Officers

Document 10/1[1]

German General Staff Training, 1944–1945

Wartime Intelligence Officer's Comments

By 1938, the German General Staff training period had been increased to three years, of which two were spent at the Staff College. It was obviously unlikely that this thorough system of training could be maintained in war, even for so select a body as the German General Staff, which is in fact a 'corps' of <u>senior</u> staff officers. Little has, however, hitherto been known of the modifications introduced.

Details have now been received from a recently captured German document of a current General Staff course, the 17th of this war. The training period for potential General Staff officers is to extend from 1 August 1944 to 1 February 1946. That at the end of the fifth year of the war, when they had for some considerable time been beset by manpower difficulties, the Germans still considered that nineteen months' training was necessary to turn an officer into a General Staff officer, is further evidence (if any were required) of the prestige, importance and privileged position of the General Staff within the German Army.

---

1. ISUM 106, 14 October 1944, extracted from *War Office Weekly Intelligence Review* No. 58.

Details of the 17th course are as follows:

(a) First Phase (1 August–31 October 1944)
Officers selected for General Staff training will be attached to division HQ for this period.

(b) Second Phase (1 November 1944–25 January 1945)
Officers attached to higher formation HQ for staff training in the branches for which they were found most suited during the 'first phase'. The period, 1–25 January 1945 is for leave and travelling to the arms of services schools (*Waffenschulen*) of the Training Army.

(c) Third Phase (26 January–4 March 1945)
If still recommended for General Staff training, officer is posted to the Staff College with simultaneous detachment to Training Army arms of service schools.[2]

(d) Fourth Phase (5 March–25 August 1945)
   Staff college course.

(e) Fifth Phase (26 August 1945–1 February 1946)
If officer successful at the Staff College, a five months' attachment to the General Staff follows. Successful candidates may be accepted for service on the General Staff at the end of this attachment.

The following reports on candidates are to be rendered during the General Staff training period:

(i) Division to OKH/Personnel branch on 1 October 1944 on suitability of General Staff candidate for further training.

(ii) Division to superior HQ (3 October 1944): a full report on the officer concerned, to be endorsed by the formation HQ Chief of Staff and copies forwarded to the OKH/Personnel branch and to the higher formation HQ to which the candidate is to be attached in the second phase.

(iii) Final report on candidate's suitability for the GS training course: from higher formation HQ to OKH/Personnel branch (15 December 1944).

---

2. The *Ersatzheer*, translated variously as the Home Army, Replacement Army and Training Army, was the service devoted to recruiting, training and replacing casualties. Every active service formation had a 'shadow' reserve unit devoted to its personnel needs.

(iv) Chiefs of Staff of higher formation HQs present a full personal report by 5 January 1944.

Changes in attachments to divisions and higher formation HQs by superior HQs are to be exceptional and then only for the purpose of bettering the training of the officer concerned. Consent of the OKH/ Personnel branch is required for this. This makes possible a complete assessment of the attached officers' capabilities by the HQs to which they are attached.

Editor's Comments

Despite being scheduled to last until 1946, the 17th wartime General Staff course only lasted until early 1945, when most students were sent to fill the many vacant staff position created by heavy fighting.[3]

Document 10/2[4]

Course Notes from Divisional Commander's Course, 1943

Wartime Intelligence Officer's Comments

When General Eberding[5] of the 64th Infantry Division surrendered, among his possessions was a notebook, which the General had kept while a student early in 1943 at the Divisional Commanders' School held at the Eden Hotel, Berlin. In it, he had jotted down in an execrable hand and in staccato fashion, his notes of what he was told.

It covers a variety of subjects, and represents the experience of the Russian front to that time. It deals with the same tactical problems that one

---

3. The previous General Staff course was prematurely ended in January 1945 and the students were assigned to various formations requiring staff officers. See Siegfried Knappe, *Soldat: Reflections of a German Soldier, 1936–1949* (New York, 1992). It is quite likely that the 17th course barely started before it was also terminated.
4. The extracts from Eberding's course notes were contained in the following ISUMs: 129, 5 November; 130, 6 November; 131, 7 November, and 139, 16 November 1944.
5. *Generalmajor* Kurt Eberding (1895–1978), commander 64th Infantry Division. Captured 2 November 1944.

of our own schools might attack for divisional commanders, although more advanced thought is seen in such topics as 'Relationship with Women of Eastern Territory', 'Care of Horses', 'The German Woman and The Foreign Worker' and 'The World Outlook'. Unfortunately no substantial part of it is a coherent statement. It is therefore proposed to discuss it in a brief series of notes in Part II of this and subsequent [Intelligence] Summaries.

The Divisional Commander

(a) *The Position of a Divisional Commander*

The most important thing is personal leadership. He must separate himself from his staff. He must give his orders asking for a report as to how they will be carried out. He thus gains an opportunity to intervene again. He must fight laziness and remove inefficiency through personal intervention. He must check punishments handed out by young COs. He must take the lead in considering the world outlook (*Weltanschauung*). He must concern himself with the care of MT and horses, with problems peculiar to officers, with the relation of his force to occupied territory, with air cooperation, with symptoms shown through censorship, and with security.

(b) *Tactical Principles and Experience*

Saving personnel means forming a *Schwerpunkt*. In attack this is easy, but in defence it is difficult because the width of the front may be 30–40 kilometres. The whole question is simply 'Where can I weaken myself?' Artillery and heavy mortar batteries must be concentrated and the ammunition reserves controlled by the divisional commander. Everything must be done to save personnel. Camouflage must be good and checked from the air. Everyone, including those in the rear areas, and horses, must be dug in. Alternative positions for all weapons are obligatory and their provision will be enforced by punishment.

Reconnaissance and observation must be continuous and thorough. Infantry and artillery observation should be joint.

There is no general rule as to what time an attack should go in and how long artillery preparation should last. Emergency units for alarms must be organized and HQ must be made into strong points in order to give additional depth.

Employment of Artillery
Wartime Intelligence Officer's Comments

Throughout his notes there are innumerable references to the artillery which at first appear as a mass of disconnected jottings written in handwriting that defies all but the most patient. These difficulties make a complete story impossible. Nevertheless, sufficient is contained therein to make it worth while publishing some of the salient features, mentioning at the same time items of interest which illustrate the general purpose of his remarks.

(1) General Principles

Artillery HQ must be with the Divisional Commander. The Divisional Commander must separate himself from his staff but should always be available to listen to the proposals as put up by the artillery commander. To implement these proposals sufficient time should be allowed for adequate preparation whether it be in the defence or the attack.

Observation of the enemy as between the infantry and the artillery must be coordinated so that duplication is avoided and information freely exchanged. The men of the artillery are specially singled out for punishment if they have not alternative positions readily available. They must not become static minded.

Finally, in order to increase the versatility of the artillery commander, it is considered that he should be ready to lead the infantry and in fact to be commander of an infantry regiment if required. So that he should be in a position to know all the mysteries appertaining to the job of infantry commander it is advised that he should accompany the divisional commander on his visits to the infantry regiments.

(2) Artillery in Preparation for the Attack

The problems of the attack appear to have been discussed in the form of a tactical exercise which envisaged a divisional operation.

The exercise deals with an attack to be carried out at dawn with the support of the divisional artillery assisted by some GHQ troops which on this occasion, consisted of:

> One Observation Unit
> Three Medium Battalions
> One Assault Gun Battalion

(*Note: The old establishment for medium battalions was one troop of 4 x 10.5 and two troops of 4 x 15 cm each. Total 36 guns. The establishment of the assault gun battalion is given by Eberding as 30 guns, 3 troops of 10 guns each*).

Assault guns are always placed under command of the infantry. They should not be dispersed when distributed since this renders them far less effective. In addition to the above support a troop of 6 Nebelwerfers is mentioned.

The process of movement is difficult to follow from the paucity of information and the lack of coordinated thought but it seems that the artillery would move in during the afternoon and begin registration after assimilation of information from air reconnaissance and forward troops.

It seems that a single gun and mortar are brought into action early, the time mentioned is 1700 hrs, in order that registration may be carried out. This method is probably employed when local air superiority rests with the enemy. On the 'Q'[6] side the divisional commander (*and this sentence is underlined*) 'must have the ammunition expenditure plan in his pocket', adding at the end that this idea is not popular with the artillery. The night before the attack all the activities must be coordinated. Whether it is harassing or defensive fire or both that is laid on it is essential to have the plan coordinated and in a sentence Eberding sums this up: 'The Russian may attack at any time! The sin of negligence.' Here he interposes the three possibilities of delivering defensive fire which are on orders from above, or on demand from below or on signal and it is the platoon commander alone who may give the signal; and a final dig at the gunners that they must be constantly ready for harassing and defensive fire without the receipt of any special and complicated order. A final exhortation is given to the artillery to have a representative present at PW interrogations. Prisoners should be asked at the time of the attack and not before, the location of hostile HQs, so that a concentration may be employed during the attack.

(3) Artillery in Preparation for the Defence

When choosing gun positions, consider their role in defence. As far as possible they should be surrounded by wire obstacles and made into strong points. The troops must be able to combat tanks from their positions and long lines of guns should be avoided for this reason. Guns

---

6. Q or Quartermaster.

therefore should be far apart. The traversing unit of the guns should be kept constantly in view since guns placed too far forward cannot cover the front adequately. Two small footnotes are added to the effect that the boundaries between formations should be adequately covered and their particular responsibility for the right boundary. Before the action starts and the attack is delivered visit the gun positions personally checking at the same time all close defensive preparations. OPs also are mentioned as worthy of a visit.

Finally, if the situation becomes obscure and a break-in commences, it should be sealed off with artillery fire brought down at the threatened point. One thing, however, is essential, namely that the whole ammunition supply for the defensive plan should be clear cut. The exact quantity of ammunition to be expended should be stated.

Security and Army Air Co-Operation

Wartime Intelligence Officer's Comments

In the notes on security which are commented on below, the General touches on a few principles discussed in a lecture by an officer of the Abwehr (German Counter-Intelligence service). There is nothing to indicate that the Germans' conception of this wide subject differs largely from ours, except insofar as contact with Jews and foreign nationals is concerned.

In the article concerning army-air co-operation, the General has jotted down a sketchy coverage of the instruction given in this subject. Enemy methods appear to differ from ours in some respects, and the notes present a rather vague idea of the German conception of army–air support.

(a) Security

The salient points, concerning leakages of information, refer to the necessity of care in dealing with confidential matters, concealing of intentions by using caution with orders and the passing of orders. It would appear that safeguarding of secret material occupies a prominent place in German security and such breaches as loss by capture of documents are severely dealt with, the death penalty being the current sentence.

More subtle security measures, such as the safeguarding of Order of Battle information are mentioned with particular reference to distribution lists. The necessity for strict wireless security is emphasized and it seems that the German order is to encode ALL W/T messages.

The Germans, knowing full well the importance of the Goebbelsian art,[7] have naturally not neglected the counter to this form of attack and mention is made of the necessity for turning in leaflets and controlling radio listening. An interesting point is the presence of the word 'disintegration' in the General's notes in reference to the effect of propaganda. One wonders to what extent the enemy fears the contingency implied in this word.

Two forms of counter measures are referred to in these notes. Firstly, the need to sever all contact between the Wehrmacht and such elements as Poles, Jews and PW. The second precaution concerns internal security within the *Wehrmacht* in so far as certain non-German as opposed to Germanic elements are concerned. Thus, troops are warned to keep an eye on so-called Foreign Legionaries, Alsatians, *Volks* Germans (citizens on probation). The security lesson learned by Major General Eberding does not appear to cover the subject thoroughly by any means. The fact does not imply of course that security in the German Army is less efficient than on our side. Lack of security which may have been noticed during the campaign results more from individual failing than from faulty handling of the subject by the appropriate organization.

(b) Army-Air Co-operation

Tactical reconnaissance in the German Army appears to be under the control of GHQ who, by exercising such close control, have possibly provoked the comment of this field divisional commander that Tac/R aircraft must fly more than twice daily. Perhaps it would be more fitting to say that German tactical reconnaissance aircraft must fly, to produce the required results for the ground troops.

The same comments would apply to air photos. Strategic reconnaissance or long range photo-reconnaissance, under the control of GHQ, does not appear to provide sufficient photos down at German Divisional level.

There appears to be no parallel arrangement for the provision of tactical reconnaissance and photographic reconnaissance for the German Army as compared with the British Army.

Ground to air signals have been for a long time both well developed and used by the enemy, coloured smoke perhaps more extensively than by the British Army.

---

7. 'Goebbelsian art', that is, propaganda and deception.

No mention is made in Major General Eberding's notes of the possible use of artillery reconnaissance. This may be attributed to one of two reasons, either it was overlooked, or because of our own predominant air superiority it was not considered worth while. Probably the latter.

Work at Divisional Headquarters

Wartime Intelligence Officer's Comments

The manuscript notes forming the basis for the following remarks do obviously not deal systematically with all the functions and duties of senior officers at Divisional Headquarters. In all probability they simply represent odd items which General Eberding thought worth jotting down during lectures in view of his own experiences in the Wehrmacht.

(a) The G Branch (Führungsabteilung)

(i) Operations (Ia)

Wherever the general goes, good communications must be kept with G Ops. The commander takes a WT section and the WT equipment with him and has a special wireless operator for his convenience. He also has a special despatch rider who has been 'broken in'. The G1 Ops (Ia) and the G2 (01) are important; they operate together and are often the only ones to be present when decisions are being made. The G2 Ops must be the best active officer available.

(ii) Intelligence (Ia)

The notes suggest that this branch does not receive as much attention as it does in the British and American Armies. They begin with a note that the G3I (Ia) shall not have 'special communications' with intelligence staffs as Corps Headquarters and continues with a remark that the use of 'special channels' presumably by I staffs, is a bad symptom.

The advice to give the situation FIRST to regiments rather than to flanking or senior formations agrees with our own practice.

Among 'other tasks' are listed: Press in the Homeland – Press officers from Corps Headquarters, – Pictures for newspapers and direct dealings with staff officers at Corps Headquarters and with certain officers of the War Ministry.

(iii) Divisional Signals Officer

'To be kept near . . . with his W/T set. One can get a lot from the Signals battalion.'

(b) The Q Branch (Quartiermeisterabteilung)

(i) The DAQMG (Ib)[8]

Capable of working independently, the DAQMG must have his divisional commander's confidence and support. He usually has a number of older officers around him (ADMS,[9] 'Intendant', etc.). Either Eberding or Eberding's professor must have been under the impression that DAQMGs are easy to replace in the German Army for the final remark reads 'Otherwise remove without consideration'. This may also be taken as an indication of the high standard required for this appointment.

(ii) The 'Intendant'

This is an official on formation staff in charge of administration of supplies, transport, financial matters, etc. The notes characterize him as a 'mixture of a judge, a soldier and an official'. He has only officials under command and has special channels of communication to the corresponding appointments at Corps and Army. He cannot, however, use these 'special channels' without the consent of the divisional commander.

The 'Intendant' deals with clothing and rations, also with appreciations of officials, transfers and requests but in these matters he may not act alone.

Presumably the divisional commander must approve.

NAAFI[10] goods were of particular interest to General Eberding and he went to the trouble of making the following entry: 'NAAFI goods are not distributed by IVa but by the divisional commander himself. Otherwise everything goes to Headquarters personnel. Forty bottles of champagne: It isn't worth while to distribute' . . . and we can all imagine what happens to them.

(iii) The ADMS (IVb)

The ADMS should normally be at Tactical Headquarters in order to be able to be informed about the current situation and to be able to take the required tactical-medical measures at once. On the other hand he must not neglect to visit the hospital and the dressing stations often. The following technical items were noted by the General.

---

8. DAQMG, Deputy-Assistant-Quartermaster-General.
9. ADMS, or Assistant Director, Medical Services, was the senior medical officer in a Commonwealth Division.
10. NAAFI (Navy, Army and Air Force Institutes) was the Commonwealth organization responsible for providing canteens and canteen goods for the troops. The Commonwealth equivalent of the USO.

Establishment of a forward chirurgical post for men who have to be operated on at once.

Preventative measures against flies: nets over beds.

Supply of extra vehicles from workshop company.

Spotted fever, de-lousing and anti-vermin solutions [illegible words]

Entire bunkers and not single men should be deloused at a time.

Establishment of a convalescent company at Division.

(iv) Divisional Veterinary Officer (IVe)

This officer usually carries the rank of Lieutenant in the German Army and the notes suggest that he often requires 'encouragement' for expressions appear such as 'not just horse inspections' or 'give tasks – if something is noticeable, orders: "you will go there for 3 days!"'.

The veterinary officer is responsible for the standard of riding and driving within the division. He will preferably use Russians for the care of horses.

(c) The A Branch

(i) The DAAG (IIa)[11]

It is expected to have a good memory for 'he must know all officers'. The only other noteworthy item under this heading refers to the existence of new regulations for promotion on recommendation. (text does not clearly indicate whether the recommendation should come from the divisional commander or from the DAAG).

(ii) The Deputy Judge Advocate General (III)

The Divisional commander should often talk with him and give him directions on how to handle cases. 'Judgements must follow a certain line' then like an ugly rock frothing in the midst of the sea the typically Nazi-like doctrine comes to the surface in the last three lines 'Name assistants to judge yourself: Men from the front: He must get at least 3 months: The judicial angle doesn't matter.'

(d) Advisors

CRA[12]

The divisional commander must keep the CRA very close by and educate him in his way. The importance of artillery is stressed by items, such as: 'When changing Headquarters the G1 Ops must not leave the old

---

11. DAAG, Deputy-Assistant-Adjutant-General.
12. CRA, Commander Royal Artillery, the senior artillery officer in a Commonwealth division.

location until the new one has an artillery officer present. Also give orders for regiments' – 'Every evening have a report submitted on expended ammunition. Concern over Allied artillery is shown by the question 'Where are new enemy gun positions?' 'Where is enemy artillery fire?' An exact and up-to-date map must be kept by the gunners.

(e) Miscellaneous

Tactical and administrative Headquarters are usually not in the same place – Tactical Headquarters should be as small as possible'.

Wartime Intelligence Officer's Comments

The remaining notes deal with movie cameras, as an aid to the recording of regimental histories, with rumours, which are said to be often hatched by clerks and telephone personnel, and finally with the outward behaviour of the ideal German divisional commander himself. Here we can visualize the 'Divisions Kommandeur' surrounded and followed by his chosen staff officers, leading a life of simplicity and setting the standard of behaviour in the common dining room. He sees to it that guests are properly treated and when reinforcements arrive he never fails to welcome them personally.

Chapter 11

Shortages of Medical Supplies, Weapons and Equipment

Document 11/1[1]

Loss of Equipment: Germany Army General Order, 12 August 1944

Wartime Intelligence Officer's Comments

The following Order of the High Command dated 12 August 1944 points to the serious shortage of small arms equipment now facing the German Army. It is significant that 1252 Coastal Artillery Regiment found it necessary to republish this drastic Order on 24 September 1944, six weeks after it was originally issued.

High Command of the Army 12 August 1944

Gen. St.d.H. Gen.Qu.
Subject: Care of weapons and equipment
To avoid the terrible losses of material I give the following Order:

    (1) <u>Everybody</u> whether officer or other rank who
        (a) loses his machine gun, small arms or respirator,
        (b) becoming a casualty leaves it behind carelessly (to be judged by the attending Medical Officer)

---

1. ISUM 108, 16 October 1944.

    (c) fails to be in possession of it when reporting to a new unit on transfer

will be punished.

(2) Loss of above mentioned weapons and equipment demands immediate disciplinary action.

    (a) Loss of leave or furlough for one year with exception of compassionate leave in case of death.

    (b) Loss of all canteen rations including any smokes for the next six months.

(3) The value is in each case to be recovered.

Cost of MG 34	120 RM (£10)
Cost of MP 44	80 RM (£6 15s)
Cost of rifle and machine pistols [submachine guns]	50 RM (£4 3s)
Cost of Pistols	30 RM (£2 10s)
Cost of Respirator	20 RM (£1 15s)

signed Guderian[2]

Document 11/2[3]

Equipment Shortage –
Seventh Army General Order, 21 July 1944

Wartime Intelligence Officer's Comments

The following is a translation of an order by General of the SS Hausser, commander of the Seventh German Army, giving further proof of the acute shortage the Germans are suffering in all types of equipment:

The Commander, Seventh Army   Army HQ, 21 July 1944

The supply situation is extremely tense.

---

2. This is, of course, *Generaloberst* Heinz Guderian, who was appointed *Chef des Generalstab des Heeres*, the effective commander of the German army, in August 1944.
3. ISUM 39, 7 August 1944, from *General Staff Periodic Report*, No. 56, 5 August 1944.

Despite the fact that production is running at high speed, new activations and regular replacement orders consume a big part of the finished products.

Therefore:

(1) Weapons and equipment that need repair will be speedily evacuated to the rear repair services of the army.

(2) Even salvage, weapons and equipment which are apparently beyond repair must be evacuated, because from two or three useless weapons of the same type, a new one can be built. Besides, extra spare parts are frequently recovered in this way.

(3) It must be completely clear to every soldier that strict saving is essential. It is irresponsible to leave behind or fail to evacuate weapons and equipment, binoculars, sighting devices, entrenching tools as well as all sorts of empty cartridge cases, ammunition boxes, and seemingly useless weapons and equipment.

(4) I expect and request from commanding generals, division commanders and below that, from every officer, that the above principles will be preached to the troops again and again.

(5) Executive orders will come from the chief of the supply services.

> (Signed)
> Hausser
> *Obergruppenführer* and
> General of the Waffen SS

Document 11/3[4]

German Problems with Medical Supplies

Many reports received in the past months show a general and increasing shortage of medical supplies in the German army in the west. In spite of all their precautionary measures, shortages of vital medical supplies

---

4. ISUM 49, 17 August 1944.

confront the Germans. In order to control the French market the Germans prevented pharmaceutical factories in France from manufacturing medicaments, with the exception of a few concerns which were acquired by Germany or came directly under German control. At the same time supplies for civilian use were cut to a minimum. In 1943 Germany could no longer supply French civilian needs and in 1944 the army faced the same shortage. Germany's loss of important stocks of medical equipment on the various fronts and the ever-increasing number of patients in German hospitals, are making the shortage serious.

German medical officers have been notified to exercise the strictest economy on medical supplies. A corps order (presumably I SS Panzer Corps) dated 23 May 1944 refers to the shortage of chemicals and medical equipment. It states that the greatest economy must be used with gauze and cellulose cotton and that washable dressings must be washed and used over again, whilst wide use must be made of paper bandages. In December 1943 it was reported that complete first aid equipment was no longer issued to motorized units, instead, a small box of essential items was issued.

The Germans have been reported as requisitioning medical supplies as far back as January 1943. In 1943 requisitioning of pharmaceutical products was reported in Marseilles and St. Raphael. In July of this year the Germans were reported requisitioning all medical and dental appliances throughout Alsace-Lorraine. Although requisitioning has been reported from a few areas it is evident that it was carried out over the entire territory.

Lack of materials and hurried production has resulted in inferior quality products. Poor quality has been reported in dressings, bandages, and anaesthetics; also reported were bad quality clinical thermometers. Certain instruments are no longer available; among those reported as practically unobtainable are the following:

Surgical instruments, drains, rubber tubes, X-Ray parts and radiographic plates.

Serious shortages have been reported in the following medicaments: Iodine products, Opium extracts, Insulin, Bismuth, Cod liver oil, Quinine, Alcohol and preparations with a vaseline base.

Document 11/4[5]

Medical Matters in 326th and 346th Infantry Divisions, August 1944

The system of evacuation of casualties in 346th Infantry Division is normal. A prisoner who was a medical orderly with III Battalion 857 Grenadier Regiment at the beginning of August, states that in his unit there is a medical orderly with each company and two stretcher-bearers to a platoon, controlled by the battalion Medical Officer (normal: one stretcher bearer to a platoon, and an orderly and stretcher bearer at company). The unit aid post was at Bassenville U1870, the nearest battalion dressing station (*Verbandplatz*) at Dozule U2673, and the regimental dressing station (*Hauptverbandplatz*, equivalent to our MDS[6]) some 30 kilometres further back. The prisoner stated that there was a base hospital (*Kriegslazarett*) at Amiens No 5. He did not know of a casualty collecting post – a stage often omitted in practice by the German medical services. No mention was made of the Divisional Field Hospital (*Feldlazarett*) though no doubt one exists, probably near the Regimental Dressing Station.

A captured order of 326 Infantry Division, with a southerly rather than easterly line of evacuation, does mention casualty collecting posts – at Putanges U12, Sees Q42 and Alençon Z38. The same order mentions military hospitals at Alençon (Number 1/612 – Specialist centre), Bagnoles de l'Orne Y99 (Surgical and General) and Evreux U77, Breteuil R84 and Chartres R30. These are static hospitals, in use for some time before the invasion. There are delousing stations at Alençon and at Brieux U22 southeast of Falaise, and bacteriological laboratories at Alençon and Perroux T80. The chemical research laboratory is in Paris.

The statements of the prisoner from 346th Infantry Division show a good state of health in the division. Apart from frequent colds, due to the damp ground the division is occupying, insect bites provide most of his business as medical orderly. The incidence of venereal disease is small – about five per cent per year, doubtless owing to the strict discipline in this matter maintained by the German Army. About eighty per cent of French women are reckoned to be infected, and men are forbidden

---

5. ISUM 42, 10 August 1944.
6. MDS, Main Dressing Station.

to have intercourse except at recognized brothels. Prophylactic stations are established near certain of these, manned by a Corporal and senior private (who checks men in and out). Each man receiving prophylactic treatment is given a dated certificate, and a man reporting sick with venereal disease who cannot produce his certificate gets 3–10 days detention and a stoppage of half his pay.

Document 11/5[7]

Medical Matters in the Wehrmacht, 1944

A group of medical officer prisoners, including the ADMS of 326th Infantry Division and DDMS[8] of 84 Corps (20 Aug) state that the system of evacuation in use is from battalion aid post (at Revier) and lightly wounded collecting post (*Leichverwundetennest*) to the main dressing station (*Hauptverbandplatz*) thence to the Army hospitals (*Kriegslazarett*). The elimination of the field hospital (*Feldlazarett*) stage in evacuation is in the interests of speed and simplicity. It was generally located near the Main Dressing Station and by passed in any case by the more serious cases. At the time of capture, the nearest *Kriegslazarett* was in Paris, and casualties were evacuated from MDS to Paris, the more serious going on to Germany. An MDS is set up by each company of the divisional medical battalion.

The *Kriegslazarett* is divided into sections (*Abteilungen*): (1) Surgical (*Chirurgie*). (2) Internal diseases (*Innere Krankheiter*). Venereal diseases (*Geschlechts Krankheiter*) and specialist sections (ear, eye, nose, throat, lungs).

Medical supplies are not admitted to be short in the field, although one of the doctors was aware of scarcity of many supplies in France. It was stated that Germany started the war with huge reserves. Re-use of bandages, and use of paper bandages where changes in dressing had to be frequent were admitted however. The officers were definite that casualties from splinters or concussion caused by artillery fire were much greater than casualties caused by bombing.

---

7. ISUM 57, 25 August 1944.
8. DDMS, Deputy Director of Medical Services.

Three other medical officers, captured between 11 and 18 August, confirm the shortage of mitigal for scabies (and other oily medicaments). Methylated spirit and alcoholic drug supplies are stated to be strictly vetted by administrative officers. These doctors had no knowledge of typhus in this theatre of war, and stated that only medical personnel are inoculated against typhus. They agreed with the others that equipment in the field was adequate.

An interesting point is that in medical equipment brought in so far, no sulpha-drugs have been found.

Prisoners of war taken between 11–18 August were found to be suffering from: scabies 23%, lice 9%, impetigo 18%, venereal disease – none. Of the seven cases admitted to hospital for ailments other than wounds, four were malarial relapses (three had contracted malaria in Russia, one in southern France). Physique and health were fairly good and no prisoners were suffering from anxiety states as a result of being in action. Some were suffering from fatigue.

Document 11/6[9]

Medical Matters in III Flak Corps

The Medical Officer of III Flak Corps, interrogated 25 August 1944, generally supported previous information given by medical personnel. The following points are worth noting:

(i) Fifty percent of the small bandages requested by Medical Officers are issued only – the balance are paper.

(ii) Insulin is very hard to get, and in some cases patients have died from lack of it. A very strict regulation of the issue has improved matters.

(iii) The most severe type of diphtheria has occurred more often than is normal. Serum is hard to obtain.

(iv) Atropine preparations are very scarce. Morphine, anti-tetanus serum, sulpha-drugs are plentiful.

---

9. ISUM 68, 5 September 1944.

(v) <u>V.D.</u> Until recently, sulphathiosol [sulfathiozole] preparations were purchased in France, and prostitutes took advantage of this and took a few tablets before being examined. Thus although infected with gonorrhea, their test proved negative, and they were allowed to carry on their trade. Men infected by these women failed to show the customary results when treated with sulphathiosol, and the percentage of cures dropped from 90% to 40% of cases cured. The coccus carried by such women became acclimatised to the drug, and was twice as hard to cure.

Document 11/7[10]

Health Problems in the German Army, Normandy

Observation of the medical condition of about 1000 prisoners (7–10 August), aided by the interrogation of medical personnel, discloses the following general condition. Prisoners were well built and appeared well nourished. They did not seem exhausted (although they had had 24–48 hours to recover since being taken prisoner). The very young soldiers – 16⅓ to 18 years old – were more poorly nourished and showed more signs of exhaustion than the older ones.

The chief disease was scabies – about a quarter of the prisoners being affected. The general opinion was that this was owing to close packing in dug-outs, lack of medical attention (as medical personnel were too busy with the wounded), and the shortage of Mitigal (the German cure for scabies). A medical officer added that it was also a result of the long opportunity for contact with civilians which the troops had enjoyed, and general inability to do a monthly inspection since the invasion. Only 1 litre a month of Mitigal was issued to a field medical officer, whereas about 4 ounces is required to cure a patient. (Mitigal is an organic sulphide made by Bayer). The scabies were often severe, and untreated for as long as three weeks.

Twelve per cent of the prisoners were lousy. The same medical officer said his regiment (987 Grenadier Regiment) was free from lice until they

---

10. ISUM 45, 13 August 1944.

got Russian reinforcements, and that this was a general observation.

Only three cases of impetigo and one of gonorrhea (doubtful) were discovered.

The medical officer also stated that the youths now being pressed into service, in spite of extra meat and fat rations, are of poor physique and incapable of the heaviest work. Medical categories in the German Army have been altered since May, whereby all men are fit for line or communications duties unless unit medical officers adjudge them unfit except for home service.

Chapter 12

Discipline, Morale, Propaganda and Tensions Between the Army and the SS

Document 12/1[1]

Discipline Problems in Panzer Group West, July 1944

HQ Panzer Group West   16 July 1944
C in C, Panzer Group West   Ops/No 441/44 Confidential

<u>Subject</u>: Discipline

1. Owing to the overstrain caused by front line conditions there will inevitably be from time to time some slackness in the behaviour of our men. As long as their fighting spirit is maintained, superficial shortcomings need not be taken seriously in these conditions.

On the other hand there is no reason why units behind the actual fighting zone (from artillery positions rearwards) should become careless in dress, bearing, or discipline. Actually, however, the state of affairs is worse there than it is at the front. The following points have been particularly noticed.

1) Far too many soldiers are idling about behind the front, although the construction of positions and the training of alarm units call for the co-operation of every single man. Idleness dulls the wits.

---

1. ISUM 35, 3 August 1944, from *Second British Army Intelligence Summary*, No. 59, 2 August 1944.

2) There is an increased number of cases of looting, cattle stealing and so-called 'purchase' accompanied by a show of weapons, etc.

3) An inexcusably large number of motor vehicles are being driven about in rear areas. As a rule these are obviously being used only to 'get organized' or to cultivate some female acquaintance – this in spite of the shortage of POL, which, by the way of contrast, is driving farmers and doctors at home to such straits that they cannot carry out their work properly.

4) The dress of some of our men is grossly neglected. Many soldiers no longer wear their caps as a matter of course. Particularly when travelling in tanks or on motorcycles they are often without headgear. Sentries often stand in good weather with the muzzles of their rifles pointing downwards or held under the arm, like a shot-gun.

5) Saluting has almost entirely ceased.

2. To remedy these abuses, which are detrimental to our good name, I order:

1) Steps will be taken to improve the present state of affairs by giving instructions to all rear units and by appealing to the German soldier's sense of honour.

2) All officers will be instructed to take measures against these abuses, irrespective of whether personnel of the army, the Waffen SS, or the Luftwaffe are concerned.

3) Patrols will be organised and sentries posted in each corps are forthwith, with the object of keeping a watch on saluting, dress, bearing and correct behaviour towards the population. These patrols and sentries will also have the duty of checking the necessity for journeys of motor vehicles and the legality of movements of cattle and foodstuffs.

In cases concerning the personnel of units of other formations, paybooks will be taken from offending soldiers and forwarded with a report to the Corps concerned.

4) Officers will be checked by special officer-patrols in the same manner as ORs.

(Signed)
Eberbach

Document 12/2[2]

Morale in 982 Grenadier Regiment, 272nd Infantry Division, July 1944

Wartime Intelligence Officer's Comments

Comments on morale from twenty PW of 982 Grenadier Regiment of 272nd Infantry Division captured at Etavaux on 21 July 1944:

All PW expressed the greatest contempt for their officers, whom they accused of sitting comfortably well behind the lines after ordering the troops to fight to the end.

Several of PW had been brought into action while unfit – one was only partly recovered from a serious abdominal wound, another had a nervous twitch of head and right shoulder from which he has suffered since childhood. In consequence, they regarded themselves as the last hope.

There were also many complaints of shortage of food – 14 Company had had NO rations brought forward for four days. Another cause of complaint was an order prohibiting any further promotion for any man who was unmarried, or, if married more than one year, had no children. The chief trouble, however, seems again to have been the continued hollow promises of heavy weapons and artillery support.

---

2. ISUM 29, 27 July 1944.

Document 12/3[3]

Allied Propaganda: Order of Commander, 276th Infantry Division

From Commander 276th Infantry Division,[4] 24 July 1944

Division Order

I have read carefully all the enemy leaflets which have been showered on us by the enemy since the attempt on the life of our beloved Führer.

They are framed very subtly and make skilful use of the situation. But what is the enemy's aim? He aims to weaken us in the moment when we are struck by the horror of this crime. He wants to mislead us from the good cause for which we have fought bitterly together with our Führer and our people at home for four and a half years. In this cowardly and filthy manner he aims at an easy victory.

In his leaflet he names all our well-known and tried generals. He does it in order to show us that these generals must know what our chances of victory are.

These generals no doubt have a good picture, but on the other hand I am convinced that they do not know as much, and certainly not more than the Führer and his staff.

And what is more decisive. I will not believe that the generals named by the English in their pamphlets belong to this band of traitors. I know most of them myself. These generals are all soldiers through and through. They went through the 9th of November 1918 and the terrible fate of all Germans in the Army and at home.

Then the German warriors put down their arms just before victory because they weakened and believed the enemy's subtle propaganda. Then fate overwhelmed us – now it would seem our complete destruction. This is my most sincere conviction and my firm belief.

Only an iron will to resist and endure will save us and lead us to victory, which in spite of everything is perhaps closer than we think. We must believe this, as the Führer believes it. Who does otherwise is

---

3. ISUM 30, 29 July 1944, from *Second British Army Intelligence Summary*, No. 61, 4 August 1944.
4. The commander of the 276th Infantry Division was *Generalleutnant* Curt Badinski (1890–1960), captured on 21 August 1944.

a scoundrel and a traitor, for he believes the enemy rather than his own commanders.

I remember a phrase frequently used by our enemies about us, not without justification: 'In their history Germans have only been defeated by Germans in the struggle for existence.' Shall we allow our enemy to be right? Who could justify this before our people and our dead?

Document 12/4[5]

V-Weapons Are Coming

The morale of German units has, according to PW, been considerably stiffened by announcements on the German radio and by officers about reprisal weapons. The following details have been given.

V.1 (*Vergeltungswaffe* 1) is of course already in use, but is supposed to mark only the beginning. In connection with this, one PW expressed his surprise that crossbow sites have not as yet been knocked out by the Allies. He said that he had heard that some of these weapons were situated, well camouflaged, in western Germany and not on the Channel coast. Rocket range is given as 450 miles. A large number of fighters are kept there at all times to shoot down aerial observers. PW gave this as an explanation for the absence of fighters on the front.

V.2 which, according to two different stories, was supposed to come into operation on July 4 or July 18 will be used against the Allied fleets and to force the Allied armies out of France. One PW said it had not yet been used because the Germans were waiting until there were more troops on the Continent to get the full effect of the weapon. An officer had told another PW that several Allied battleships and cruisers had already been destroyed.

V.3 exists but PW knew no details, except that its effect would be even more devastating.

V.4 has a single (and ambitious!) purpose. It is designed to sink the British Isles.

---

5. ISUM 23, 18 July 1944, from *Second British Army Intelligence Summary*, No. 37, 11 July 1944.

Document 12/5[6]

Morale Boosting in 276th Infantry Division

A PW from 6/988 Grenadier Regiment relates how his company commander treated the entire company to a 'pep' talk a few days ago. '276. Division', he said, 'is to take part in the great counter-offensive. It will be supported by 3,000 aircraft which are even now being concentrated and prepared, and this is why the Luftwaffe has not been in evidence over the battle front in the recent fighting. We shall eject the Anglo-American tools of Bolshevism by the 21st of July.'

The same company commander gave lurid details to his men of the success of the V-1 (pilotless 'plane) over England. All southern England is repeatedly on fire and 12,000,000 people have so far been killed!

Document 12/6[7]

Absence of German Airpower:
A Reply from the Luftwaffe High Command

Wartime Intelligence Officer's Comments

Herewith a translation of a document reproduced by 16 German Air Force Division on 15 July from the original from the Chief of the General Staff of the German Air Force:

Various units in the army have been complaining of a lack of air support in the fighting on the Invasion Front, and the opinion has also been expressed in various quarters that the success of the Air Force has been exaggerated in the press and on the radio.

Naturally the individual in his sector of the front cannot survey the activity of the Air Force. In particular he cannot see how supply ships and

---

6. ISUM 23, 18 July 1944, from *Second British Army Intelligence Summary*, No. 33, 7 July 1944.
7. ISUM 30, 29 July 1944, from *1st Corps Intelligence Summary*, No. 33.

troop transports are sunk or damaged, so that the enemy troops, tanks and supplies on them never reach the battle zone, causing the enemy considerable losses and lightening the weight of the enemy along the whole of our front. Care must be taken therefore that this is explained, in order to avoid a misunderstanding between the different services.

It must be seen to that through an exact explanation each individual soldier at his post is convinced that the Air Force is doing everything to support him in the hard land battle.

Document 12/7[8]

An Effort to Boost Morale

Wartime Intelligence Officer's Comments

The following is a translation of a leaflet found at St. Martin 9860 on the 6 August 1944.

Now to Hold – Then to Charge

Only after years of painstaking intensive preparations have the Anglo-Americans dared to invade the new Europe – on the orders from Stalin. According to plans found on PW they intended to destroy our coastal fortifications and occupy the whole of Northern France all in the space of a few days.

In That They Have Not Succeeded

Our battalions along the coast have fought extremely well; our coastal fortifications have held up the enemy for a long time. For every inch of soil the enemy pays heavily in life and blood.

In this small space on the northern coast of France the youth of Britain and America die for the communist world revolution of Stalin.

---

8. ISUM 38, 6 August 1944.

This Small Invasion Beachhead . . .

We must keep enclosed with a ring of steel. We all know that this task is tremendous until such time as the full power of our armies and our counter measures can be brought to bear upon the enemy. Our enemies count on their temporary superiority in men and materials, and try to destroy your heroism and bravery through cold steel. Right now they have to train their naval reserves for infantry tasks:

> BECAUSE they have tremendous casualties

> BECAUSE their infantry is cowardly and no good

> BECAUSE their armoured troops can not stand up against the pluck and bravery of our comrades of the tank corps

The enemy infantry man dares to attack you – the bravest soldiers in the world – only after the heaviest artillery barrage.

Only recently your divisions were mentioned in despatches for their bravery.

The Enemy Has Enormous Casualties

You may notice it on your small sector of the front, but PW interrogation and our reconnaissance proves it again and again. But now the enemy has learned to know your prowess in battle. Their lying leaders in England and America had promised them a holiday excursion through France into Germany. You will spoil this pleasure trip for them as you did

At Dunkerque in 1940

Every man <u>must</u> hold his slit trench, every section its position, every battalion its sector. If you leave your trench for what you think may be safety, then the hail of shrapnel is sure to get you.

Be Wise! Cover Your Trench And Camouflage It Well

Comrades! Think Of The Fatherland

We must hold our positions. If we don't, we imperil final victory. If we do not win, Bolshevism will engulf Germany. Then we lose everything: Honour, Freedom and Bread.

The enemy hates the German New Order, National Socialism, which brings to every labourer work, bread and a happy future. In their hatred against everything German, they have proclaimed to the whole world:

> The workers will be sent as slaves to Siberia

The intelligentsia will be castrated or killed

The German youth will be educated to communism by Jewish teachers

Our women will be easy prey for lewd, dirty Jews and savage Negro bastards of the army of occupation. You will still remember this from the time of our disgrace when the Ruhr and Rhine were occupied. You have seen with your own eyes at the eastern front the murders of all non-communists by the communists.

Therefore: <u>WE MUST HOLD</u>!

Document 12/8[9]

Awards of the Iron Cross

The Norddeutsche Zeitung *for 31 August 1944 gives the following information about awards of the Iron Cross.*

Up to August 1944, the following number of Iron Crosses, higher grade, were awarded:

Knight's Cross	4800
Oak Leaves to the Knight's Cross	539
Swords to the Knight's Cross	83
Swords and Diamonds to the Knight's Cross	18
Great Cross	1

The following are recipients of the Swords and Diamonds to the Knight's Cross:

Oberstleutnant Werner Moelders
Generalmajor Adolf Galland
Major Gordon Gollob
Oberleutnant Hans-Joachim Marseille
Generalfeldmarschall Erwin Rommel
Korvettenkapitän Wolfgang Lüth

---

9. ISUM 121, 28 October 1944.

Hauptmann Walter Nowotny
Oberst Adalbert Schultz
Major Heinz-Ulrich Rudel
Oberst Hyazinth, *Graf* von Strachwitz
SS-Gruppenführer und Generalleutnant der Waffen-SS Herbert Gille
Generaloberst Hans Hube
Generalfeldmarschall Albert Kesselring
Oberstleutnant Helmut Lent
SS-Obergruppenführer Sepp Dietrich
Generalfeldmarschall Walter Model
Oberleutnant [Erich] Hartmann (*Staffelkapitän* in a fighter
'Geschwader')

The Great Cross of the Iron Cross has been conferred only on *Reichs-marschall* Hermann Goering.

The Führer, personally, signs each diploma from the Knight's Cross upwards. The holder of the diamonds receives the Oak Leaves with Swords covered with a number of diamonds. In addition, he receives a replica with imitation diamonds to be worn on service.

Document 12/9[10]

Boosting Morale in 1040 Grenadier Regiment, 226th Infantry Division

1040 Grenadier Regiment   *25 August 1944*
NSF Branch[11]

NEW ORDER

(1) For the second time in a generation, Germany is facing the necessity of recognising the truth of Moltke's words that a future war may last seven or possibly thirty years.

---

10. ISUM 71, 8 September 1944.
11. *Nationalsozialistischer Führungsstab des Heeres*, National-Socialist guidance staff of the army. This branch was established in the spring of 1944 to control Nazi doctrine in the army and promote fighting spirit.

(2) Everything that happened in former wars fades into insignificance compared with the new infernal hatred of everything that is German.

(3) You know what you have suffered. Remember, the enemy is no better off and often much worse.

(4) Compare crisis periods of the Seven Years War and accentuate the moral courage of Frederick the Great.

(a) The Battle of Kolin of 18 June 1757. Beaten by Austrian troops twice as strong, Frederick the Great cannot see the war being brought to a quick decision. Nevertheless he finds the courage to withdraw from Prague with bands playing. He writes in a letter to a general: 'In our misfortune it is up to our good morale to mend things . . . My heart is broken. However, I am not depressed and at the first opportunity I shall make good this loss.' In another letter he writes: 'I am shaken and harassed from all sides. Accidents at home, bad health, general public distress, outbreak of new diseases, this is my daily bread. But don't think I shall give in. Should all elements break loose, I would let myself be buried under the ruins in cold blood just as I am writing you this letter. In such terrible times one has to have guts of iron and heart of steel. I am determined to save my poor country or to go under with it.'

(b) In 1760 Berlin is occupied by the enemy. Frederick remains unshaken. He states: 'I shall never survive the moment which will compel me to conclude an unfavourable peace. No reason will force me to sign anything dishonourable. I repeat, never will my hand sign a shameful peace.' Eight days later the King won the brilliant victory of Torgau.

For years the King of Prussia had carried on a practically hopeless war. From a normal objective standpoint, he hardly had a chance to win the Seven Years War. Nevertheless he never admitted defeat. His endurance, his courage and his confidence in himself were stronger than his misfortune.

He remained victorious because his will was stronger than the acid test that fate imposed upon him.

signed Benes
Lieutenant-Colonel and Regimental Commander

Document 12/10[12]

Boosting Morale in 3rd Parachute Division, August 1944

The Commander   Division HQ 14 August 44
3 Parachute Division

To all men of the 3rd Parachute Division

Foul rumours are the same as bad odours, BOTH ORIGINATE FROM THE REAR.

I have occasion to point out that contrary to rumours which are brought up to fighting troops from the rear, there is no reason for concern about the situation. It is rumoured that the division is encircled by the enemy. Although I cannot go into details, I want to state that all rumours of this kind are false. They are to be classed as enemy propaganda which intends to discourage our paratroopers in battle.

The army, British or American, which can encircle or capture our Division does not exist. Even if the enemy should succeed in interrupting our communications for a short time, that is no reason for paratroopers to lose heart who are trained to jump into the midst of the enemy.

It is certain that we will finish this war victoriously just as certain that the glorious 3rd Parachute Division will never cease to fight and will do its duty unvanquished to the end of the war.

Whoever thinks or speaks differently will be slapped across the face.

SCHIMPF[13]

---

12. ISUM 56, 24 August 1944.
13. *Generalleutnant* Richard Schimpf (1897–1972), commander of 3rd Parachute Division. WIA 20 August 1944.

Document 12/11[14]

Morale Problems in an *Ersatz* Battalion

Wartime Intelligence Officer's Comments

Extract from an undated document found in a file of an Ersatz Battalion.

(i) Enemy propaganda leaflets which are lying about in our positions should have been collected long ago by dutiful NCOs, since <u>even a corporal</u> should know the destructive influence of the clever enemy propaganda. This lack of interest is partly responsible for our present predicament.

(ii) When soldiers say that they cannot go on anymore after marching 5 km in marching order, transport should not be provided for them but they should be made to go on. Since rations are sufficient to keep a soldier fit, he is evading his duties if he does not want to continue marching.

(iii) Soldiers who are suspected of being shirkers should not be disposed of as undesirables but should be the first to go into action. It cannot be tolerated that the good soldier will bear the whole burden while the shirker plays dumb and (this goes especially for older men) remains shiftless after having it easy all his life.

---

14. ISUM 59, 25 August 1944.

Document 12/12[15]

Guidance for the Award of Decorations, May 1944

Wartime Intelligence Officer's Comments

After five years of war and promiscuous awarding of Iron Crosses to the men of Infantry divisions, the OKH, in a SECRET order dated 16 May 1944 and signed by Schmidt, has finally issued a guide for division commanders to follow, that there will be a more even distribution of Iron Crosses in the army.

The following is the table set up to show the number of Iron Crosses 2nd Class to be awarded per division (of 75% battle strength) and the requirements for their receipt:

On a quiet front, disturbed only by skirmishes with partisans: 50–100 Iron Crosses 2nd Class per month

On a quiet front with active reconnaissance activities: 100–200 Iron Crosses 2nd Class per month

During continuous heavy battle and moving front situations: 200–400 Iron Crosses 2nd Class per month

During great battles and offensives: 400–500 Iron Crosses 2nd Class per month

Special conditions have been laid down for the awarding of the Iron Cross 1st Class. The Iron Cross 1st Class is meant for front fighters only. If too many 'rear fighters' receive this decoration, the OKH fears that the effect will be damaging to the morale of the front line infantrymen.

Wartime Intelligence Officer's Comments

The importance attached to the awarding of Iron Crosses was vividly illustrated on the 9 September 1944 when the Commander of the Blankenberghe Garrison, in the midst of a heated defensive battle, sent in an urgent request for two Iron Crosses 1st Class and eleven Iron Crosses 2nd Class.

---

15. ISUM 74, 22 August 1944, from *SHAEF Intelligence Notes*, No. 26.

Document 12/13[16]

Morale Boosting, 6th Parachute Regiment, September 1944

Wartime Intelligence Officer's Comments

The following extract has been taken from a long document written by Lieutenant-Colonel von der Heydte[17] (Commander 6 Parachute Regiment) on the proposed re-forming and retraining of his regiment during the month of September 1944.

I demand of every soldier the renunciation of all personal wishes. 'Whoever swears on the Prussian flag, has NO right to personal possessions'. From the moment he enlists in the Paratroops and comes to my regiment, every soldier enters the new order of Humanity and gives up everything he possessed before and which is outside the new order. There is only one law for him henceforth – the laws of our unit. Each soldier of the regiment is no longer an individual but a member of our community. He must abjure every weaker facet of his own character, all personal ambition, every personal desire. From the renunciation of the individual, the true personality of the soldier arises. Every member of the regiment must know what he is fighting for.

He must be quite convinced that this struggle is a struggle for the existence of the whole German nation and that no other ending of this battle is possible than that of the victory of German arms. He must, because of this, know the reasons for this war and the aims of the nations who are at war. He must learn to believe in victory even when at certain moments logical thinking scarcely makes a German victory seem possible. He must know that history has given us more than one example of how a nation which has already appeared beaten, has nevertheless been victorious in the long run by its own power of resistance and in joy of sacrifice.

But he must be quite clear at the same time that victory is only possible if every German gives up everything and that everyone is equally responsible. I demand that every soldier of my regiment shall become

---

16. ISUM 90, 28 September 1944, from *30 Corps Intelligence Summary*.
17. *Oberstleutnant Freiherr* Friedrich von der Heydte (1907–94) was the commander of the 6th Parachute Regiment.

as fanatical in his belief as men were at the time of the Crusades of the Knightly Orders.

Only the soldier who is schooled in philosophy and believes in his political faith implicitly can fight as this war demands that he shall fight. This is the secret of the success of the *Waffen* SS and of the Red Army – and lack of this faith is the reason why so many German Infantry Divisions have been destroyed.

Document 12/14[18]

Problems between the Waffen SS and the Army

Further evidence of dissension between Wehrmacht and SS personnel has been given by a PW from 83 *Werfer* Regiment who was captured on the 14 August. This account also indicates that there are still members of 12th SS Division who have no compunction in shooting such Allied PW unfortunate enough to fall into their hands.

On the 12 August a British fighter plane was shot down in the area of Courcy. The pilot bailed out and dropped northwest of Courcy near Hill 62. Pilot's jump was observed by a Lieutenant and a Sergeant-Major of III/83 *Werfer* Regiment, and also by an *Untersturmführer* and a corporal of the SS. All four rushed to the scene but the *Werfer* lieutenant arrived first and took the flyer to his orderly room. The SS arrived about three minutes later and bursting into the army HQ tried to get the pilot into their custody. The *Werfer* lieutenant insisted that the PW would remain where he was, and thereupon the SS officer and corporal began to struggle in an attempt to get the prisoner into their hands. The army officer locked the pilot in the orderly room, and the SS thereupon rushed the door shouting 'this man must be shot immediately'. However seeing that the army personnel stood firm and that their efforts were useless the SS finally gave up and returned to their units.

---

18. ISUM 53, 19 August 1944.

Document 12/15[19]

Tension between the Waffen SS and the Army

Recent PW reports have indicated the possibilities of a major rift between the Army and the SS on the fighting front. While at present there are only sullen grumblings between the two, a marked distrust has grown between these factions of Germany's fighting force. The SS apparently feel the need for standing behind army divisions and keeping them in line with waving pistols, while naturally enough the army resents this attitude. Complaints against the obviously better equipment and treatment accorded SS divisions have begun to be heard, and with the deterioration of the German military position the volume of these moans is likely to increase.

On 2 August two PW of I/98 Fusilier Battalion of 89 Infantry Division told their interrogators:

Yesterday morning the SS with pistols in their hands drove us into battle with the cry, '*Geht los Ihr Hunde*' ('Push on you dogs'). One *Unterscharführer* of the SS threatened to shoot our corporal, *Unteroffizier* Hartmann, because he did not advance fast enough with his group.

The use of such methods to keep the forward troops in the line was verified by this statement from a PW of 13/300 *Flak Sturm Regiment*:

I overheard the officers of my Unit say that we were to fire at our own forward infantry should they try to withdraw and thus force them to stick to their positions.

Verification of this statement was given by an officer PW Captain Bartras of *Flak Sturm Abteilung* 13/300 who did not deny having issued an order to fire at forward troops should they withdraw. His claim is that with a wall of heavy guns behind them, troops must hold on to their positions, and if they don't they must be forced to do so. These flak units are composed of Luftwaffe personnel under command of 1 SS Panzer Corps on our front.

Another PW, this one from 8/1089 Grenadier Regiment of 89th Infantry Division spoke at considerable length on the cleft between the army and the SS. He was taken on 11 August and at that time he claimed that the state of morale in the division was deplorable. The SS, he said, were kept in the rear areas withholding support they could well give, and

---

19. ISUM 67, 15 August 1944.

restricting their activities to a considerable extent to pushing up into the line any army personnel who were inclined to 'drift back'. The anger at this attitude of the SS had created a great deal of trouble in the formation.

Indignation with the SS was expressed by a PW of 6/978 Infantry Regiment of 271st Division who complained that the SS always left them in the lurch, while the poor infantry had to march and march and march. And he probably had not heard of 89th Infantry Division who came into battle on their flat feet all the way from Amiens.

Then to make matters worse were men of 12th SS Division [who] with typical German tactlessness jibed the arrival of II/978 Grenadier Regiment of 271st Infantry Division at the front on their bicycles and horse-drawn wagons with the not very bright remark '*Geht Ihr zum Markt?*' (Are you going to market?).

Chapter 13

Casualties and Casualty Replacement

Document 13/1[1]

Casualties and Desertion Problems in 2nd Company, 26th SS Panzer Grenadier Regiment, 12th Waffen SS Panzer Division

A nominal roll for this company gives its strength on the 29 June 1944 as 98 Other Ranks and a month later on the 30 July 1944 this strength had been reduced to 50 Other Ranks. The casualties suffered during this period were attained as follows:

Wounded	Missing	Killed
47 (38 Germans)	20 (14 Germans)	26 (22 Germans)
(9 Ukrainians)	(6 Ukrainians)	(4 Ukrainians)

From a pad of carbon copies of reports of the 2 Company sent to its Battalion HQ, these two interesting items are extracted:

30 July

The enemy has broken into our position in front of St. Martin (022606) but has been repulsed. Opposite us are the Canadians. The company needs hand grenades, rifles, anti-tank grenades and *Panzerfaust*. The enemy again attacked at 1810 hrs and was repulsed. Small arms ammunition is urgently needed.

---

1. ISUM 34, 2 August 1944.

31 July

The company sector is only thinly manned during enemy attack since the Ukrainian volunteers can only be kept in the trenches by force of arms and will desert the first opportunity they are not under observation. Consequently, the enemy is able to infiltrate nearly everywhere in St. Martin. The enemy opposite is the *Régiment de Maisonneuve* of Canada.

Document 13/2[2]

Wehrmacht Volunteers (HIWIs)[3]

Wartime Intelligence Officer's Comments

The following interrogation report of 27 Russians from 979 Grenadier Regiment of 271st Infantry Division, indicates some of the persuasive methods used by the Germans in obtaining 'volunteers'.

All PWs, with the exception of three, had not been in the Soviet Army, as they were too young, ages ranging from 17–20.

In February 1944, as the Germans were retreating through the Ukraine, they employed Cossacks and Kalanucks to round up all the males from fifteen to fifty years of age, as well as young girls and women without children up to the age of 30 for evacuation to Poland and Germany. The women were raped and the men, should they show any signs of disobedience, were shot on the spot.

The above mentioned PW were separated from the women after a march of 35 km, and, having received new guards, some of the women were sent back to their homes. The men, 740 in all, entrained and were sent to Przemisl, Poland, where they remained for approx 20 days. While there, they were called out in groups of 100, and a German officer spoke to them – asking them to fight against their common enemy. The other alternative, which, however, was not mentioned, was death by bullets or

---

2. ISUM 27, 26 JULY 1944.
3. *Hilfswillige* (Voluntary Assistants) or HIWIs were Russians who joined the Wehrmacht as auxiliaries and were used for a multitude of minor duties and sometimes for combat. Their fate, if recaptured by the Soviet army, was not very good.

starvation. Having been tipped off to this effect, they all volunteered, and thus became HIWIS ('*Hilfswillige*').

The volunteers were then sent to an Army Camp at Warsaw, where they were issued with German uniforms. They left Poland for the south of France on 1 June, and arrived at Sete on 26.

At Sete, they were divided among the various companies of 979 Grenadier Regiment in such a manner that they had never more than 2 or 3 Russians per section. They remained there for 2 days, and on 30 June they proceeded to the Front, where they arrived on 12 July.

They were issued with rifles, but were mostly employed to dig slit trenches, carry ammunition, and bring up food from the kitchen, which was approximately 2 km further back. On several occasions, they were persuaded – with a pistol in their back – to defend themselves against the advancing British troops.

Not speaking German and not having been with the Regiment for more than a few days, they had no knowledge of organization or weapons.

Document 13/3[4]

Availability of Officers in the German Army

Wartime Intelligence Officer's Comments

Two documents have been received which throw considerable light on the German problem of finding suitable officers to command units and formations in the field. The first of these is in the form of notes made by Dr. Freytag, IIa of LXXX Corps, at a conference held in Paris on 4 and 8 February 1944 for adjutant-generals, which give a comprehensive picture of losses of officers and anticipated requirements.

(a) Officer Casualties up to 20 January 1944

Killed: 23,776
Wounded: 67,488
Missing: 18,805 (exclusive of 5,000 officers lost at Stalingrad)

---

4. ISUM 98, 6 October 1944, from *SHAEF Intelligence Summary*, 28, 30 September 1944.

(b) Losses by ranks up to 1 January 1944

	Genls	Cols	LCols	Majs	Capts	1st Lts	2nd Lts
Killed	33	104	138	575	2000	6563	17,546
Wounded	39	200	281	1084	4752	15,561	44,326
Missing	25	76	110	957	960	2,866	4,194

(c) Relative Losses by Arm of Service

The highest losses of officers were among Panzer grenadier units followed by Panzer, Infantry, Engineers, Artillery, Signal and Supply troops in that order.

(d) Future Requirements

18,000 were needed for new formations.

(e) General Staff Officers

The 1900 General Staff appointments were filled by 964 General Staff officers, 233 officers assigned to the General Staff, 90 former General Staff officers and 500 reserve officers.

(f) Divisional Commanders

Command of a division can only be gained by front-line service. Regimental commanders not fit to command a division to be promoted only in the normal way. Command of a training division to be given only to former commanders of active divisions who have been wounded or fallen sick.

(g) Regimental Commanders

Were urgently needed. 240 regimental commanders were casualties in 1943.

(h) Intelligence Officers (Ic)

Intelligence officers to be given accelerated promotion only if they have held an active command previously. The NSFO[5] is not subordinate to the Ic.[6]

---

5. NSFO, or *Nationalsozialistischer Führungsoffizier*. NSFOs were assigned to Wehrmacht units in 1944 to ensure that Nazi ideology was disseminated throughout the armed forces.
6. In the German staff system, the IC was the officer in charge of intelligence. The IA was the operations officer and the IB the supply officer.

Wartime Intelligence Officer's Comments

The second document contains the conclusions of a conference for adjutant-generals held by the OKH on 16 and 17 June 1944 and forwarded by the adjutant-general of the First Army to the adjutant-generals at Corps with the express proviso that it was not to be transmitted in writing below Corps. The following are the main points of interest.

(a) Difficulties have arisen in the general personnel situation mainly in filling positions of company commander and higher ranks, especially regimental commanders.

(b) Young officers may not be immediately employed under trying battle conditions. They must at first be carefully directed, even if the posts of company commanders must be filled by NCOs.

(c) All staff must again be examined with a view to determining whether the Führer's order that NO officer of the age group of 1914 and younger can hold staff positions, has been carried out. Report to Army headquarters by 18 July 1944.

(d) Average age of regimental commanders at the present time is 30 years. Efforts will be made to raise the age to 32 years.

(e) Graduates of colleges (*Abiturienten*[7]) must be considered for officers' careers. A decree is in preparation which will exclude from admission to the universities all those graduates who failed to become officers.

(f) There is an urgent need for army commanders. The Führer has requested the names of ten generals who are fit for the command of an army to be submitted to him. Age is 45.

(g) Medical officers who have not been properly employed as well as finance officers who have not yet been employed at all will be reported to Generalmajor Michaelmann to be sent to the front.

(h) Colonels who have been in charge of divisions at the battle front as acting commanders may be promoted to the rank of general within two months.

(i) Employment of staff officers at the front. Troops over and over again request that older staff officers be offered an opportunity of commanding

---

7. The *Abitur*, granted after a secondary school student had passed a series of government exams, was a combination high school diploma and university entrance examination. It was a necessary prerequisite for higher education or entrance to a profession.

troops. All officers before being posted to staff appointments should have commanded a company for 6 months at the front, before promotion to lieutenant-colonel a battalion for 3 to 6 months and before promotion to *Generalmajor* a regiment, and before promotion to *Generalleutnant* a division.

(j) No exchange between the eastern and western front will take place in the future.

(k) The number of officers at present is 240,000 (1,200 general officers).

(l) Particular concern is at present felt over <u>cases of corruption</u> on the largest scale, extending into the highest ranks. Such cases are apt to influence attitude and morale of the people and may have decisive consequences for the outcome of the war.

(m) The chief of the Army Personnel Office urgently requests that all officers down to the lowest rank become familiar with the order concerning <u>Seydlitz</u>.[8]

(n) Extremely strained conditions in the replacement of officers requires a constant examination of all officers, regimental, battalion and company commanders, who are qualified to be promoted to the next higher rank. They must be transferred.

(o) Immediate report to the Personnel Office in the event of a son of a general being killed in action.

(p) <u>NSFO</u>. Of 740 existing positions only 450 have been filled.

(q) Youngest officers in the various ranks:

1st Lieutenant	20 years of age
Captain	21 years of age
Major	24 years of age
Lieutenant-Colonel	25 years of age
Colonel	32 years of age
Generalmajor	38 years of age
Generalleutnant	42 years of age
General	47 years of age
Colonel General	48 years of age

---

8. *General der Artillerie* Kurt von Seydlitz-Kurzbach (1888–1976) abandoned his corps command and crossed into the Russian lines in early 1943. He became a Soviet collaborator and was sentenced to death *in absentia* by Hitler.

Document 13/4[9]

Ages of Personnel in 12th Waffen SS Panzer Division, July 1944

The extreme youthfulness of the personnel of 12 SS Panzer Division is strikingly illustrated by a recently captured nominal roll of I/25 SS Panzer Grenadier Regiment. The document dated the 12 July 1944 showed a strength of 672 all ranks, but many of the names had been crossed off and a health state dated 1 August 1944 showed the unit's strength reduced to 459 at that time. The listed birthdays indicate the following age groups:

Age	Officers	NCOs	ORs	Percentage
18	0	1	433	65
19	0	2	112	17
20–25	7	66	31	13
25–30	1	8	1	1.5
Over 30	2	8	0	1.5

Document 13/5[10]

Problems with Reinforcements, 1st and 12th Waffen SS Panzer Divisions

Details are now available from PW of recent method of reinforcing 1st SS and 12 SS Panzer Divs

(i) A group of Austrian and Polish deserters from 1st SS Panzer Reconnaissance Battalion were all previously members of 9 Panzer Division. They believed they had left 9 Panzer because of German fear of foreign elements in the ranks and the desire to keep these elements under most stringent control. The official reason given, however, was that 9 Panzer had too many troops and too little transport.

---

9. ISUM 46, 14 August 1944.
10. ISUM 46, 14 August 1944, from *Second British Army Intelligence Summary*, No. 79, 13 August 1944.

March Battalion[11] 'Elizabeth' was formed on 2 July of 1000 men from 9 Panzer, 90% of them non-German. It travelled via Sedan, Jarascon, Nimes, Toulouse, Bordeaux and Le Mans and was split up among the companies of 1st SS Panzer Division and a third unknown division on 4 August, 1st SS Panzer Reconnaissance Battalion receiving 72 men from the March battalion.

1st SS Panzer Division is reported to have sent reinforcements to 12 SS Panzer Division but the extent of these, the date and the reason for them was not known.

(ii) A deserter from 25 SS Panzer Grenadier Regiment has described how he was among 3000 German air force personnel transferred to the SS in March 1943. Many of them went as reinforcements to 1st SS Panzer Division which had suffered heavy losses at Kharkov. This PW deserted and after serving one year of a sentence of five years' imprisonment was sent to 1st SS Training and *Ersatz* Battalion near Berlin.

A March battalion of 250 men, half of them *Volksdeutsche* and most of them ex-Luftwaffe personnel and men returning from hospital was formed in July. All were infantrymen and were destined for 12 SS Panzer which was said to be in greater need of reinforcements than 1st SS Panzer. This may explain the statement about reinforcement for 12 SS Panzer made by the PW from March Battalion 'Elizabeth'.

The battalion travelled via Magdeburg, Pagny, Paris to Marville les Bois, where it did a short period of training with a 1st SS battalion and was split up into two groups. PW went with 32 others to II/25 SS Panzer Grenadier Regiment and went into action on 8 August.

---

11. A *Marschbataillon* was a temporary unit created to transfer replacements to the front line units. In an emergency they were sometimes pressed into a combat role.

Document 13/6[12]

The Bottom of the Barrel:
276 *Festungs* Machine Gun Battalion

Wartime Intelligence Officer's Comments

The gutters of Germany are being thoroughly scraped to supply all the available manpower for the rapidly dwindling Wehrmacht. This fact was strikingly illustrated by an interrogation report of a second lieutenant of 3 Company, 276 Festungs *Machine Gun Battalion.*

Organised in Ingolstadt in Germany towards the latter part of August 1944, the unit left on 27 August and arrived in Boulogne on 2 September 1944. The battalion consisted of an HQ Company and four rifle Companies, each of about 20–30 men. The equipment was woefully inadequate, with 3 Company having what was believed to be the only mortar in the battalion. No MMGs were known to be in the battalion, and each platoon had three LMGs.

On 3 Sep, 3 Company was sent into a position at St Etienne astride a road and a railway, and Battalion HQ was about 2 kms behind. Four days later, PW's platoon was sent about 500 metres further south in a forward platoon position, and was out of connection with the company except by runner.

On arrival at this outpost, the NCOs and men plainly told the Lieutenant that they did not intend to fire a shot and that on the approach of the first enemy patrol they would surrender. Since they were out of contact with anyone else, the officer claimed he could do nothing but give in to this demand, and all gave themselves up that day.

The officer, in explaining his actions, claimed that it was unreasonable to expect men to fight without proper weapons or training. The type of soldier in his unit was aged 35–40, with little or no training and 90% were in the physical category for only garrison duty at home with the balance coming straight from the hospital. Amongst this almost pure-German unit was one man with a stiff arm and another with a glass eye. It was the PW's firm belief that the battalion had no desire to fight and, furthermore, could not if it had wanted to.

---

12. ISUM 71, 19 August 1944.

Chapter 14

The Effects of Allied Artillery and Air Bombardment

Document 14/1[1]

Effect of Allied Artillery and Air Bombardment, 271st Infantry Division, July 1944

PWs of 979 Grenadier Regiment, 271st Infantry Division, captured in the Maltot salient on 22 July 1944:

(i) Lance-Corporal

'I fought in Poland, France, the Balkans and Russia. I can honestly say that I have never in the whole of my experience as a soldier experienced anything which remotely compared to British artillery fire.'

(ii) Corporal

'I arrived at the front firmly believing in the Führer and a German victory. A few hours of British artillery fire and the sight of British tanks, together with the faultless organization behind it all, was sufficient to make me realise how matters stand. Now I am confused, and don't know what to believe, but one thing I do know – there is no greater hell than British artillery fire.'

---

1. ISUM 52, 20 August 1944.

(iii) Private

'I have fought on all fronts, but I have never seen such artillery. It was withering. For accuracy and strength, it far surpassed anything I have ever experienced.'

Document 14/2[2]

Effects of Allied Bombing and Shelling

(a) General

PWS who have experienced a bombing attack, think that artillery fire is not as bad as bombing. Those who have not been directly in the bomb area and have experienced the full weight of the British artillery think that artillery fire is worse.

(b) Splinters and Casualties

Most PW seem to think that the splinter effect of artillery shells causes more casualties and damage than the actual bombing. They stated that after the bombing attack nearly all personnel, though badly shaken-up, were unwounded, while, after shelling, there were casualties. A German officer explained that well-dug slit trenches form very good protection, but out in the open away from cover and protection, personnel were often killed or wounded.

(c) Warning of a Bombing Attack

PW stated that the warning of a night bombing attack is the dropping of flares in the target area. Thus they always had time to take cover.

(d) Damage to Equipment

Any equipment lying out in the open is put out of action by bombing. Therefore guns are well dug in and usually are in working order after bombing attack.

---

2. ISUM 44, 12 August 1944.

(e) Rocket-firing Typhoons

These are more feared than any other form of 'Weight Dropping'. Accuracy is deadly and officers and men have great respect for it.

Document 14/3[3]

The Effects of Allied Air Attacks (1)

This report is based on the interrogation of Germany Army PW by British and American Officers of the Air PW Interrogation Unit. The object was to assess the effect of the Allied Air Offensive against troops in the Falaise–Vire–Mortain–Mayonne–Alençon salient and to obtain first-hand stories of their experiences.

During the period of the interrogation, August 12th to 17th, some 5/6,000 prisoners passed through the various cages and this report is based on about a ten per cent sample taken from all fronts, and including all major formations. With PW passing through the cages so rapidly, any statistical analysis is impossible and therefore this report is largely made up of Interrogators' impressions backed by individual stories.

General

Most of the PW who have so far been captured are from units which the German High Command is sacrificing while the main Artillery and Armoured forces extricate themselves. These PW are of a low type, including a very high percentage of foreign elements, and men of such low morale that they can be classed as deserters even though they may not actually have deserted.

These troops were often stationed within the Allied Bombline and therefore have not been subjected to direct air attack. These PW can thus only give indirect testimony to the efficacy of the air offensive through their stories of food, water and ammunition shortage.

At the beginning they fought stubbornly but as they came to realise that they were virtually surrounded and in fact were later told by their

---

3. ISUM 51, 19 August 1944, from *Air PW Interrogation Unit – 84 Group RAF.*

officers that bombing was cutting off their supplies, their fighting spirit fell rapidly.

The remainder of the PW are those who were captured nearer the 'bottle-neck'. This category includes tank crews and, somewhat surprisingly, few tell stories of being knocked out by air attack. Rather, it was a general realisation of the position, coupled with petrol and ammunition shortage, which caused them to blow up their tanks, whether damaged or not, and attempt to escape either in a smaller vehicle or on foot.

A junior officer of 363 Infantry Division, who surrendered on August 13th, crystallised this attitude with the words, 'You have bombed and strafed all the roads causing complete congestion and heavy traffic jams. You have destroyed most of our petrol and oil dumps, so there is no future in continuing to fight.'

It seems that Carpet Bombing by heavy bombers is the most feared attack of all and it is also this type of attack which causes the greatest damage and casualties. MG and cannon fire is still feared because of its very personal nature against the individual, while only in one case did PW rate RP[4] as the most devastating; a salvo of rockets had hit his slit-trench.

Concealment

Some units ascribe their comparative or complete immunity from air attack to their good camouflage and concealment well inside woods and under trees. The Luftwaffe formations, such as the Parachute Divisions are, perhaps naturally, outstanding in this respect, and according to PW of the 5th Parachute Regiment they were only attacked twice since D-day – once on 11 June when moving into the St Lô area and then at 1600 hrs on 30 July when a tank from another unit took refuge in 'their' wood but did not draw completely under cover.

As soon as a unit halts, the vehicles, if any, are dispersed and hidden, while the personnel scrape one man 'foxholes', not in the open fields where they can be seen but in ditches and under hedges.

Look-outs are always posted, both on the move and at the halt, but the nervous tension is such that every man is his own spotter. As soon as an aircraft is seen or heard they go to ground. No attempt at identification is made; all aircraft are assumed to be hostile.

---

4. RP, rocket projectiles.

Road Movement

It is no exaggeration to say that road movement, whether by night or by day, is a nightmare for the Germans. Constantly tribute is paid to the hawk-like qualities of Allied fighters, who will pounce down even on a single vehicle or motor cyclist.

The majority still stick to by-ways even though these may treble or quadruple the distance to be covered. For instance, one party withdrawing on August 8 from Vire to Tinchebray took the route via St. Germain, Le Fresne Poret and St. Cornier des Landes, the journey taking eight days. This column was constantly attacked by Lightnings, which bombed and strafed, but their only casualties were at Le Fresne Poret, where they lost seven horses and three men.

The belief is growing that Allied fighters concentrate on the first and last vehicles of a convoy, with the object of immobilising the whole column, which can then be handled at leisure. One Commander sent a protest to his division regarding the compulsory use of narrow secondary roads and asked permission to use main roads, where other vehicles could pull out and pass any which had been knocked out.

Petrol Shortage

By 12 August the petrol situation was acute, not only in the battle area but also in France generally. 84th Infantry Division, which moved from Belgium at the beginning of August, was told to leave their vehicles in Rouen owing to petrol shortage and to continue on foot or on bicycle. The only vehicle allowed was that belonging to the doctor and when this ran out of petrol he too had to carry out his duties on foot.

Most impressive of all, however, are the stories of tanks which have been blown up by their crews because they had run out or were short of petrol.

Food Shortage

It is perhaps the absence of rations which has brought home most clearly to the infantry soldier the hopelessness of his position and thus lowered morale. It was something which impacted upon him personally, although he could only vaguely ascribe it to the disruption of the area behind him by bombing.

In the later stages water also became a problem, which seems surprising in a terrain so well supplied with streams and rivers. One *Feldwebel* from the Falaise sector so far forgot himself as to beg the interrogator for a drink from his water bottle. He had had nothing to drink for twenty four hours.

Ammunition Shortage

In the early stages, that is according to PW captured on 10 August to 12 August, there was no hint of any shortage of ammunition. No matter what else gave ground for complaint, ammunition supplies were apparently ample.

Then, with the capture of the first tank personnel, came stories of shortage. It seems that the shortage was of the specialist types of ammunition for tank guns or even – the demoralisation in some cases was so great – it may have been invented as an excuse for abandoning the tank and blowing it up.

The story was told by a PW of 752 Regiment in the Falaise sector, of how two tanks were sent into a minor counter-attack, one with eight shells and the other with only one.

Tank Casualties

The subject of tank casualties cannot be dismissed without making the observation that no PW have been interrogated whose tank was knocked out by aircraft. This may be due to 'professional pride', not wanting to admit to an Air Interrogation Officer to a defeat at the hands of the Air Force, or it may be due to the German predilection for finding a scapegoat. 'We were never beaten in battle, our supplies failed us' – another version of the 'stab in the back'.

It may also be that tanks which are hit from the air yield no survivors. If so, that is a problem which lies in hands other than the Interrogator's.

Nevertheless, the fact remains that numerous tank crew personnel have said that a direct hit from a bomb is required to 'kill' a tank. Cannon and even small arms fire apparently penetrates the weaker spots in tank armour not infrequently, but seldom causes vital damage. So far there have been no stories of tanks having been knocked out by RP.

Personnel Casualties

Due to the instant dispersal on receipt of an air alarm and also no doubt to short memories during the confusion which must follow air attacks, the impression is gained from PW that air attack does not cause serious casualties.

Even bombs which fall within a position cause surprisingly few casualties, although the effect of such an attack on morale is such that it may be said to cause 'temporary casualties' if not the will to desert.

Artillery Fire

Any survey of this kind should not exclude mention of artillery fire. Although offensive fighter patrols may create a sense of being haunted, although carpet bombing may have an anaesthetic and numbing effect, and although the general air offensive may be acknowledged by PW as the one factor which has caused all the disruption and its attendant lowering of morale, there is no doubt that it is artillery fire which strikes the greatest terror and which looms above all else in their minds.

Gunfire seems to be aimed directly and personally at your own position. In this it may be likened to cannon and MG fire from aircraft, but unlike the latter, artillery fire is of long duration, the missiles are larger, more deadly, and the accuracy seems more remorseless.

Document 14/4[5]

The Effects of Allied Air Attacks (2)

Wartime Intelligence Officer's Comments

The following is added to the report based on interrogation of German Army PW by the Air PW Interrogation Unit which appeared in First Canadian Army Intelligence Summary Number 51 dated 19 August 1944 [this is a reference to Document 14/3 above].

Tank Casualties

Since the main report was written, stories have been received of tanks having been knocked out by aircraft.

The first is from an *Oberfeldwebel* of the 6th Parachute Division. He had previously been an officer, but had been reduced to the ranks for

---

5. ISUM 52, 20 August 1944.

some crime and was therefore very disgruntled. In spite of careful re-interrogation he stuck to his stories, even though they sound exaggerated.

On about August 12th, while lost in the Vire sector, he hitch-hiked in a Panther tank. They were attacked by four fighter aircraft with small arms fire, bombs and RP. One RP scored a direct hit at the back of the tank and blew off both tracks, broke the driving axle and penetrated the rear armour to render the engine u/s.

At about the same time, at St Clement in the Vire sector the same PW witnessed an attack by about 20 RP fighters on a group of 32 Panther tanks, which were in staggered rows with half-tracks in between. The aircraft attacked the half-track first with cannon fire and destroyed several. Then they attacked the tanks with RP and knocked out 30 out of the 32. The damage included tanks burnt out and others with their tracks off.

Also about the same date, or possibly earlier, he was in the Avranches sector and witnessed an RP attack on 15 Tigers which were taking cover in a road cutting. All the tanks were put out of action – some by fire – with the exception of two, and these could not extricate themselves from the jam of wreckage.

A *Gefreiter* of the 2nd Panzer Division was a gunner in a Mark IV on the move (date and place unknown), when they were attacked from the air by fighter bombers. The bombs all missed narrowly, but several cannon shells pierced the armour in front of the turret, killing the W/T operator and one other. The engine caught fire, so the crew abandoned the tank and watched it burn out.

An *Obergefreiter* of the same division had his own tank destroyed by a Sherman and the replacement, which arrived in two days, was destroyed by artillery fire. While tank-less, he observed a Tiger tank brought to a standstill by cannon fire from the air, which ripped off the tracks.

Chapter 15

Miscellaneous and Humour (Such as it Was)

Document 15/1[1]

Eyes Right!

The following is an extract from a German District Order:

Again and again I meet soldiers in the Department EURE who, as cyclists, do not keep their legs stiff when saluting. This is against orders when the bicycle is free-wheeling and the journey is not up-hill.

signed Gollnitz, Colonel

Document 15/2[2]

Pay Day for *Feldmarschall* Kesselring, June 1944

The pay voucher for the month of June for *Feldmarschall* Kesselring. Total pay for the month of June 1944 – 2,886.60 RM [Reichsmarks]

---

1. ISUM 67, 4 September 1944.
2. ISUM 23, 18 July 1944. from *21st Army Group Intelligence Summary* No. 146, 16 July 1944.

Deductions

Income Tax	630.00	RM
Pay Tax	894.60	"
Old Age Pension	9.31	"
Rent (no garage)	197.40	"
Bonds	26.00	"
Air Force Club	1.50	"
Welfare Organization München	5.00	"
Bavaria Foundation	9.55	"
Alliance Insurance	5.00	"
Total Deductions	1,778.36	"
Net Balance	1,108.24	RM

Document 15/3[3]

Wehrmacht Humour

Wartime Intelligence Officer's Comments

The following is a translation of a German poem found on 17 August 44. The reference to 'MEYER' is based on upon a statement once made by Göring that, 'if the RAF ever bombs the REICH, my name will be Meyer'.

Evening Prayer

> Tired and sleepy I say my prayer,
> Bombs are falling everywhere.
> Ack Ack gunners look out well
> O'er the town in which we dwell.
> Look down on us, oh dear Gott
> On the havoc Tommy's wrought,
> All the neighbours from Schulz to Meyer
> Lost their houses through bombs and fire
> And everyone I've ever known

---

3. ISUM 52, 20 August 1944.

Has rubble instead of a home of his own.
As the moon looks down upon us all
We await '*Vergeltung*'[4] and hope ere long
That Tommy will get it good and strong.
Oh dear Gott please help 'Meyer' out,
Give him more Vs[5] to put to rout
The RAF and remove the stain
From the name of Göring again.
Amen

Document 15/4[6]

Etiquette for the German Soldier

Wartime Intelligence Officer's Comments

A document captured from 191st Grenadier Regiment[7] sets out a complete guide to correct social behaviour for the German soldier in almost any situation. The following are extracts.

Example 1

A soldier is sitting with a girl on a bench in the park. A superior goes past.

- (a) The soldier 'busies himself further' with the girl as if he has not seen his superior <u>or</u>
- (b) Lets go of the girl and sits up quickly.

Both wrong

<u>Correct</u>: The soldier stands up and salutes correctly.

Example 2

A soldier enters a bar. How should he conduct himself? He removes his cap and gives the Hitler salute to the whole company. Likewise on leave.

---

4. Revenge or retaliation, a reference to the long-await V-weapons.
5. 'V's' were *Vergeltungswaffe*, or retaliation/revenge weapons such as the V-1 flying bomb and the V-2 missile.
6. ISUM 98, 4 October 1944, from *Allied Forces Headquarters Intelligence Notes* 74.
7. Probably the 191st Fusilier Battalion of the 91st Air Landing Division.

Before going into a room he knocks, takes off his cap and, when told to come in, gives the Hitler salute in the room. It is stupid at this point to ask for permission to enter. He has already been called in and is standing inside the room.

Example 3

A soldier sits in a beer-house and a superior enters.

(a) The soldier intentionally looks away <u>or</u>
(b) makes the Hitler salute <u>or</u>
(c) jumps up (and knocks over his beer!)
All wrong

<u>Correct</u>: The soldier puts down his knife and fork or his glass of beer, takes his hands off the table and turns towards the superior.

Document 15/5[8]

The Sight and Sound of Ground Attack

Wartime Intelligence Officer's Comments

A German soldier's letter vividly describes the anti-tank tactics of a rocket-firing Typhoon:

'Tank on road – clank, clank, clank;
Aircraft approaches – m-m-m-m-m-a-a-r-r-;
SCHRUMPF!
Tank in flames.'

---

8. ISUM 66, 3 September 1944.

The Wehrmacht Retreats from Dieppe, August 1944

A French View[1]

During the last three days the Germans had been requisitioning all the rolling stock available in the region. On Wednesday 30 August 1944 it became a real collective hysteria: they moved away by all possible means. Some by foot, others in horse carts; a few sailors had found a tractor; they hitched a cart onto it and to this they attached the shaft of a grocer's cart. The whole paraphernalia then departed under the ironic gaze of the population. Everywhere groups of Germans were struggling with old lizzies trying to get them going. New cars often did not work better than old ones (strange coincidence). A German told a man of Dieppe he was convinced that nine-tenths of the vehicles they were forced to abandon would function again on the very day of the arrival of the English.

At breakfast time, on Wednesday, a regular raid was organized by the sailors of the harbour. Half undressed, dirty, with long hair, a scarf around their neck, they proceeded by small groups to steal bicycles in the streets and in the houses. If any simple minded person tried to discuss the matter in the street or attempted to request the control of the *Kommandantur*,[2] the soldier pulled out his revolver and the excuses he used suddenly became very weighty.

During the afternoon, collective looting took place the same way as it did in 1940. As soon as a furnished house was vacated by the troops, the crowd, aroused by a spirit of jealousy and easy gain, would dash inside the place and remove the last pieces of furniture the troops had left for the unlucky proprietor. Fortunately, the Dieppe police, taking quick action, put an end to these regrettable scenes.

---

1. ISUM 70, 7 September 1944, from *La Vigie Nouvelle*, a Dieppe newspaper, 5 September 1944.
2. *Kommandantur*, the local commandant's headquarters.

Tuesday night explosions resounded in the entire region. During the night of Tuesday to Wednesday large explosions lit the horizon in a westerly and south westerly direction while unending convoys of horses and carts stolen from the French, moved northwards, packed with men and materials. Wednesday morning pillboxes were blown up at Janval, at Golf, in the Arcques Forest, etc. The demolitions were carried out without stop during the night of Wednesday to Thursday.

But it is on Thursday morning that the last troops indulged without any curb in the savage joy of destruction. All the pillboxes were blown up one after the other and the smallest bridges underwent the same treatment. At 0630 hrs the quays were destroyed and this was followed by the destruction of the 'Grand Pont'. Finally, a crime clearly bearing their signature, a clumsy and gross crime, the 'Tour St Remy' the finest building in Dieppe, the most obvious and decorative one, began its slow agony. The Germans had the delicate and Teutonic idea of transforming it into an ammunition dump. During the entire day the explosions followed one another; under the repeated shocks the roof of the old and noble building gradually began to sink. Each time and explosion took place, surrounding with a cloud of smoke the wonderfully weathered tile roof, the people of Dieppe anxiously waited for this veil to disappear so that they could still see whether or not this masterpiece of men and time was still standing. Luckily the base of the tower built by our ancestors was wonderfully solid and its strong architecture withstood the violent explosions.